God's Schools

God's Schools
CHOICE AND COMPROMISE IN AMERICAN SOCIETY

MELINDA BOLLAR WAGNER

RUTGERS UNIVERSITY PRESS
New Brunswick and London

Permission to use previously copyrighted material is gratefully acknowledged:

"Christ Is the Greatest Puppeteer." Copyright © 1990 by Boyd Amason. All rights reserved. Used by permission.

Born Again: Life in a Fundamentalist Baptist Church, James Ault and Michael Camerini, 1988. James Ault Films, 71 Fifth Avenue, Suite 1100, New York, New York 10003 (212) 799-5052.

"The Family of God," words by William J. and Gloria Gaither, music by William J. Gaither. Copyright © 1970 by William J. Gaither. All rights reserved. Used by permission.

"What to Give to Jesus," James McKeever, *END-Times News Digest,* December 1986:1–8.

Educating for Eternity, Claude E. Schindler, Jr., and Pacheco Pyle, Whittier, Calif.: Association of Christian Schools International, 1979.

Library of Congress Cataloging-in-Publication Data

Wagner, Melinda Bollar, 1948–
    God's schools : choice and compromise in American society /
Melinda Bollar Wagner.
        p.   cm.
    Includes bibliographical references (p.).
    ISBN 0-8135-1606-4 (cloth)   ISBN 0-8135-1607-2 (pbk.)
    1. Church schools—United States—Case studies.   2. Church and
education—United States.   3. Christian education—United States.
4. Educational anthropology—United States.   I. Title.
LC621.W34   1990
377'.0973—dc20   90-32431
                                                                      CIP

British Cataloging-in-Publication information available.

Dedicated to

Lida Jean McDowell Bollar,
mother, teacher, confidante, booster, and friend

Contents

List of Figures and Tables

Preface

The purpose of anthropology is to help people with different backgrounds, beliefs, and life-styles to understand one another; the anthropologist translates from one culture to another. The anthropological enterprise is a collaborative one; the ethnographer forms a partnership with her informants, who tell her, and let her see, how they live their lives—the rules they use for living and the meanings that lie behind those rules. An anthropologist who has promised anonymity to those generous and invaluable informants finds herself thereby in the position of not being able to thank them adequately in print. Administrators, teachers, parents, and students at the nine Christian schools in "Southeastern Valley" and "City" graciously opened their doors to me and spent much time teaching me what they knew about Christian education. I especially want to thank those from "Grace Christian Academy" and "Dells Christian School"; administrators "Kathleen Mitchell" and "Rebecca Webb," and teachers "Nancy Sherwood" and "Janeen Turner" spent the most time with me. They were informants, and are friends. I want to thank the schools and Christian communities, too, for allowing me to use their printed materials within this book, especially "Living Waters Christian Community" and "Springfield City Christian School."

Concerning the pseudonyms I gave the students, the reader will notice that diminutives are very rarely used. That is, John is John, not Johnny; Sandra is Sandra, rarely Sandy. That aspect of the pseudonyms is true to what I observed. One characteristic of some of the children's names was lost, however, when pseudonyms were created; several had biblically derived names that made it clear that their parents had been conservative Christians long before they enrolled their children in Christian schools.

Besides the several administrators and teachers to whom I owe a debt of gratitude, personnel from national organizations—A Beka Book, Accelerated Christian Education, Alpha Omega Publications, the American Association of Christian Schools, and the Association of Christian Schools International—talked to me extensively and allowed me to attend their professional meetings.

Many institutions and individuals contributed resources and effort to this study. This material is based upon work supported by the National

Science Foundation under Grant No. BNS8520070. The National Science Foundation's generous grant allowed me to undertake one year of full-time participant observation research within the Christian schools. Another semester for analysis was granted by the Radford University Faculty Development Leave Program. Seed money for the equipment and resources necessary to write the research proposal was provided by the Radford Foundation Faculty Professional Development Program.

Many colleagues kindly wrote recommendation letters for me, and several reviewers have contributed helpful suggestions at various points in the study, from proposal to early drafts. I wish to thank Dwight B. Billings, Joseph P. Fichter, Roland Mushat Frye, Luther P. Gerlach, Jeffrey K. Hadden, Conrad P. Kottak, Meredith McGuire, Alan Peshkin, Roy A. Rappaport, Wade Clark Roof, Ellen M. Rosenberg, and other anonymous readers for their support and kind reviews. Gertrude Enders Huntington provided the first materials I obtained concerning Christian education, and has been a helpful voice and ear as the fieldwork and analysis progressed. Stuart Plattner, Program Director for Cultural Anthropology at the National Science Foundation, wrote in an early letter to me: "Part of my job is to facilitate your work and help you to see it through to a successful conclusion"; he most certainly fulfilled this aspect of his position. Rutgers University Press and Marlie Wasserman, Associate Director and Editor in Chief, Managing Editor Marilyn Campbell, and copyeditor Adaya Henis were most professional, enthusiastic, and helpful in their handling of the manuscript.

Any findings and conclusions expressed in this publication are, of course, those of the author and do not reflect either the views of the National Science Foundation or those of the various reviewers listed here.

At Radford University, Janet Hahn, grants officer, provided encouragement and aid of every variety in the proposal process. My department chair, Stephen H. Lerch, encouraged my research and worked to provide a smooth transition away from and back to my teaching duties. Our secretary, Pat Rupe, kept my life uncomplicated by expertly handling paperwork on the school front. My teaching replacement, anthropologist John Michael Coggeshall, and colleague C. Clifford Boyd, did an excellent job of keeping the home fires burning in cultural anthropology classes while I was away. Student assistant Holly Kelly carefully entered numerous codes into computer files. Reference librarians David Hayes and Larry G. Pollard were valuable research assistants, pointing me to pertinent information, retrieving demographic information, and searching for reference citations. Manuscript secretary Carolyn Sutphin performed the valuable services of transcribing audio tapes, checking references, and general cleaning of the manuscript. Graduate student Susan Dodson, herself a Christian school pupil in her early years, helped to trim the number of ethnographic examples that found their way into the manuscript. Carolyn Turner, photocopy technician, made numerous professionally printed copies of the manuscript in its many variations.

My family deserves much praise for dealing with the concentrated effort required by participant observation research, not to mention writing a book. My husband, Stephen Everett Wagner, supported my efforts in every possible way. The pride that my mother, Jean Bollar, and my mother-in-law, Dorothy Wagner, take in my work is a motivating force.

A parent at Grace Christian, to whom I had talked at length, told me that she and her husband had been musing about what my report would be like. "At least she got to know us," she said. I hope that the people who graciously taught me what they know will feel that I did get to know them, and have reported their activities without bias, objectively, toward the end of helping people understand one another.

God's Schools

Introduction

Picture the Christian school of your mind's eye. What do you see? Children standing in rows, wearing red, white, and blue uniforms. The girls' skirts cover the knees; the sleeves of their blouses reach below the elbows. The boys sport white shirts, blue dress slacks, and navy ties. All are wearing black leather shoes that gleam with a spit-and-polish shine.

The teacher calls out that it is time to go to chapel, and the children turn in their line as if they are one organism. But for knees raised not quite high enough, you would say they marched into the sanctuary where chapel is held. They quietly take their places: little ones in front, big ones in back; girls on the left, boys on the right. The chapel service will be led by the male pastor and principal, who lurks in the halls, never far from the paddle in his office.

Now please follow me to the window of another school, and guess, as you look in, what kind of school it is. Is it a public school, a Christian school, or a secular private school?

As we look through the window we see:

A teacher standing in front of her class of twelve students, leading them in unison chants of "Aaa Aaa Apple" and "Ih Ih Indian." Up high on the classroom walls are hung pictures of everyday items used to teach the vowel and consonant sounds—apples, balls, cats, dogs, and Indians. The young blond teacher is wearing a skirt printed with huge red and yellow flowers. Her red high-heeled shoes are open-toed, revealing dark red toenails which match her shiny fingernails.

Later she asks students to come to her desk and read to her from their reading books, one at a time. When it is his turn, John comes up to the teacher's desk, and wiggles so that his back faces her, his head peeping over his shoulder. "I can't read it!" he says. The teacher reaches for him (since he seems to be trying to make a getaway), as she says, "That's what we're here for, to *learn* how to read it."

The teacher, Mrs. Sherwood, is sitting on a chair made for first graders; as John stands beside her, his head is level with hers. She enfolds him in her arms, holding the book in front of him. It looks like a loving embrace, but it also reduces the blond-haired boy's wiggling and keeps his eyes focused on the book (Field Notes 10/31/86).

When some of the students at their seats talk too loudly, the teacher says, "If you don't be quiet, Mrs. Sherwood will put your name on the board, and you'll have to sit at recess."

We leave this window and step inside another classroom. Here we see: A kindergarten teacher watching as her charges prepare to take a nap. The children take off their shoes, all of them a variation of running shoes. Those with Velcro fasteners are out of their shoes in a flash. The shoe-stringed ones need some assistance from each other or from the teacher. Five-year-old Sandra asks me to untie a particularly ratty knot. I think for a moment and decide that this would not be intruding too much on my desire to be inconspicuous and not to present a challenge to the teacher's authority. I bend and untie the knot. Sandra looks up at me with her dark eyes set in a square face ringed with curled thick brown hair. "Thank you, Mrs. Wagner," she says.

Eventually they lay on mats laid side-by-side and end-to-end in the classroom. The mats, brought to school by each child, are stored in a nearby room. Two of the students are assigned to bring them out and take them back every day. The mats have a variety of motifs: A yellow one sporting happy faces belongs to chubby dark-haired Peter; Sandra's cousin Holly, brown-eyed with short bobbed hair, has a blue one with Velcro fasteners to help it roll up for storage. Douglas takes his glasses off and burrows completely inside his sleeping bag which is shaped like a Crayola box, making his blond unruly hair even more so; now we can't even see his head. Sandra lies on Snoopy's picture printed on a beach towel.

Sandra's skirt flips up and shows her ruffly panties as she hoists up her legs to play with her socks. She is the only one wearing a skirt. The other girls are wearing jeans. The boys are wearing jeans or chino pants and striped knit shirts.

While the little students are taking a nap for an hour, Douglas and David actually go to sleep. The other eight find ways to amuse themselves. One ties his shoelaces together. Another ties his neighbor's shoe to his desk. Still another finds a screw at the bottom of a filing cabinet and sets to work trying to loosen it. Holly gets up six times to straighten her mat. A girl and boy whisper and giggle, louder and louder. "Gena, turn your mat the other way. Put your head up here," the teacher admonishes. One boy pushes another with his feet—tap, tap, tap—harder and harder. As the teacher rises to intervene, we leave the classroom (Field Notes 9/8/86).

We move back to a vantage point in the first-grade classroom, where the children are taking their recess indoors. Two boys and one of the girls are building an elaborate castle out of cast-off computer paper, gluing strips of it together.

Eric:	This the grocery store. I own that. I own from here to here.
Timothy:	I own this prison.
Diane:	I'm making furniture.
Eric:	This is the hot tub. And I'm putting a cover on the shower room—it's also my kissing room. . . .
Eric:	Look at my fancy car. I'm making a sports car with a secret shower room. I'm making a kissing car.

Eric and Timothy's good friend Andrew walks into the room. He isn't supposed to stay to play, since he is not yet finished with his schoolwork. Eric teases him about being slow with his work, and a tussle ensues. It ends with Eric exclaiming, "You stepped on my beautiful limo!" (Field Notes 10/14/86).

Now we go out onto the playground, where third, fourth and fifth graders are having physical education. The class begins with laps around the building; they must run for three minutes. The teacher is looking at his stop watch. As they round the corner, nearly every student pants, "How much longer?"

After the run they gear up to play soccer. The physical education teacher is dividing them into teams. Marvin, a red-haired fourth grader, yells, "No, no, you can't put them together; they'll always win! That's no fair! We want to be together." The teacher explains that he is trying to make balanced teams, and that he may make adjustments later, after he watches them play for a little while (Field Notes 10/30/86).

We see some seventh graders walking from one classroom to another, changing classes. Today is "Sixties Day," proclaimed as such by the seventh graders themselves. They are wearing their mothers' and fathers' castoffs from the sixties, although some seem to have gone back to the fifties, sporting poodle skirts and angora yarn wound around their fathers' class rings. At the same time, they haven't entirely rid themselves of modern accoutrements, still wearing at least one Swatch apiece.

Dawn asks a blond-haired boy who is dressed in eighties' jeans, "Samuel, why aren't you dressed up?"

"Well, Andrea called me and told me to, but I didn't believe her. I called James and he didn't know anything about it."

"We didn't tell *him!*" (Field Notes 10/3/86).

Let's look at these scenes in our "mystery school" once more, with a fuller eye. There are some items of context omitted from the descriptions which would have given away the fact that they are everyday scenes at Christian schools.

The reading lesson and indoor recess take place in a combined classroom of first and second graders. While not unheard-of in public schools, the combined classroom is common in small Christian schools. The classroom walls are filled with figures of Snoopy—some with scripture, some without—and large-headed big-eyed children created by Joan Walsh Anglund, Harry and David, and Precious Moments. The behavior modification forms of discipline (such as sitting during recess) are used very frequently, but Mrs. Sherwood might also say, "What does God say about that?"

Before reading time began, the class has had a Bible lesson. Likewise, in the kindergarten class, nap time is sandwiched in between Bible story time and the prayer that ends the school day. The teacher of the physical education class is a volunteer. He begins and ends the class with a prayer. If students get hurt he prays for them.

Perhaps your preconception of Christian schools was not as extreme as the strict and conservative picture I painted at the beginning of this chapter (although it was derived from comments made to me by colleagues as I undertook to learn about Christian schools). But by observing some scenes inside Christian schools, you have seen that the culture found there is a tapestry woven from strands of American mainstream *popular culture, professional education culture,* and elements of *Christian culture.*

UNDERSTANDING CHRISTIAN SCHOOLS IN AMERICAN CULTURE: CHOICE AND COMPROMISE

Liberals regard the conservative Christians as a bunch of threatening intransigents; their schools are seen as places where children in uniform are indoctrinated into fundamentalist dogma, and taught little else.

Indeed, the rhetoric of the conservative Christians themselves is one of polarization and what they call "separation from the world." "Be ye not unequally yoked together with unbelievers" (II Corinthians 6:14) is a favored expression. Accelerated Christian Education (producer of self-paced curriculum materials) states that "our material is *not* written with conventional viewpoints in mind" (Randall 1988, emphasis in original). Conservative Christian writings show that they include among their devil-inspired enemies, the secular humanists and the "New Agers," who are castigated in books like *The Hidden Dangers of the Rainbow* (Cumbey 1983), which posits a New Age conspiracy to take over the world. Separate, polarized, devoid of compromise—this is the picture painted both by the conservative Christians themselves and by their detractors.

The equivalent in social science terminology to the separation the conservative Christians claim to have is the *total institution*. The classic total institution—the prison or the traditional convent—controls nearly every aspect of people's lives, stripping them of any accoutrements of identity save those offered by the institution itself. Well-researched studies of Christian schools have said that the conservative Christian church and school is a total institution (see Peshkin 1986, 1987).[1]

Like my colleagues, I thought that I would find fundamentalist ideology—and only fundamentalist ideology—clearly played out in every aspect of the Christian schools. What I found, instead, was that despite the rhetoric of "being not yoked" with unlike people and ideas, the Christian schools are far from the all-encompassing total institution. They are fraught with compromise with the American popular culture that surrounds them. The Christian alternative school is not as alternative as it could be.

While today's conservative Christians carry the *ideal* of living by "black and white," they themselves say that their schools, homes, and churches are "not heaven," and that compromises are made while living on this earth. Accordingly, I saw a "gray" amalgam of conservative Christian ideals, American popular culture, and professional education techniques braided together at the schools. This supports Hunter's (1983, 1987) contention that conservative Christians have undergone a good deal of accommodation to the surrounding culture (see also Rose 1988, 198ff; see Ammerman 1987 for a different view). We will describe Christian schools by unbraiding this cultural plait to reveal strands of American popular culture, professional education culture, and conservative Christian ideology. Examining the context within which the Christian schools function is the first step.

THE CONTEXT: TIME, PLACE, AND PEOPLE

The Time

The 1980s were an exciting time to be learning about—and from—conservative Christians in America. In early 1987, evangelist Oral Roberts was threatening to die, announcing that God might "call him home" if he didn't raise $4.5 million for his ministry, and Gary Trudeau's Doonesbury cartoon went on an "Oral Roberts death watch." Jerry Falwell threatened to move his ministries and industries from Lynchburg, Virginia, to Atlanta, unless the city provided relief from taxes (which it did). Jim and Tammy Faye Bakker were threatened with disclosure about past scandals and left their PTL (Praise the Lord and People that Love) ministry. Jerry Falwell took over the troubled ministry for a time, blurring distinctions between charismatic Christians (the Bakkers) and fundamentalist Christians (Falwell), and causing newspapers to run page-long taxonomies of denominational affiliations and "who's who" in the conservative Christian world. In 1988 the Bakkers' accuser, Jimmy Swaggert, was himself caught in a web of sexual allegations. In the late 1980s, the Southern Baptist Convention fought a battle between fundamentalists and moderates, with the fundamentalists gaining in leadership positions. In 1986 Pat Robertson, founder of the Christian Broadcasting Network (CBN) and CBN University, asked God whether he should run for President of the United States. In 1988 he did.

The courts were full of church and education controversies. In 1986 a judge in Greeneville, Tennessee, ruled that a public school could not require children to read books which would be found objectionable in their fundamentalist Christian homes; in 1987 this ruling was reversed by the U.S. Circuit Court of Appeals. In another case in Mobile, Alabama, a federal judge who had previously upheld prayer in public schools banned over forty textbooks, claiming that they advanced and promoted humanism and thereby violated the Constitution's First Amendment, which prohibits the state from advancing religion in public schools. The case revolved around the expert testimony from sociologist James Davison Hunter (1986) that humanism could be counted a religion, and from psychologist Paul Vitz that the textbooks did have a humanistic bias.[2] In 1987 the U.S. Supreme Court (by a seven to two vote) declared unconstitutional a Louisiana law requiring that creationism be taught alongside evolution.

The news media struggled to make sense of the evangelical cultural scene. Columnists and cartoonists had a field day. Religious pluralism seemed to be headed toward religious polarization. At one pole stood the increasingly vocal and politically astute conservative Christians, chagrined by and distancing themselves from the scandals with which they were being identified. At the other pole were the groups they identified as their nemeses, which they labeled "New Age." Shirley MacLaine's reincarnation experiences were featured on television. On-the-job seminars incorporated meditation and other New Age practices.

Yet most of America stood in the middle. Most lived, perhaps, in the "Village of the Darned" (Larson, "Far Side"), neither bad enough to be damned nor particularly virtuous. Gallup (1981, 85) polls show that most Americans (over 90%) believe in God, 70 percent believe in an afterlife, and 44 percent of Americans believe that "God created man pretty much in his present form at one time during the last 10,000 years" (Gallup 1983). So we are not willing to sign the "Humanist Manifesto," which declared that "we are convinced that the time has passed for theism, deism, modernism, and the several varieties of 'new thought' " and that "promises of immortal salvation or fear of eternal damnation are both illusory and harmful" ("Humanist Manifesto" I and II). But we're not ready to attend church whenever the church doors open, either. Polls show that nearly 70 percent of Americans claim to be members of churches, but 40 percent of Americans attend church regularly. Somewhere between one-fifth and one-third of Americans—more than 50,000,000 people—say they are "born again" Christians (Ammerman 1987; CBS "48 Hours," 4/14/88; Gallup 1981; Hunter 1983; Los Angeles Times 1986; Quebedeaux 1978).

The scandals that have rocked the conservative Christian world have served to make it a laughingstock, in the same way that the Scopes "Monkey Trial"—about the teaching of evolution in public schools—did in the 1920s. On the other hand, some of the objections of conservative Christians to public school education and textbook content have garnered an assortment of strange bedfellows, who at least partially agree with them. For example, Lynne Chaney, the chair of the National Endowment for the Humanities has made pronouncements which could very well have come out of Christian educators' mouths. She worries that the educational system's "preoccupation with global education" erodes the concept of America's greatness. "I find it hard to imagine that there's a story more wonderful than [the Pilgrims'] being driven by the desire to worship freely, to set off across that ocean, to make a home out of this wild and inhospitable land." She blames, as do the conservative Christians, the onset of "progressive education in the 1920s." (Los Angeles Times 1987). When he was secretary of education, William Bennett said that American schools should be teaching "more about the evils of communism and less about the consequences of nuclear war. . . . Social studies classes should not shrink from making judgments on other societies and political systems" (Lawrence 1986). "Our values as a free people and the central values of the Judeo-Christian tradition are flesh of the flesh, blood of the blood. . . . The fate of our democracy is intimately intertwined—entangled, if you will—with the vitality of the Judeo-Christian tradition" (Will 1985). Speaking at Jerry Falwell's Liberty University, Secretary Bennett said that "absolute moral values should not be left out of public education" (Chamberlain 1986). Bennett was also the keynote speaker at the national convention of the Association of Christian Schools International.

In 1987 a group that included William Bennett and his sometime nemesis, People for the American Way, along with Walter Mondale, Jimmy Carter, Gerald Ford, leaders of teachers' unions, and representatives from the National Association of Evangelicals, all agreed that "we fear that many young Americans are growing up without the education needed to develop a solid commitment to those 'notions and sentiments' essential to a democratic form of government." A conference sponsored by People for the American Way made it "clear that politically liberal groups had moved toward their conservative counterparts in advocating that schools should teach civic virtue and take clear positions on right and wrong behavior" (Vobejda 1987; see also Nord 1986 concerning textbook content).

So it was an exciting time to study religion and its relationship to education in America. The piles of newspaper clippings grew as a new educational issue was discussed in the media nearly every day. The headlines suggest that the parameters of the perceived current crisis in public education include: ineffective teacher training programs producing poorly paid teachers who lack morale (Jones and Chamberlain 1986; Stipp 1986; *Time* 1986); poorly written, boring, "dumbed down" textbooks ("Boring Books: Researchers Say Bad Writing Is Why Johnny Can't Read" [Associated Press 1986a]; Billings 1987; Buchanan 1987; Cohen 1986; Desilva 1986); "teacher-proof curricula" which stifle creativity in the classroom (Hechinger 1986, 1987); "teaching to the test," which further reduces the teacher's role in deciding what to teach; "drugs," "lack of discipline" (Associated Press 1986b); and lack of parental concern (Fiske 1986).[3]

At a time when public school education is coming in for nearly daily criticism, Christian schools are an educational alternative to which increasing numbers of parents are turning. These schools "constitute the most rapidly expanding segment of formal education in the United States" over the last twenty-five years. They also "represent the first *widespread* secession from the public school pattern since the establishment of Catholic schools in the nineteenth century" (Carper 1984, 111, emphasis his). During this period when the number of public schools has decreased (in response to a declining school-age population), the number of Christian schools has increased. It has been estimated that enrollment in these schools doubled from 1965 to 1975, and that it now includes 1.5 million children.

The Place

The Southeastern United States is the home of those who make national headlines: Jerry Falwell and Pat Robertson in Virginia, the Bakkers and their Heritage USA resort in North Carolina, Jimmy Swaggert in Louisiana, and the parents in the textbook court cases in Tennessee and Alabama.

To understand Christian schools from the inside out, I undertook participant observation research in all of the schools in "Southeastern Valley," as the study area is called. The area, the schools, and the people are given pseudonyms in order to protect the anonymity and confidentiality of those who graciously gave of their time to help me understand why they do what they do. (Any resemblance to actual people or places bearing these names is purely coincidental.) Besides all of the seven Christian schools in Southeastern Valley, two schools in the nearest large city (population 250,000) were observed. The "City" is frequented by shoppers from Southeastern Valley, and some parents from the Valley send their children to school there.

Trips were made in a two hundred-mile radius in every direction to attend national conferences and conventions of Christian educators, courses for Christian school teachers, to make short visits to other schools, and to visit Christian resorts. Full-time participant observation was underway from August 1986 though August 1987.

Southeastern Valley encompasses one county and one incorporated city, with a total population of about 112,000. The largest town in the Valley has a population of about 30,000 in the winter and 10,000 in the summer, because it is a college town. The area also includes another smaller college town, a county seat, bedroom suburbs, and rural areas. Thus, its culture is both rural-native and urbanized, because the two universities prompt a constant influx of professors, staff, and students from across the country. It is a growth area, experiencing a development and building boom.

This is an area in which the Central Intelligence Agency recruits frequently. They say it saves them time to do so, because background checks on potential employees turn up little besides patriotism. It's "apple pie and motherhood" here, they say (Local TV News 11/86). Blue laws which prohibit stores from opening on Sunday are still in effect in City. The blue laws in the county under study were repealed by referendum in 1986.

The area's churches include all but one of the religious "families" delineated by Melton (1977, 1978) and Piepkorn (1978): Liturgical (Catholic), Anglican (Episcopalian), Lutheran, Reformed-Presbyterian, Liberal (Unitarians, and so on), Pietist-Methodist, Holiness, Pentecostal, Free-Church (Mennonites and Brethren), Baptist, Independent Fundamentalist, Adventist, New Thought, Psychic, and Magical. Eastern Orthodox are the only churches missing in the area. According to Johnson et al. (1971), 35 percent of Southeastern Valley's residents are members of a variety of churches whose national organizations report membership statistics. (This is lower than its neighboring counties which do not house college towns.) Methodists, Southern Baptists, and Presbyterians lead, with forty-five churches and 64 percent of this type of church membership. Catholics, Church of Christ members, and Lutherans each make up about 5 percent of this population. Church of God, Episcopal, Pentecostal Holiness (with eleven small churches), Brethren, Seventh-Day Adventist, Unitarian-Universalist, and Friends church memberships account for a lesser proportion. But these figures omit a variety of independent Baptist and nondenominational churches and their members.

Parents acknowledge that the local public schools "aren't bad." They win awards from the State Department of Education and are nominated for honors in the U.S. Department of Education's School Recognition Program, which cites schools "for exceptional progress in education, trying innovative ideas and showing positive results for students." However, conservative Christian parents are engaged in a pitched battle against a proposed family life education curriculum.

The People

What's in a name? Who are the conservative Christians? In "labeling" and "categorizing" the people that I am describing, I desire to use the labels other authors have used, in order to fit my study into the overall scheme of understanding Christian religious life in America. Yet, as an anthropologist whose method is to listen to the people, I am ambivalent about using labels they themselves do not use. The people who served as my informants, graciously allowing me to enter into their lives, eschewed labels and categories, as most people do when they are applied to themselves.[4]

FAMILY TREE. All of the denizens of Christian schools labeled *themselves* simply "the Christians." This did have some of the ethnocentrism, born in this case of their conviction of rightness in God's eyes, that self-labels often do. Similarly, *Homo sapiens* means "man the wise"; the Navajo word for themselves, NaDene, and the Eskimo word for themselves, Inuit, both translate to "The People."

I will use the term *conservative Christians* because its common meaning is the same as the meaning that I want to convey. It serves as an umbrella term, covering all the types of Protestants I studied. There are others that would have served. Hunter (1987) and Quebedeaux (1978) use Evangelical this way; Hadden (1981; Hadden and Shupe 1988) uses New Christian Right (see also Wilcox 1986). *Conservative Christians* has the added ethnographic advantage of incorporating the term they use for themselves; yet, it serves to distinguish these particular Christians from more liberal mainstream ones.

It is important to know that the schools in Southeastern Valley represented all strands of conservative Protestant Christianity. In the words used by other authors, they were evangelical, fundamentalist, and charismatic, and they were part of the older Holiness and Pentecostal traditions. To develop a taxonomy of these groups is a process of unpacking a box, within a box, within a box.

All of the conservative Christians believe in the literal truth of the Bible, although Hunter (1987) found that a minority of students in a sample of evangelical colleges are softening on this position. Nearly all consider it important to share their faith with others.

They all believe that a personal relationship with Jesus Christ is necessary in order to be "saved" and to have eternal life in heaven.[5] Their own definition of Christian is clear from this exchange between two teachers: "Is she a Christian?" "Well, I know she goes to church, but I don't know if she has a personal relationship with Jesus" (Field Notes 3/10/87). As the charismatics put it, "If a person believes in his heart and confesses with his mouth that Jesus Christ is Lord and that God has raised Him from the dead, that person shall be saved." The alternative is the lake of fire in hell.

In conservative Christian ideology, when God brought Jesus Christ to earth, and allowed him to die to atone for the sins of humankind, he offered salvation, by his grace, to all who would choose it. This choice, it is thought, is proffered by God's grace and no amount of good deeds, or "works," people might do can ever make them good enough for heaven. Here the conservative Christians say they differ from mainline liberal Protestantism, which, they say, uses a "balance-scale" approach—weighing people's good and bad attributes and behavior—to determine their after-death fate.

If people choose to be saved, it is thought that God is not obliged to give them a good life here on earth, but that they will go to heaven. If, however, they endeavor to "walk the Christian walk" and to do the Lord's will, then this life will be good, as well as the next.

In general, *evangelicals* are taken to be more conservative than the liberal mainline churches and less conservative than *fundamentalists.* Evangelicals are more likely to embrace ecumenism; fundamentalists are viewed as more separatist and exclusive. *Charismatics* believe in the gifts of the spirit, such as speaking in tongues and spiritual healing, as do the older *Pentecostals;* fundamentalists believe that, although these gifts were used in Biblical times, they are not meant for human use today. Some *Holiness* churches are Pentecostal, and some are not.

Holiness churches, which grew out of the Wesleyan Methodist tradition, disagree with fundamentalist Baptists (and with the new charismatics), who believe that once you have taken on the personal relationship with Jesus then you are saved, and nothing you can do will prevent you from going to heaven; this is called "security of salvation" or "eternal salvation." Wesleyan and Holiness churches believe that your behavior can "backslide" to the point that you would again become "lost." As one teacher at a Holiness school said to me, after ascertaining that I wasn't a Baptist, "Well, you know Baptists believe that you couldn't do anything to harm your salvation. And you know that just doesn't make sense. That can't be true" (Field Notes CCCA 5/6/87). The Wesleyan and Holiness beliefs allow for humankind's fall from grace, and also for its perfectability. The evangelical Presbyterian Church in America (PCA) holds to a Calvinistic doctrine of "total depravity" of humans and "unconditional election" by God to a saved state (Field Notes 7/22/89).

Those are the basics. There are many other more subtle doctrinal differences to be found within the conservative Christian milieu, as just two examples—concerning the beginning and the end of the world—will show. There are several conservative interpretations of Genesis. The Institute for Creation Research uses a "short earth" interpretation, with the earth being created less than six thousand years ago. But the Dakes Bible, and Jimmy Swaggert, teach a "long earth" interpretation, with the earth (and dinosaurs) existing before Adam and Eve were created.[6]

Most of today's conservative Christians are premillennial, believing that this world will end, and Jesus will return to reign on earth. But they differ with regard to how much of the devastating "end times" the saved Christians will be called upon to live through. They talk of "pre-trib," "mid-trib," and "post-trib" exegeses, which refer to being "raptured out" to heaven at the beginning, in the middle, or at the end of the tribulation. Some believe that in these times "to the just will go the spoils of the wicked," so that the saved will live in luxury; others vehemently deny the scriptural soundness of this interpretation. These differences do not stay within the evangelical, charismatic, or fundamentalist lines.

Some markers may help to identify the various strands which make up the conservative Christian milieu. According to Dollar (1973), a fundamentalist author from Bob Jones University, evangelicals are associated with the National Association of Evangelicals, the Fuller Theological Seminary, Billy Graham, *Christianity Today,* the *Moody Monthly,* and *Christian Life.* These give support to "ecumenical evangelicalism," which fundamentalists are unlikely to sanction (see also Fowler 1982; Quebedeaux 1978; Simpson 1983). Markers for fundamentalism are Bob Jones and Bob Jones University, The American Council of Christian Churches, the *Christian Beacon,* and *The Christian Crusade* (Marty 1976). Jerry Falwell used to be identified with fundamentalism, but Bob Jones II decries Falwell's entrance into politics and his loosening of older fundamentalist exclusivity in order to be more effective in the political realm (D'Souza 1984; Guth 1983). Falwell's reaching out to the PTL ministry, identified with charismatics, must have solidified Bob Jones II's negative feelings. Markers for charismatics include Oral Roberts, Pat Robertson, Jimmy Swaggert, Jim and Tammy Faye Bakker and the PTL Ministry, and *Charisma* magazine. Markers for the liberal, mainstream Christian institutions, which are criticized by all of the above, are the National Council of Churches and the *Christian Century.*

Others have written fine histories and typologies rendering the long and complicated history of the conservative Christian movement comprehensible.[7] The conservative Christians identify *themselves* with the early Christian church, but the labels and distinctions that serve to categorize them today did not exist until they began reacting to and against modernism, especially with regard to the teaching of evolution, the restructuring of the family, and the kind of scholarship that challenges the inerrant nature of the Bible.[8] Thus, the split between fundamentalists and evangelicals (then called modernists) arose in the late 1800s when the latter began to redefine Christianity to accommodate modern culture (Cole 1931). But the word "fundamentalist" was not used until the 1900s, following the publication from 1909 to 1915 of a set of twelve books containing ninety articles entitled "The Fundamentals." They delineated the elements of traditional doctrine, which included: (1) The Bible was created from divine inspiration and is authentic and unerring; (2) following the Bible is absolutely sufficient for man's redemption; (3) Christ is the savior, born of a virgin. He died for humans' sins and was miraculously resurrected (Cole 1931; Marsden 1980; Sandeen 1970).

The split between fundamentalists and evangelicals hardened in the

1940s, when many of the organizations we have listed as markers were formed (Gasper 1963; Marty 1975). The Pentecostals were new in the 1900s. The new charismatics sprang up in the 1960s (Lewis 1973; Marty 1976). (See Marsden 1980 concerning the relationship between fundamentalism and Pentecostals.)

New labels arose in the 1980s—"The New Christian Right" or "The New Religious Political Right" (Hadden and Schwann 1981; Hadden and Shupe 1988; Hill and Owen 1982). These labels reflected the academic interest in the political leanings of the fundamentalists and evangelicals. Markers for the New Christian Right include Jerry Falwell's Moral Majority (phased out in 1989), Pat Robertson's Freedom Council (shut down in October 1986 during Robertson's campaign for the 1988 presidential election), *Christian Voice*, the Religious Roundtable, Tim LaHaye and his several books, and Richard Viguerie's direct mail operation. Those who do *not* want to be labeled New Christian Right, because they don't want to be political, or they don't want to be that far right, include Billy Graham, Carl F. H. Henry, Wheaton College, Calvin College (Reformed tradition), and the Fuller Theological Seminary (Hill 1981, 16).

Some markers to the Christian schools movement would be these: The American Association of Christian Schools (AACS) is the most exclusive in its "Statement of Faith." The statement which an aspiring member must sign states that the AACS does not allow membership by those "associated with, members of, or in accord with the World Council of Churches, the National Council of Churches, the Modern Charismatic Movement, or the Ecumenical Movement." (These groups are defined as too liberal by the AACS.) The Association of Christian Schools International (ACSI) is more inclusive. Oral Roberts University Educational Fellowship caters to the charismatic branch of conservative Christendom. Christian Schools International (CSI) has long been associated with schools in the Reformed tradition. The American Christian Consortium for Education and Accreditation is "a new consortium of accrediting agencies," formed in 1986 "at the suggestion of the U.S. Office of Education, with the goal of more rapid governmental recognition." Its member organizations are ACSI, AACS, and the Trans-National Association of Christian Schools (for colleges) (ICR 1986). (In addition, some denominations have internal organizations such as the Wesleyan Education Association of America, but their schools may also belong to multidenominational organizations.)

As we will see, these labels—fundamentalist, evangelical, charismatic— do not manifest themselves in clearcut differences in the Christian schools sponsored by these various segments. We have been discussing *beliefs;* indeed, most taxonomies have been based on theological beliefs. I find in

Marty (1976) a soulmate in the thought that it would be instructive to attend to both belief and praxis when trying to see the commonalities and differences among Christians. The evangelicals and charismatics accuse the fundamentalists of being too "legalistic" in their rules for behavior. The Holiness and Pentecostal churches hold their adherents to norms of behavior and dress that tend to set them off from the rest of the American population. The newer charismatics abide by few of these strictures.

It is especially important to look at both belief and behavior when trying to understand the place of a subculture within a larger culture—in this case, the place of conservative Christianity within American culture. People in the subculture can have very ordinary *behavioral* lives, and very extraordinary *belief* lives (see Wagner 1983). Within the Christian schools sponsored by the various branches of conservative Christianity the stated beliefs were very much alike, and extraordinary when compared to mainstream America. The behavior—the praxis—in the schools was somewhat more varied and, to varying degrees, ordinary. Certainly, the behavior in the schools is not nearly as extraordinary as it is thought to be, or as it could be.

DEMOGRAPHIC CHARACTERISTICS. A common way of explaining the differences between the conservative Christians and their more liberal counterparts, and later the differences between fundamentalists and evangelicals, was that the more conservative were rural, with all the accompanying isolation and anti-intellectualism thought to go along with that (see Niebuhr 1931, for example), which is a caricature in itself (see Eller 1982). Clarence Darrow, the lawyer for the evolution-teaching defendant at the 1925 Scopes trial in Dayton, Tennessee, did much to promote this view, as he questioned his opponent, William Jennings Bryan. And in truth, Bryan did not make the task of making himself look ridiculous particularly difficult. Journalist H. L. Mencken followed Darrow's lead and described the fundamentalists, with their insistence on a literal translation of the Biblical version of creation, as absurd bumpkins trying to salvage the last vestiges of their ignorance. "Scopes was found guilty of teaching evolution (the decision was subsequently reversed on a technicality). But in the trial by public opinion and the press, it was clear that the twentieth century, the cities, and the universities had won a resounding victory, and the country, the South, and fundamentalists were guilty as charged" (Marsden 1980, 186).

The view of fundamentalism as solely a phenomenon of rural and isolated populations has been laid to rest historically (Barr 1978; Sandeen 1970). The millenarians (believers in the second coming of Christ), who Sandeen (1970, 266–267) posits had a major influence on fundamentalism, "were most strongly represented in the eastern, mid-western, and far-western states. They were especially strong in the Boston, New York, and Pennsylvania area of the East, and around Chicago and Los Angeles."

Using Gallup's (1981) figures, today's evangelicals, compared to their proportion in the population of the nation as a whole (19 percent), are overrepresented in the South (33 percent of the South's population is evangelicals) and in rural areas (26 percent evangelical). Hunter's (1983, 55) careful comparison of the income, educational, and occupational statuses of evangelical Christians with those of other religious groupings concluded that "evangelicalism remains based within the middle and lower socioeconomic echelons of American life—lower overall than the other major bodies yet clearly not within the lowest reaches of social and economic life." Still, the conservative Christians who run and populate the Christian schools today are not mossbacks. As anyone who has been watching the news throughout the Reagan and Bush administrations knows, there are people of evangelical and charismatic persuasions at the highest levels of government. Rose (1988) found behaviors linked with class differences *within* the conservative Christian community, as did I. No longer will a simple dichotomy of rural versus city, lower class versus middle and upper class wholly suffice to predict fundamentalist or modernist, conservative or liberal ideas and behavior. Now the conservative Christians' desire for separation from the world often translates into desire for separation from the rabble, and from the "assembly-line mentality," in the words of the school administrators.

In the Southeastern Valley, the parents who sent their children to Christian schools reflected the demographic characteristics of the population surrounding them, and in some cases had a higher socioeconomic status.

At the Southeastern Valley schools sponsored by independent Baptist and Holiness churches, the population was largely (but not totally) technical, clerical and sales, farm, or blue collar. But at the schools sponsored by parents who were largely from Full Gospel (charismatic) churches, a Charismatic Renewal community, and the Wesleyan church, the parents were more well-off economically than the surrounding population. At Grace Christian Academy (GCA) and Dells Christian School (DCS), sponsored by mostly charismatic parents and a Wesleyan church, respectively (63 families combined), 38 percent of the fathers are professionals (professors, accountants, architects, business owners, and pastors), 5 percent are graduate students training for professions, 14 percent are managers and administrators, 5 percent are in clerical or sales jobs, 34 percent are in blue-collar or service jobs, and 5 percent are unemployed. This compares to 18 percent of the labor force of Southeastern Valley who are professionals, 8 percent are managers and administrators, 26 percent who are in clerical and sales, 15 percent who have blue-collar jobs, 25 percent who work in service occupations, 2 percent on farms, and 6 percent who are unemployed.

Two-thirds of the DCS and GCA mothers work full time, compared to about 48 percent of the women in Southeastern Valley. Thirty-three percent of the working mothers at the two schools are in professions (owning a day care center, nursing, teaching), 2 percent are students, 5 percent are managers, 35 percent work in clerical and sales jobs, and 26 percent in blue-collar and service jobs. Nine of the thirty-six homemakers have bachelors' degrees (many in the education field); four more have attended college for two or three years. In Southeastern Valley, 24 percent of the employed women are professionals, managers, or administrators; 39 percent work in clerical, technical, and sales jobs; and 36 percent are in blue-collar or service occupations (U.S. Bureau of the Census 1983, 1988). Rose (1988, 114, 68) says that the parents of the students who attended the Baptist-run Academy she studied were "farmers, skilled laborers, truckers, secretaries, and housewives." The young families who made up the charismatic community which built the other school she described were "college professors, farmers, skilled laborers, businessmen, and social workers."

At Grace Christian Academy and Dells Christian School 25 percent of the families have experienced divorce (16 out of 63). In the population of Southeastern Valley, about 7 percent of the population is currently divorced or separated (U.S. Bureau of the Census 1983).

Racism has been posited as a reason for opening and populating the largely white Christian schools by some commentators and discounted by others (Nordin and Turner 1980). But demographic statistics would suggest that it doesn't play much of a role in the county and city which comprise the Southeastern Valley, where the public school population is 94.8 percent white. The minority population in the public schools is 3.9 percent black, 1.0 percent Asian or Pacific Islander, 0.2 percent Hispanic, and 0.1 percent American Indian or Alaska Native (Triennial School Census 1984). One Christian school had black teachers and several schools had a few black students; the schools in City had a few more black students and a few Asian students.

THE GROWTH OF CHRISTIAN SCHOOLS

As today's conservative Christians are wont to point out, the original school system in America was founded by Protestant Christians, as were the first institutions of higher learning (Field Notes ACE 11/10–11/86; ICR 8/11–15/86; see also Hunter 1987). When these became secularized, Christians opened Bible Institutes, colleges, and seminaries in the first half of the twentieth century (Gasper 1963). Many of these later became Bible colleges and Christian colleges with a broader liberal arts emphasis (Hunter 1987).

After the Civil War, increasing secularization prompted conservative Christians to open primary and secondary schools. In 1918, a plea went out from a conservative Christian journal to "MAKE THE COUNTRY SAFE FOR CHILDREN," because "in the public schools the Devil was dispensing 'a Satanic poison that threatens the very foundations of the Republic' " (Marsden 1980, 160).[9]

The first national organization for conservative Christian primary and secondary education was formed in 1947. The National Association of Christian Schools was formed by the National Evangelical Association "to meet the growing demand for fundamentalist primary and secondary education and to combat the secularism in public schools instruction" (Gasper 1963, vii). (In the 1940s, children from evangelical and fundamentalist homes were attending schools affiliated with Reformed-oriented Christian Schools International schools. It was this that provided the impetus for the National Association of Evangelicals to form its own organization.)

"Since the mid-1960s, [conservative Christians] and their churches, . . . have been establishing Christian day schools at a phenomenal rate." Some proponents have claimed "that Christian schools are being established at the rate of nearly two per day" and some researchers say that for a time, Christian schools opened at the rate of three or even four per day (Carper 1984, 111; National Center for Education Statistics 1976–1988; Synthesis Project 1984; Turner 1979).

During the last twenty-five years of rapid growth for Christian schools, somewhere between four thousand and eighteen thousand schools have been founded. As Gerald Carlson (1987, 23–24), then Executive Director of the American Association of Christian Schools, noted: "No one knows exactly how many schools exist because of the fiercely independent nature of all of our Christian schools"; thus, there is wide variety in the estimates of the number of Christian day schools and the numbers of children enrolled within them. However, nationally collected statistics and Christian school organizations seem to agree that "based on the best available data, an estimate of between nine thousand and eleven thousand schools with a student population of approximately 1 million [1.5 million now] seems reasonable" (Carper 1984, 115; Carlson 1987 agrees; see also Cooper et al. 1983; National Center for Education Statistics 1988).

As of 1987, a slowing of school openings was noted by some national organizers. AACS's Carlson (1987, 24) wrote that "my evidence indicates that very few new schools are being established." However, due to the independent nature of the schools, slowing of growth is as difficult to track as growth itself. The Association of Christian Schools International, the largest Christian school organization, has reported growth in the years 1980 to 1986 from 1,482 member schools to 2,468 (a 67 percent increase), with enrollment rising from 289,001 to 416,061 (a 44 percent increase) (ACSI 1987).

Using the conservative guess of nine thousand Christian schools with 1.5 million students, Christian schools make up 35 percent of the nation's private schools, and 8 percent of all schools. Nationwide, 26 percent of private school enrollment is in Christian schools, and 3 percent of all students are enrolled in Christian schools.

In the Southeastern Valley, there has been a 50 percent increase in Christian schools over the last five years. Following the national trend, the seven Christian schools there, enrolling 376 children, account for 2.8 percent of the area's school population. But in the Southeastern Valley, Christian schools account for 69 percent of all private schools, and 87 percent of the enrollment in private schools.

Today, the support and supply of Christian schools is big business. Taken together, there are close to one hundred support organizations, publishers and purveyors of curriculum materials, and journals and magazines for Christian educators. For this study, information from each of these sources was collected and analyzed, from 1985 to 1989. That's not counting the myriad of books on Christian education published by Christian publishing houses, nor the conservative Christian media (cable TV, videos, magazines, books) meant for home consumption and used as resource material in the schools by Christian teachers. Information from about one hundred of these conservative Christian, but not necessarily education-oriented, sources was also collected and analyzed.

INTERPRETING THE COMPROMISES

Why do we find a syncretistic culture, rather than a total institution within the schools? Why do we find the particular compromises that we do? This is the question in the minds of anthropologists as they observe a culture. Why are these traits here? What causes this culture to look the way it does? When that culture is inside the larger American society, we seek to discover the interplay the two have with one another.

On another level, we plumb the relationship between the culture and the people living within it. This research is a case study reckoning this relationship. We know that people are affected by their culture; how do the culture-bearers turn into actors and effect change in their culture? Sherry Ortner (1984, 159) paraphrased this concern: "Society is a system; the system is powerfully constraining; yet the system can be made and unmade through human action and interaction." The question is, how do humans "make and unmake" their cultural surroundings?

CHRISTIAN SCHOOL BUILDING AS A REVITALIZATION PROCESS

When the conservative Christians set about to build a Christian school, they are making a new culture. It would be instructive to view the creation of a Christian school as a revitalization process. In Wallace's (1966, 39) terms, a revitalization movement is "any conscious, organized effort by members of a society to construct a more satisfying culture. . . . A revitalization is the process by which cultural materials which have hitherto appeared to the members of a society as dissonant are analyzed and combined into a new structure" (Wallace 1966, 211).

The interpretation of Christian school building as a revitalization process is close to the way the Christians themselves view their task. Their ideal culture, as they see it, is the original Christian one; they have adhered to the articles of the faith, while others in modern Western society have abandoned them. Conservative Christians "feel that they are fully incarnating the general shape and intention of the Bible and especially of the first generation of the Christian church" (Marty 1976, 84). They wish to follow in the footsteps of sixteenth-century Protestant evangelicals.

In Wallace's (1966, 160) terms, the conservative Christians' model of an ideal society would be their *goal culture*. When I asked them to describe the goal Christian culture, they readily and consistently referred to "no competition, forbearing and forgiving, and the fruits of the spirit" as described in Galatians 5:22–23—"love, joy, peace, longsuffering, gentleness, goodness, faith, meekness, temperance." "Contrasted with the goal culture is the *existing culture,* which is presented as inadequate or evil in certain respects" (Wallace 1966, 160, emphasis his). For the conservative Christians, the American way of life, and particularly secular humanism, is the denigrated existing culture. "Connecting the existing culture and the goal culture is a *transfer culture*—a system of operations which, if faithfully carried out, will transform the existing culture into the goal culture" (Wallace 1966, 160, emphasis his). The Christian schools themselves are the transfer culture, the crucible of change. Inside the Christian schools the revitalization process—"the process by which cultural materials . . . are analyzed and combined into a new structure"—is ongoing (Wallace 1966, 39, 211).

As we will see, the rhetoric of the conservative Christians is one of separation from the world. Yet, they are not prone to creating (or as they would see it—re-creating) their desired culture by building self-contained communities where they actually separate themselves from mainstream society. We will certainly see attempts to manifest Christian culture, but we will also see many compromises with competing cultural strains in American society. In the Christian schools, therefore, we can see how decisions are made, consciously and unconsciously, when people go about the business of creating a culture. How do they decide what to keep and what to eschew? How are choices and compromises made in "God's schools?"[10]

The chapters to come describe how these compromises are made. They analyze the ideological boundaries that inform the decisions, and analyze the decision-making process itself, from both the outsider's point of view of the social scientist and from the perspective of the conservative Christians themselves. Chapters 1 and 2 describe the Christian schools observed for this study. Chapters 4, 5, and 6 explore the goal culture that conservative Christians wish to create. Chapters 7, 8, and 9 analyze the compromises that are made within the syncretistic Christian school cultures. Chapters 10 and 11 will examine the decision-making process that produces these compromises.

Christian Schools in Southeastern Valley

Christian schools come in all stripes. Mainstream churches—Presbyterians (USA), Lutherans, and Episcopalians, for example—sponsor schools. The Catholic church has a long tradition of maintaining parochial schools (see Fichter 1958). The longest-lived support organization for Christian schools, Christian Schools International (CSI) (founded in 1921) is associated with the Reformed-Presbyterian tradition. Many of its schools are in the Great Lakes states, founded by the descendants of settlers from the Netherlands who carried this ideology with them. But the schools which have come to be identified as Christian schools are those sponsored by conservative Christians and their churches. Even within that category, there is much variety.

The largest Christian school, Pensacola Christian School, is also known in conservative Christian circles as the most strict; it is defined as such by teachers who have visited it and by those who have merely heard of it. Located in Pensacola, Florida, the school has been in existence for over forty years and enrolls 2,800 students (Dollar 1973). It, along with Pensacola Christian College, is the home of the A Beka Book curriculum for Christian schools. Parsons (1987, 6–7) describes his visit to Pensacola Christian School:

Second graders paraded two-by-two down a hallway. . . . Talking isn't permitted in the hallway. Instead, the teacher gives hand signals to start and stop the line of children. . . . [My guide] and I rounded a corner and reached an intersection of hallways. A long line of children silently walking two-by-two toward the cafeteria dissected our path. I slowed, but [my guide] kept walking so I stayed with him. Sure enough, just like the waters of the Red Sea parting for Moses, the line of children parted just as we reached it, with the preceding twosomes walking on and succeeding twosomes coming to a perfectly timed halt to let us through without one step's delay. Not a word had been spoken. The hallway was quiet except for the soft patter of shoes. We walked on, and I couldn't help but glance back in amazement. The two parts of the line had reunited by now, in straight rows that would make a drill sergeant proud.

One of my informants, using Pensacola as a benchmark for strictness, said that "at Pensacola you would see sharpening pencils only at certain times—things like that" (Field Notes GCA 5/4/87). And indeed when I attended an A Beka in-service seminar, the schedule was dictated by a very large digital clock on the lecturn at the front of the sanctuary where lectures were held. The talks began and ended precisely at the time scheduled, whether or not the speaker had finished her thought.

On the other side of the ledger, the school described by longtime Christian educator Bruce Lockerbie (1972), Stony Brook School in New York, teaches from the perspective of "Christian Humanism." Lockerbie (1986) is critical of the A Beka curriculum, noting that A Beka had gone quite far in keeping under wraps things which it considers indecent, even covering a piece of Michelangelo's statue of David when it was pictured in one of their books. Lockerbie disapproves of self-paced Accelerated Christian Education because "the exchange of ideas is almost altogether lacking, [and] the necessity of articulating what it is you think you've been taught . . . has been eliminated by this method, which also, in fact, eliminates the teacher" (Crescenti 1982, 26).[1]

As more data accumulate on what Christian schools are like inside (Ammerman 1987, chapter 10; Parsons 1987; Peshkin 1986; Rose 1988), the places of similarity and difference among the schools become clearer, and the degree of risk associated with generalizations can be better judged. We can say that Christian schools differ with respect to degree of regimentation, from virtually none to quite a lot. However, we cannot say that if we know the denominational affiliation of the sponsoring church or parents, then we know what the school will look like. Schools sponsored by a single denomination will belong to varying supporting organizations, will use varying curriculums, will have varying *attitudes* toward rules, and will indeed *have* varying rules. They will, in fact, have varying organizational entanglements with a sponsoring church, Christian community, or body of parents. Some will desire change; others will resist it. The conservative Christians who taught me about Christian schools felt that social class was a major determinant of school style; Rose's (1988) research supports their opinion.

In order to learn as much as possible about schools affiliated with all branches of the conservative Christian family tree, four samples of material were used in gathering data for this report. One sample consists of the population of all seven Christian schools in Southeastern Valley plus two larger schools in nearby "City." These were the schools I attended on a daily basis. One was my home school, where I attended all functions from the August pre-school workdays to the post-school workdays in June. At the first Parent-Teacher Fellowship (PTF) meeting I was introduced as "sort of on staff"; at the graduation ceremony I was made an honorary graduate. I attended all morning faculty prayers, faculty meetings, all PTF meetings, board meetings, and sat in on classes from three to five days a week. I went along on all field trips, attended the parties, went to faculty luncheons and dinners, and talked to parents. At the other schools I sat in on classes and chapels, went on field trips, and attended ballgames, Christmas programs, and graduation exercises. It is easier to measure the data accumulated from the fieldwork in the Southeastern Valley and City in linear feet than in numbers of pages. It accumulated to over eleven feet of primary data, artifacts, and field notes handwritten on 8½-by-11-inch paper, six inches of computer disks, and ninety-nine hours of tape recordings.

Another sample is a "snowball" of information gleaned about other schools by corresponding with personnel I met at regional and national conferences (seventeen schools altogether).

A third source of data were meetings, seminars, student contests, and courses sponsored by organizations that support Christian schools. The organizations included A Beka Books, Accelerated Christian Education (ACE), the Association of Christian Schools International (ACSI), the American Association of Christian Schools (AACS), and the Institute for Creation research (ICR). Added to these were discussions with leaders of the national organizations, regional sales representatives and national marketing managers of curricula for Christian schools. This added another half dozen three-inch notebooks of field notes, and sixty hours of audio and video tape.

Finally, in order to gauge the extent to which Christian educators could rely on Christian rather than secular materials, an inventory was made of organizations that support Christian schools, booksellers, purveyors of curricula, and magazines for Christian educators. Primary printed information was collected from each of these. This was done in snowball fashion, beginning with the organizations and magazines familiar to the Southeastern Valley school personnel, and obtaining information from any advertisers mentioned. Nearly one hundred organizations of this nature were identified; their materials, together with Christian school textbooks, accumulated to another eight feet. For background, I read conservative Christian books, listened to Christian radio and television, and visited Heritage USA, home of the PTL empire founded by Jim and Tammy Bakker.

CHARACTERISTICS OF SOUTHEASTERN VALLEY'S CHRISTIAN SCHOOLS

The Christian schools in Southeastern Valley and surrounding area are quite varied in some respects (see tables 2.1 and 2.2). The schools listed as Valley and Near in locale make up all of the schools in a contiguous area of four counties and one incorporated city (population 150,000). The schools are affiliated with five different denominations. They use seven types of curricula. They are affiliated in a variety of ways with four support organizations. For example, only one school (Springfield City Christian School) is actually accredited by the Association of Christian Schools International (ACSI). The personnel at this school are highly involved in ACSI activities, and they act as members of teams that judge the suitability of other schools for accreditation. Ten other schools are members of ACSI, and two more have faculty who attend ACSI meetings. The demographics of schools that are members of the American Association of Christian Schools and the Association of Christian Schools International in this region have been added for comparison with the Southeastern Valley and surrounds sample (see table 2.2).

Variables of age, number of grades served, tuition and enrollment, will be compared among only the seven schools in the Southeastern Valley sample; such other variables as the pool of parents the schools have to draw from, their incomes, and denominational affiliations are thus held constant. In the Southeastern Valley, the "median" Christian school would be nine years old, serving grades kindergarten through twelve, with an enrollment of forty-seven students and an equivalent of five full time and one half time teachers, charging $630 per year in tuition, with a discount for more than one child from one family.

The schools use the major types of Christian school curriculum materials—A Beka, Bob Jones University—and most of the types of self-paced instruction available—Accelerated Christian Education (ACE), Alpha Omega, and BASIC. Springfield City Christian School uses a variety of secular and Christian materials, including materials from Christian Light, which are geared toward Anabaptist philosophy. A Beka's video program of instruction is used for Spanish at Abundant Life Christian Academy; other schools are considering using the video instruction.

The churches and parents who sponsor the schools come from a variety of denominations. The Full Gospel, Charismatic Renewal, and Independent Pentecostal congregations would be considered charismatic. The Wesleyan church and the Presbyterian Church in America (PCA) would

Table 2.1 Christian Schools in Southeastern Valley and Surrounds, Affiliations

ABBREVIATION	LOCALE	SCHOOL	DENOMINATION OF SUPPORTING CHURCH[1]	ORGANIZATIONAL AFFILIATION[2]	CURRICULUM[3]
CCCA	Valley	Calvary Cross Christian Academy	Holiness	None	SP:BASIC
DCS	Valley	Dells Christian Schools	Wesleyan	ACSI(M)	Traditional
GCA	Valley	Grace Christian Academy	Full Gospel	ACSI(C), ORUEF	A Beka
HCA	Valley	Hamlin Christian Academy	Ind. Pentecostal	None	SP:ACE
LWCA	Valley	Living Waters Christian Academy	Charismatic Renewal	ACSI(C)	Traditional
MCA	Valley	Maranatha Christian Academy	Ind. Baptist	AACS	A Beka/SP:ACE
PCA	Valley	Porter Christian Academy	Holiness	None	SP:AlphaO
HCS	Near	Hope Christian School	PCA	ACSI(M)	A Beka/BJU/CSI
NWCA	Near	Narrow Way Christian School	Ind. Baptist	AACS	SP:ACE/A Beka Video
PVCA	Near	Pine Valley Christian Academy	Ind. Baptist	AACS	SP:ACE
RCA	Near	Reedsville Christian Academy	Ind. Baptist	AACS	A Beka/SP:AlphaO
ALCA	City	Abundant Life Christian Academy	Ind. Baptist	AACS	A Beka
SCCS	City	Springfield City Christian School	Ind. Baptist	ACSI(A)	Traditional

[1]Ind. = Independent; PCA = Presbyterian Church in America.
[2](A) = school is accredited; (M) = school is a member; (C) = teachers attend conventions.
[3]SP delineates a self-paced curriculum. Schools with "traditional" curriculum use a variety of Christian and secular materials. CSI = Christian Schools International.

Table 2.2 Christian Schools in Southeastern Valley and Surrounds, Demographics

ABBREVIATION	SCHOOL	FOUNDED	TUITION[1]	GRADES[2]	ENROLLMENT	TEACHERS
CCCA	Calvary Cross Christian Academy	1967	$300	K–12	70	6
DCS	Dells Christian Schools	1981	$985	K–3	17	2
GCA	Grace Christian Academy	1983	$600	K4–7	50	6
HCA	Hamlin Christian Academy	1977	$850	K–12	45	5
LWCA	Living Waters Christian Academy	1983	$630	K–11	47	7
MCA	Maranatha Christian Academy	1976	$650	K4–12	112	8
PCA	Porter Christian Academy	1978	$324/495	K–12	35	4
HCS	Hope Christian School	1982	$1,000	K–9	53	7
NWCA	Narrow Way Christian Academy	1973	$770	K–12	80	4
PVCA	Pine Valley Christian Academy	1977	$495	K–12	45	5
RCA	Reedsville Christian Academy	1979	$750	K4–12	47	5
ALCA	Abundant Life Christian Academy	1974	$1,300	K4–12	319	22
SCCS	Springfield City Christian School	1973	$1,395	K–12	530	30
	American Association of Christian Schools survey of member schools in state[3]		$530–1,625		14–330	2–30
	Association of Christian Schools Int'l. survey of member schools in SE region[4]		$1,315[5]		1–100 = 32%[6] 101–250 = 32% 251–500 = 23% 501–750 = 11% >750 = 2%	

[1]Tuition listed is the amount charged for grades one through five; often the figure is lower for kindergarten and higher for upper grades. Most schools offer discounts for more than one child in a family. For Porter Christian Academy, the lower figure is used for members of the sponsoring church.

[2]K4 refers to kindergarten for four-year-olds; K refers to kindergarten for five-year-olds.

[3]Survey by AACS state affiliate sent to their 62 member schools had a 32% response rate.

[4]Survey by ACSI Southeastern Region (AL, FL, GA, MS, NC, SC, TN, VA) sent to 155 member schools had a 53% response rate.

[5]Median for seventh grade. Median for third grade was $1520, for tenth grade $1825.

[6]32% of the schools in the ACSI survey had enrollments of 1–100 pupils, etc.

be evangelical. Independent Baptists are usually thought of as fundamentalist. Holiness churches also sponsor some of the schools.

But as you can see, the denomination of the sponsoring church is not a good predictor of how the school chooses to operate. Denomination does not determine curriculum materials. A Beka books are used in schools which have charismatic, Baptist, and PCA sponsors. Bob Jones University is thought to be a fountainhead of fundamentalist thought, but their curriculum materials are written in such a way that they appeal to a broader audience, including those we have classified as evangelical and charismatic. This is true of the materials of nearly all the curriculum publishers. They cannot afford to provide materials that appeal to only a narrow segment of the conservative Christian market; therefore, their materials are generic conservative Christian. Self-paced instruction is used in schools sponsored by independent Baptists, by Holiness congregations, and by independent Pentecostals.

Smaller schools might be thought to be the most likely to use self-paced, relatively teacherless instruction packages, but even the size of the school cannot predict the use of a self-paced curriculum: Maranatha Christian Academy, the largest school in the four-county area designated as Valley and Near, uses ACE. The smallest school, Dells Christian School, uses a variety of Christian and secular materials, including Bob Jones University and Economy. The self-paced schools tend to be those including kindergarten through twelfth grade. They don't necessarily have fewer teachers, but their student-teacher ratio is slightly higher. The ratio varies from 6.7 at Living Waters Christian Academy to 14.0 at Maranatha. The lower student-teacher ratios (6.7 to 8.3) belong to schools using a classroom approach. The higher student-teacher ratios (8.8 to 14.0) are in schools using self-paced systems.

Since the denomination of the sponsoring church does not predict how the schools operate, I will avoid labeling them as Baptist schools or Holiness schools. They do not label themselves this way; none are __ Baptist Academy; all are __ *Christian* Academy. Although there are Christian schools which serve one congregation, all of the schools I visited emphasize that they do not want to serve one congregation, or even one denomination. This has contributed to the ways in which syncretistic cultures within the Christian schools have evolved, a point we will examine later.

To further explore these schools, we will illustrate statements of belief, and then examine rules for behavior. The distinction between belief and behavior is one the Christians themselves would recognize, although perhaps not label, as such. Time and time again, conservative Christians from a variety of denominations said: "We really all *believe* the same way; maybe we dress differently, but we'll all be together in heaven."

BELIEF: A GENERIC STATEMENT OF FAITH FOR CHRISTIAN SCHOOLS

In fact, the conservative Christians don't all believe the same things, but they do have a core in common. It is this core which the schools, trying to appeal to children of more than one church, present to the world in their statements of faith.

All of the schools (except the Holiness schools) and many of the support organizations for Christian schools have printed statements of their philosophy. For the schools, they usually appear in the student handbook, or in the application form for employment. For the various support organizations, they may appear in the membership applications or advertising brochures.

An analysis of statements of faith of schools and organizations with a wide variety of denominational affiliations showed that there is indeed much unanimity in belief. The analysis included ten schools, five sponsored by fundamentalist Baptist churches: Maranatha Christian Academy (MCA), Narrow Way Christian Academy (NWCA), Springfield City Christian School (SCCS), Ebenezer Christian School, and Herald Christian School (the latter two located in a nearby state); two by charismatics: Grace Christian Academy (GCA) and Living Waters Christian Academy (LWCA), one by an evangelical Wesleyan church: Dells Christian School (DCS), one by an evangelical Presbyterian Church in America: Hope Christian School (HCS); and one upholding Holiness-Arminian doctrine: Baldwin Gate Christian School (in a nearby state). It included twelve support organizations: American Association of Christian Schools, Acorn (curriculum materials associated with Jerry Falwell's Liberty University), Accelerated Christian Education, the Association of Christian Schools International, Alpha Omega curriculum, CBN University, Central Wesleyan College, Coalition on Revival, American Christian Consortium for Education and Accreditation, Grace Theological Seminary, Oral Roberts University Educational Fellowship, and the Trans-National Association of Christian Schools (an organization for colleges). The latter four had simple statements which did not include the point-by-point recitation of beliefs characteristic of the other statements of faith.

In order to give the reader an idea of the central beliefs these schools and their supporting organizations operate under, a generic statement of faith includes what all of their statements had in common, and in words that they used. No two statements were worded exactly alike, yet the content was much the same and certain wordings did recur. These, then, are their fundamentals, to which all of the Christian schools I visited and the various supporting organizations would adhere.

1. *The Bible:*
We believe that the Bible is the Word of God, inerrant in the original writings, and that it is the final authority in faith and life.
2. *The Nature of God:*
We believe that there is one God, eternally existing in the Father, the Son, and the Holy Spirit.
3. *The Deity of Jesus Christ:*
We believe in the Deity and virgin birth of Jesus Christ.
4. *The Nature of Man and Salvation:*
Salvation is attained by the grace of God through the blood of Jesus. Whoever believes in Christ and will accept Him as Lord shall receive eternal life.
5. *The Holy Spirit:*
We believe the Holy Spirit applies the redemption purchased by Christ. He convicts of sin, draws to the Savior, enables men to answer the call of the gospel, and indwells continually every believer.
6. *The Return of Christ and Judgment:*
We believe in the personal return of the Lord Jesus Christ. There will be a resurrection of both the just and the unjust resulting in the everlasting conscious blessedness of the saved and the everlasting conscious punishment of the lost.

The above six articles of faith were agreed upon by all of the schools and organizations, whether charismatic, evangelical, fundamentalist, or Holiness in sponsorship.

Not surprisingly, only the two schools sponsored by charismatics mention the gifts of the spirit (in these cases, speaking in tongues and healing) in their statements of faith. Two of the organizations, the American Association of Christian Schools and Grace Theological Seminary, specifically opposed them.

RULES FOR IDEAL BEHAVIOR: A GENERIC HANDBOOK FOR A CHRISTIAN SCHOOL

We have seen that if the sponsors of Christian schools have doctrinal differences, they mute them in their schools' statements of faith. It wasn't difficult to create a generic statement of faith to which all would adhere. Surprisingly, it also isn't too difficult to create a generic handbook for Christian schools which lists the philosophy, rules, and regulations for the schools.

An analysis was made of nine handbooks, four from schools sponsored by fundamentalist Baptist churches, one by an evangelical Wesleyan church, one by an evangelical Presbyterian Church in America, one by charismatics, and two by Holiness churches. The handbooks used were from: Abundant Life Christian Academy (ALCA), Calvary Cross Christian Academy (CCCA), Dells Christian School (DCS), Grace Christian Academy (GCA), Hope Christian School (HCS), Maranatha Christian Academy (MCA), Narrow Way Christian Academy (NWCA), Porter Christian Academy (PCA), and Springfield City Christian School (SCCS) (see table 2.1). By analyzing schools that are all in the same geographical and cultural area, we are holding these variables constant. That way we can see whether there are *ideological* differences among the schools. We can see whether it is the particular *doctrine* of the sponsoring church that informs the choices made when administrators, teachers and parents undertake the revitalization process of creating the Christian school culture.

No two handbooks were exactly alike, although they contained entire passages and pages in common. This is because a newer school would borrow a handbook from an older school and use what it liked. (The borrowing does not follow denominational lines. Thus, an evangelical Wesleyan-sponsored school borrowed passages from the handbook of a fundamentalist Baptist-sponsored school, and in fact advertised the Baptist school in its own handbook, recommending it to students in grades higher than those served by the Wesleyan school.) Another reason for the similarity is that schools using the ACE curriculum repeat some passages from ACE's own generic handbook. Finally, the number of scriptures concerning education is, after all, finite.

To be precise we would need to create two different forms of generic handbooks. One would be a single sheet of paper, listing the rules of the school, and requesting parents' signatures at the bottom. The schools sponsored by Holiness churches had this type.

The other style would be a handbook, most commonly labeled "Student Handbook," consisting of some ten to forty pages, and typically stapled into a 5½-by-8½-inch cover. The front cover would tell the name of the school, generally followed by "a ministry of ＿ Church," and include a picture of the school's logo, more often than not containing a reference to scripture. The handbook might be composed on a computer, have right-justified margins, and contain no errors, or it might bear the telltale jagged right-hand margin of the "plain old typewriter," and a few typographical errors and misspellings.

Despite concerns, generally discussed in the dress code section, about men being and looking like men and women being and looking like women, the handbooks of two schools (both sponsored by Baptist churches) had capitulated to nonsexist language and used "him/her" when referring to students and teachers.

The handbooks contain scripture to explain their philosophy of education, and sometimes to justify discipline policies and dress codes. (The most scripture-full handbook belonged to the Wesleyan-sponsored school.) The only other quotations used in the handbooks were from news commentator Paul Harvey, Christian educator and author Bruce Lockerbie, and James Dobson, the Christian psychologist who is widely known as a spokesperson on family issues.

The message of the handbooks can be abstracted to this: Christian education must be God-centered and authoritative in its approach, and taught by Christian teachers, in order to produce children who embody Christian character by following the school's policies of operation, following the academic policies, obeying the rules for conduct inside the school, dressing like Christians, and by protecting their testimony off campus. The student should be grateful that they secure their education at a sacrifice to parents and teachers.

To expound on that message, a twenty-seven-page handbook (the median size) for "Faith Christian Academy" would begin with eight and one-half pages of information concerning the philosophy of the school. These principles of Christian education are similar to the philosophy presented in books by Christian educators, and indeed are often indirectly gleaned from them (Byrne 1977; Gaebelein 1968; Kienel 1977; Lowrie 1980; Rushdoony 1985; Schindler and Pyle 1979).

Christian Education Must Be God-Centered

In our generic handbook we find the theme, played with variations, that "All truth is God's truth"—the source of which, though not known to all who use it, is Gaebelein (1968, 20) and that "the fear of the Lord is the beginning of knowledge" (Proverbs 1:7). The message is buttressed by scriptures: "Hear, O Israel: The Lord our God is one . . . teach them diligently unto thy children . . ." (Deuteronomy 6:4–7; see also Romans 13:1); "But rear them tenderly in the training and discipline and counsel and admonition of the Lord" (Ephesians 6:4; used only by the three non-Baptist schools). The curriculum, then, should be "Bible-based."

CHRISTIAN EDUCATION IS BIBLE-BASED: All Truth Is God's Truth.

> God and His Word are the only source of truth and wisdom (Colossians 1:12–22). (ALCA)

> In the belief that man's chief end is to glorify God and to enjoy Him forever and that the way to do so is found in the Word of God alone, ... Therefore, God and His Word, the Bible, will be the unifying principle of the whole curriculum and program of instruction to the end that the children may learn to bring into captivity every thought to the obedience of Christ, that they may glorify God and enjoy Him forever. (HCS)

Below the "Christ-centered" illustration shown in figure 2.1 is the explanation that:

> With the basic understanding that all truth is God's truth, we strive to see that every subject is founded on the absolutes of God's Word and acknowledge the preeminence of Jesus Christ in all things. With the control of the Holy Spirit, the teachers seek to relate truths from

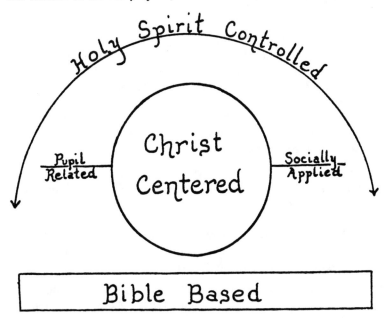

Figure 2.1 Christ-Centered Education (Springfield City Christian School Home-School Guide)

a Christian world viewpoint in such a way that the pupil in turn applies his learning within the context of his society. (SCCS, 1)

Each subject can be taught as a manifestation of God. Thus,

English	HIS WORD
mathematics	HIS ORDER
science	HIS CREATION
heritage studies	HIS STORY
physical education	HIS TEMPLE
music	HIS SONG
arts/crafts	HIS BEAUTY (DCS)

THESE ARE GOD'S SCHOOLS. The schools are thought to be founded by God's command.[2]

We are commanded in Deuteronomy 6:5–7 to teach our children. The objective of Faith Christian Academy is to obey scripture. In Proverbs 22:6, we are told to "Train up a child in the way he should go." (NWCA)

We have God's promise for eternal success in this area; therefore our faithfulness to the task is the declining factor. May God grant us—Staff, Parents, and Students—a determination to accomplish our goal for the glory of God, and the preservation of Christian leadership and freedom for future generations. (MCA)

Thus, the founders of the schools believe that they are following God's will. One of the purposes of the school is to help young people find and fulfill God's will for their own lives.

LEARN TO DO GOD'S WILL AND HAVE SELF-CONTROL. It is necessary to bend children's wills to the authority of the school, so that later they will bend their wills to the Lord's.

Education, in terms that are Christian and biblical, is twofold: (1) to reveal God, and (2) to bring students into conformity with God's revealed will for their lives. (NWCA)

Self-control is important in life and in the classroom. And the Christian life is not merely self-control but CHRIST-CONTROL. True joy is found in submitting our will to His control. It is by outward control that we learn to submit to Christ. Each student's conduct should be brought into harmony with the principles of God's Word. (NWCA)

The handbook might use this desire to fulfill God's will to encourage young people to study. Under the heading "Proper Study Habits," the handbook says:

> Young person: God's will for you at this period of your life is mastery of your school subjects. You should give yourself as earnestly to your studies as you will later give yourself to life's work. You will not succeed in school without good study habits. Good study habits begin with a proper attitude in the heart. Consider your assignments as from God, and do them "heartily as unto the Lord" (Colossians 3:23). (NWCA)

This is followed by nine study habits which the student is bidden to follow. They are all of the ordinary secular variety, such as "Schedule a regular time for study. . . . Concentrate on the work at hand," except for these two:

> Before beginning your work, commit your study time to God in prayer. You are His child and you are studying to honor Him. Place this time and yourself into His hands. . . .

> Be dissatisfied with any effort which falls short of your God-given ability. (NWCA)

THERE IS NO SEPARATION OF SACRED AND SECULAR. In the view of the Christian school, there should be no separation of the secular and sacred realms of life.

> [The purpose of] Faith Christian Academy is to promote the understanding and application of biblical principles to every part of daily life. (DCS)

WE ARE USING GOD'S PROPERTY AND CHRIST'S NAME. "A Christian school bears his name." That the school belongs to God is further manifested in admonitions to students to take care of the school property; for ultimately, it belongs to God.

> We will recognize God's ownership and control of all things. (DCS)

> Faith Christian Academy is God's property, having been provided by Christian people to provide Christian education. (SCCS)

WE ARE SEPARATED FROM THE WORLD. The handbook may note that its own God-centered orientation makes it different from the "man-centered," "humanistic" orientation of the public schools.

35

In the same vein, and for the same reasons, most of these schools eschew accreditation: "Contrary to government rhetoric, accreditation does not mean quality, it means control. We, at Faith Christian Academy, are not interested in governmental control of what we teach" (MCA).

Christian Education Must Be Authoritative in Its Approach

In order for the child to wrap his life around concern for the Lord's will, and to bend his own will to God's, "Absolutes must be taught: i.e., what is right is right; what is wrong is wrong" (GCA).

> We believe that all authority comes from God and in school the authority of the parent is extended to the school and in turn to the teacher. This authoritarian philosophy permeates every area of school life. We believe strict discipline is basic in Christian school and imposed discipline has as its aim, self-discipline. (ALCA)

Thus, a child who is obeying his teachers is obeying his parents, and ultimately is obeying God. To break the rules of the school is to sin. (GCA; HCS)

> Let every soul be subject unto the higher powers. For there is no power but of God: the powers that be are ordained of God (Romans 13:1). Whosoever therefore resisteth the power, resisteth the ordinance of God: and they that resist shall receive to themselves damnation. (Romans 13:2)

Parents (and their helpmates, teachers) will be held accountable at the Judgment for how they have allowed students to behave. "Obey them that have the rule over you, and submit yourselves: for they watch for your souls, as they that must give account, that they may do it with joy, and not with grief: for that is unprofitable for you" (Hebrews 13:17) (MCA).

You Are Taught by Christian Teachers

The philosophy of Christian education stresses the importance of the teacher as a role model—an exemplar of Christian character. "A student is not above his teacher, but everyone who is fully trained will be like his teacher" (Luke 6:40 NIV).

Here the handbook lays out the school's policies on the qualifications of teachers. Their spiritual requirements range from being "a Christian" to being an active member of a particular church. Academic qualifications range from high school to college degrees: "Be assured that all teachers and staff members are born-again Christians committed to providing children with a quality academic program in a totally Christian environment" (GCA).

You Should Embody Christian Character

The handbook describes the kind of person the school is trying to produce. The school wants to affect the whole person's "spiritual, intellectual, physical, social, moral and emotional" attributes.

Like a super scout, the Christian student should respect authority and obey it promptly and cheerfully, be courteous in word and deed, have self-control and self-discipline, and have a will that is bent to the Lord. He should be prompt, clean, and truthful, and he will not complain or "gripe." He will respect others and will be a good citizen, embodying "Christian Americanism," which "places emphasis upon the greatness of America's heritage and the sacrifices of her heroes. America's constitution guarantees liberties to educate in order to preserve freedom. We unabashedly teach the Biblical doctrines of self-discipline, respect for those in authority, obedience to law, and their natural outgrowth, love for flag and country" (MCA).

Here the handbook includes the Pledges, said every school day:

Pledge of Allegiance to the American Flag
I pledge allegiance to the flag of the United States of America, and to the Republic for which it stands, one nation, under God, indivisible, with liberty and justice for all.

Pledge of Allegiance to the Christian Flag:
I pledge allegiance to the Christian flag, and to the Savior for Whose kingdom it stands, one Savior, crucified, risen, and coming again, with life and liberty for all who believe.

Pledge of Allegiance to the Bible
I pledge allegiance to the Bible, God's Holy Word. I will make it a lamp unto my feet and a light unto my path. I will hide its words in my heart that I might not sin against God.

YOU MUST FOLLOW THE POLICIES OF OPERATION. In this section of our generic handbook we find school hours, medical information, and policies for fire drills, transportation, and inclement weather. These are standard procedures like those used in public schools, secular in content and style of presentation.

YOU MUST FOLLOW THE ACADEMIC POLICIES. Here begins the second long section of information—about academic policies—which includes admission and graduation requirements, grading, probation, records, homework, schedules and calendars, and sometimes study habits. Schools using the Accelerated Christian Education (ACE) self-paced curriculum may include the "trail of a PACE," to show how the ACE system works. For the most part, this section is secular in orientation and tone. The schools followed the state requirements for public schools with regard to curriculum, number of school days, and so on, even though the state has no requirements for private schools.

The handbook has a discrimination disclaimer detailing policies on admissions:

> Faith Christian Academy wishes to accept students of any race, color and national and ethnic origin to all rights, privileges, programs, and activities generally accorded or made available to the students at the school.

> It does not discriminate on the basis of race, color, and national and ethnic origin in administration of its educational policies, admission policies, scholarship and loan programs, athletics and other school administered programs. (NWCA)

YOU MUST OBEY THE RULES FOR CONDUCT INSIDE THE SCHOOL. This is a long section of rules for behavior inside the school. These pages are labeled Deportment and Conduct of Pupils, Discipline Code, Conduct and Expectations, Code of Conduct, or Biblical Standards. ACE schools might include an extra section on rules for the Learning Center, as the cubicle-lined classrooms are called. The handbook makes it clear that "attending this school is a privilege, not a right"; students who do not hew to the school's rules may lose the privilege.

Scriptural references are provided to explain the need for the rules. They range from the simple admonition that a person should walk honorably before all men, or Paul's admonition that "Love . . . does not behave itself unseemly" (I Corinthians 13:4) (used only by Baptist-sponsored schools) to more specific references, such as the often used "All things should be done decently and in order" (I Corinthians 14:40).

The handbook might specifically enlist the aid of the Bible in justifying bureaucratic procedures. "The Matthew 18 principle" finds voice as policy:[3]

1. If another believer offends you, go and tell him his offense privately. Don't share it with others (Matthew 18:15).
2. If he will not heed, take one or two persons with you to establish every word before witnesses (Matthew 18:16).
3. If he still will not heed, explain the situation to the person who is in authority over you (Matthew 18:17a).
4. If he still will not heed, the necessary disciplinary action will be taken in accordance with established disciplinary policies (Matthew 18:17b) (DCS; SCCS).

In the handbooks, the list of rules for prescribed and proscribed behavior within the schools is long for all the Baptist-sponsored schools, the PCA-sponsored school, and the Wesleyan-sponsored school (whose list is the longest of all). It is shorter for the school sponsored by charismatics.

The prescribed behavior follows the "model student" character outlined above. The student is to show proper respect. (Some of the handbooks require that students show respect for staff and faculty by using "Ma'am" and "Sir" (MCA; SCCS)). Students should have respect for the property of the school and of other people, use proper speech, be honest, and cheerfully conform to the rules of the school. They should be prompt and come to class equipped with supplies and books. They should be quiet in class, raise their hands to speak, not interrupt others, walk in the buildings, and eat with proper manners (HCS). One school requires the "six-inch rule" between boys and girls (NWCA).

It is likely that the "thou shalt not" lists of proscribed activities listed in some of the handbooks grew as students violated the teachers' idea of decorum. Thus, teachers sitting around a table creating a handbook wouldn't think to include "shoes are not to be taken off in the schoolyard" and "no throwing of snow"—until bare feet were spotted, and until a spate of snow-throwing broke out one winter day—and the next year's handbook included these prohibitions. Thus, the proscribed behavior is an indicator of what children in Christian schools are doing—what deviant behavior they have which must be corralled into the school's norms.

Proscribed behavior includes boisterousness, roughhousing, and rowdiness; running in the halls and yelling, chewing gum, throwing snow, spinning car tires, being loud and making a mess in the lunchroom, personal grooming in the classroom, talking or writing notes to other students during class, using the office telephone without permission, and possessing radios, playing cards, tape players, knives, comic books, guns, or matches (ALCA; NWCA; SCCS). Also prohibited are griping, vulgarity, profanity, lying and slang:

> Language is given by God. Therefore, its use must please Him. Students are expected to use proper language—profane and/or dirty talk is not allowed. Philippians 4:8 is the pattern for our thinking as well as our speaking (HCS).

> Finally, brethren, whatsoever things are true, whatsoever things *are* honest, whatsoever things *are* just, whosoever things *are* pure, whatsoever things *are* lovely, whatsoever things *are* of good report; if *there be* any virtue, and if *there be* any praise, think on these things. (Philippians 4:8)

YOU MUST DRESS LIKE A CHRISTIAN. Each school had some kind of dress code (at least as stated in the handbook). They ranged from the strict rules of one of the Holiness schools—sleeves below the elbows, skirts below the knees, no jewelry, no makeup; for certain occasions, girls' hair must be worn up in a bun, French roll, or French braid; although girls aren't required to refrain from cutting their hair, those who follow the Holiness code do (CCCA)—to simply prohibiting shorts (but not culottes) for high school students (HCS). In between was the charismatic-sponsored GCA, allowing pants for girls, but prohibiting T-shirts with pictures or writing, sleeveless muscle shirts, halter tops, bare midriffs, shorts, and cutoffs. Ten of the thirteen schools in Southeastern Valley and surrounds required that girls wear dresses or skirts. Only one school required uniforms (Hamlin Christian Academy). Almost all of the schools' rules proscribed jeans. (But jeans were actually worn at all of the schools, even the one requiring a uniform.)

Schools sponsored by Baptist, Wesleyan, and PCA churches justified their dress codes scripturally, calling for these traits in dress:

1. Modesty
In like manner also, that women adorn themselves in modest apparel, with shamefacedness and sobriety; not with braided hair, or gold, or pearls, or costly array (I Timothy 2:9).
2. Distinction (between the sexes)
The woman shall not wear that which pertaineth unto a man, neither shall a man put on a woman's garment: for all that do so are abomination unto the Lord thy God (Deuteronomy 22:5; also I Corinthians 11:14–15).

3. Identification with the Lord and not the world
Love not the world, neither the things that are in the world. If any man love the world, the love of the Father is not in him. For all that is in the world, the lust of the flesh, and the lust of the eyes, and the pride of life, is not of the Father, but is of the world (I John 2:15–16; also Romans 12:1–2).
4. Appropriateness
But take heed lest by any means this liberty of yours become a stumbling-block to them that are weak (I Corinthians 8:9; also I Corinthians 8:12–13; 9:19–27; 10:32–11:1) (DCS; HCS; MCA).[4]

YOU MUST PROTECT YOUR TESTIMONY OFF CAMPUS. This section of the handbook would contain rules for behavior outside the school grounds. Here the generic quality of our handbook is lost, for the schools do differ in the degree to which they deem it appropriate to reach into the home life of the student.

The schools sponsored by Holiness churches have the most strict dress rules, emphasizing a look that is separate from the world. But at the same time, the administrators of the Holiness schools make no attempt to monitor what the students do when they leave campus. Although they would like for students to behave themselves when off school grounds, they do not think it appropriate or possible to control.

> We have no control over the students when they leave here. We would like for them to remember that they [go to school here] and the things that they do should reflect well on the school, but that's a request, not a demand. That would be like letting the cows out the barn door and then trying to tell them where to go. (Field Notes PCA 4/8/87)

In a mirror image of this policy, the Baptist-sponsored schools have made various in-school compromises to fashion and the availability of certain kinds of clothes, yet are the most desirious of students following certain rules outside the school walls.

> As long as a student is enrolled in the Academy, he represents this school both on and off campus. If the testimony of the student either on or off campus is detrimental to Faith Christian Academy he may forfeit the privilege of being a student. (ALCA)

The Wesleyan, PCA, and charismatic-sponsored schools capitulate in their efforts to mold the child, saying that it is the parents' place to guide the child in the home. Thus these schools are more circumspect about their expectations for students outside the school. The school sponsored by a Wesleyan church says:

> While Faith Christian Academy policy regarding discipline applies to students while they are on campus, or at recognized school activities, and while behavior at other times or places is an individual and parental responsibility (and not the responsibility of FCA), BEHAVIOR THAT IMPAIRS THE TESTIMONY OF THE SCHOOL CANNOT BE TOTALLY IGNORED, and will be considered as to its severity and impact on the school's objectives and reputation. (DCS)

The PCA and charismatic-sponsored schools are even more willing to leave these matters to parents.

> Exposure to movies, music, television, and literature should be carefully chosen and supervised by the parents in accordance with Philippians 4:8. (HCS)

> The school, as such, is intended to supplement the training of the Christian home; it will, therefore, seek to abide by the teachings of the word of God, the Bible, and will expect the parents to undergird these efforts. (GCA)[5]

You Are Here at a Sacrifice to Parents and Teachers

The last page of the generic handbook concerns tuition fees and their payment in a timely manner. It might go into some detail regarding the sacrifices parents must make to send their children to a Christian school; at the same time it provides assurance that the scriptures require that parents do so (DCS; MCA). It also discusses the teachers' sacrifices, noting that they see their work as a ministry, not a vocation, and that their salaries most often reflect that they are "working for the Lord."

We end our handbook with the school song:

> Faith Christian Academy, we're pressing on to victory.
> Faith Christian Academy, the most loyal we will be, Rah, Rah, Rah.
> Gold and Blue, with hearts all true,
> To highest standards we will cling.
> Faith Christian Academy, Our pledge to Jesus Christ Our King.
> (NWCA)

3

Through Classroom Windows

We now return to the classroom windows where we stood briefly in the introduction. In all, I observed eleven schools, with a combined enrollment of nearly 2,000 students with 135 teachers, and I talked to some 40 school administrators. Not all of these will be introduced here. More of their voices will be heard in later chapters. (See also Ammerman 1987, chapter 10; Parsons 1987; Peshkin 1986; Rose 1988 for descriptions of Christian schools.)

The school where I spent the most time, and became the most attached, was Grace Christian Academy (GCA). GCA was founded in 1983, after the administrator, Kathleen Mitchell, approached the minister of her Full Gospel church about her "vision for a school." It began with twenty-one students in six grades (kindergarten through five), Mrs. Mitchell and Mrs. Sherwood as teachers, and Mrs. Turner handling before and after school child care. Three years later it broke away from its ties with the sponsoring church, and incorporated under a parents' board of directors; Mrs. Mitchell said no changes in school curriculum or policies resulted, other than the operation of finances. In 1986, the school had six teachers for fifty students in kindergarten (for four and five-year-olds) through seventh grade. That made it just above the median (forty-seven students) for the nine Christian schools in Southeastern Valley. It charged $600 annual tuition, just below the median of $630. The school was, for four years, housed in a residential area in two buildings spaced one block apart. One building housed kindergarten through second grade. The home of grades three through seven was two duplex apartments which had been converted into six classrooms, plus an office, two locker areas, and a kitchen used both as a lunchroom and as a home economics classroom.

The school day at GCA begins between 8:00 and 8:15 for the teachers, who gather for the morning prayer. They meet in the administrator's office, or downstairs in the kitchen which adjoins the third- and fourth-grade classroom.

The administrator, Mrs. Mitchell, is a dedicated and skillful teacher, with a bachelor's degree in education; she continues to take courses at local universities. She had twelve years' experience in public schools when she left a secure position to begin Grace Christian Academy. While she does not want the school to be seen as her school (it is, rather, "God's school"), her input and work have been greatest of all those who support the school. She is quick and efficient, both at work and at home, with a schedule that includes twenty minutes for getting herself ready (including makeup) and making the beds in her house each school-day morning. On Mondays she does two loads of laundry before leaving for school, and on Monday and Tuesday nights she does her ironing. She likes to read one of her many Bibles in the evening; "then the mind can dwell on it in the night." She is an avid reader, particularly of Christian and educationally oriented sources, and with children in junior and senior high school, she wouldn't like to stay at home. Although she says she likes to keep house and do needlework, "I guess I get that done, and I'm bored" (Field Notes 8/10–15/86).

As the teachers gather in the morning, the informal time together serves the latent function of providing a time for them to meet and exchange greetings. "That color looks good on you." "Look, we're all wearing blue today!" It allows for exchange of information among the teachers—about teaching and disciplinary techniques—and about how individual students are doing in various subjects. As the teachers and the administrator laugh and chat, suddenly Mrs. Mitchell reaches out her hands to the teachers standing on either side of her. At that cue, all join hands and become quiet.

The prayer itself brings a variety of concerns "before the Lord," in an idiom reflecting Biblical language. These concerns could affect the school as a whole, or any individual connected with it. While it is made clear that God is in control of the school, the prayers are not simply recitations of "God's will be done." Rather, God is to *show* the teachers his will for specific situations. And Mrs. Mitchell suggests to God what he could do, asking specifically for good weather on particular days, and help in obtaining and stretching finances, for example. God is thanked, too, for all it was thought that he has provided, including such things as heat for the buildings (Field Notes GCA 2/2/87).

Father, we just come before Your presence this morning in thanksgiving for the beautiful, beautiful way that You manage this school (Field Notes GCA 10/2/86). We thank You Father, that You have established this place for Your children in this area (Field Notes GCA 10/24/86). And Father, we just know that none of this would be, without You. (Field Notes GCA 10/21/86). We know that we can't do anything; we are totally and ultimately in Your hands, Father. We know that You will lead, guide and direct us, if we'll step aside (Field Notes GCA 10/17/86). And Father, we give You the glory (Field Notes GCA 10/24/86). And Father, I just thank You that You are watching over and protecting all the things that [concern] us. (Field Notes GCA 10/21/86)

Father, continue to guide us as we move into [parent-teacher] conferences. . . . Father, You work around us and go around us . . . as the parents come in, and let only those conversations that are pleasing to You be said this coming Monday night. . . . Let us do [the conferences] well, Father, and to glorify You. And Father, [we ask] that the words that are said be taken into the hearts of the parents, and be received, Father and not as condemnation, but as a weaving of home and school together. (Field Notes GCA 10/24/86) Show them Father, that this is not a man-made school. That it's not a school that is anything except under Your wings and under Your shelter, and under Your watchful eye, Father. (Field Notes GCA 11/3/86)

Watch over every activity that anybody in this school is involved in (Field Notes GCA 10/24/86). And Father, I lift up the singles [at Mrs. Sherwood's church] as they went to City with Nancy and Larry today. Give them a day, Father, that is full of You. . . . And Father, I just thank You that You will protect them and You will restore them, and place the angels 'round and about them and keep them safe. (Field Notes GCA 10/24/86)

Father, we rejoice now that we can come to this place today Father, secure, knowing that we could speak Your word, and pray, and hug these children and show Your love in this place today. . . . Father, I thank You for the privilege of coming in here, and not having to go to work—not having to be in bondage—to the world system, Father. I just count it an honor.

And I thank You, Father, for the diligent teachers that You have sent into this school. Father, let us never take each other lightly. . . . But just allow us, Father, to lean on each other, as we lean on You. And to give encouragement to each other, Father. Show us ways—just a word in the process of the day—might lift someone else up.

And Father, I believe that You are warding off the fiery missiles that Satan would throw nigh our dwelling. And we trust that Your blood is poured over this place and that those missiles cannot come nigh our dwelling; that we're under the shelter of the Almighty God.

We know it's a miracle the way You handle the electric bills and the water bills. And Father, I *know* the bills, Father, that we have are being taken care of supernaturally by You. I know that, Father. And I thank You for Dale, [the treasurer]. Thank You that You have given him the wisdom to work with the money in this place. (Field Notes GCA 11/3/86)

Heavenly Father, . . . we lift up the Music Program. . . . And Father, we pray that You would go forth, and that You would make that [rehearsal] day a nice day for us to move back and forth [between the school and the borrowed church sanctuary] and that You would provide vans to use, Father, and that people will be right there to help us, Father. And we just dedicate this program to You, to Your glory.

Whatever it is that we need to do [with these children], You *show* us, Father. (Field Notes GCA 12/2/86)

Thank You that You are here today; we will do what You tell us to do. We trust in You moment by moment (Field Notes GCA 11/3/86). And Father, we just know that You are right there. We are with You, Father. We are yoked with You, Father. The next move, as You move we'll move easily with You. (Field Notes GCA 2/24/87)

In Jesus' name, Amen.

The teachers go their separate ways, into their classrooms. You have already met Mrs. Sherwood, GCA's first- and second-grade teacher, while she was giving a reading lesson to grades one and two in chapter 1. One of the two original teachers at GCA, Mrs. Sherwood began teaching there after earning a degree in elementary education from a secular university. She maintains her state teachers' certificate, even though it isn't required for teaching in private schools, "just in case" she may need it in the future. In order to keep her certification, she takes continuing education classes; for example, she has taken several courses in cognitive instruction which she puts to use in her classroom.

You have also met GCA's kindergarten teacher, the ever-patient Mrs. Turner, as she supervised nap time in chapter 1. Mrs. Turner has a high-school degree. She began her teaching career by operating the before- and after-school child care that GCA provided in its first year of operation. In subsequent years she was put in charge of the kindergarten class, which now includes both four- and five-year-olds. Mrs. Mitchell and Mrs. Sherwood shared with her teaching tips they had learned in classes and by experience. She was a willing student, who also attended teachers' conferences and read books the other teachers recommended. She has two children who are students at GCA. Mrs. Turner was more likely to speak in the local vernacular than were the other teachers, and her grammar was not always as perfect as that of Mrs. Mitchell, who even used the subjunctive correctly in speaking. Mrs. Mitchell corrected Mrs. Turner if she said, for example, "We was . . ." Once in awhile, even a student came forth with a correction, as happened on the day Kevin and Gena were washing the blackboard, and Kevin dumped the chalk into the water. Mrs. Turner said, "Kevin honey, don't warsh Mrs. Turner's chalk. It doesn't write as well when you do that." Terrell said "Can't you say 'wash'?" Mrs. Turner obligingly said "Don't *wahsh* the chalk. Is that better?" Terrell, still not satisfied with this version, which seemed stilted to him, said, "Say 'wush' " (Field Notes GCA 11/6/86). Mrs. Turner's writing was impeccable, whether on the classroom blackboard or in informal notes to me.

These two teachers and Mrs. Dobbins stay in their "contained classrooms" all day. Mrs. Dobbins, a twenty-five-year veteran of public schools, teaches third and fourth graders during her first year at GCA. Mrs. Dobbins, who attends a Baptist church, has also taught at Dells Christian School, where at one time she was assigned to teach grades one through five to sixteen students. Her church has doctrinal differences with those who sponsor the schools where she has taught, but they have no bearing on her teaching, and have caused no problems within the schools.

As the teachers go their separate ways, Mrs. Mitchell goes into her office. We hear her cry out, "Praise God, I found that lipstick; I've looked for that for a year" (Field Notes GCA 8/86). In a few minutes she is outside her office door again, near the top of the stairs, watching the fifth- through seventh-grade students as they come up the stairs into their homerooms.

Mrs. M:	Hello Tina. How is Tina today?
Mrs. M:	Hello Denise. What a pretty bag. That's like Joseph's coat of many colors!
Mrs. M:	Hello Samuel. Did you have a good weekend? Get rested up?
Mrs. M:	Hello Patricia. How's your mother? Is she feeling better?

The children smile and make their slight replies, as they trudge past with their loaded backpacks slung from their shoulders.

Today we follow the seventh graders into their homeroom. You met a few of the seventh graders as they dressed up for their self-proclaimed "Sixties Day" in chapter 1.

Their homeroom is crammed full of ten students' desks and a teacher's desk. During the pre-school teacher workdays before school began, Mrs. Halsey had stapled handmade and commercial bulletin board items onto the wallboard walls. The decorations reflect the teacher's specialization in mathematics or convey an optimistic Christian message translated into the vernacular of popular American cartoon characters. On the classroom door Snoopy on a skateboard is holding balloons with a student's name in each one. A big balloon at the top proclaims "Mrs. Halsey's 7th graders." "Are we having fun yet?" Snoopy asks. Beside a world map, a large cardboard ruler showing fractions turns one corner of the room, and the teacher jokes about "bending the rule." A large thermometer with Fahrenheit and Celsius figures and the legend "Hot, Warm, Cool, Cold," asks: "How warm is your friendship with God?" Another sign demands "Measure in Metrics." A huge rainbow with hearts pouring out from it takes up several feet of wall space, along with a large "God is Awesome" sign. In the hallway Snoopy says "Beloved, Let us Love One Another"; "A Candy Shop for Jesus" holds two apothecary jars full of the boys' and girls' names, respectively. On the bathroom door Snoopy, looking joyful, says "Rejoice in the Lord, Again I say Rejoice." Nearby sits a "Father we (heart) you" sign.

The students empty out some of their bulky book-bag materials and put them in their homemade wooden lockers in a room adjoining their homeroom. Their locker doors are personalized (on the inside) with bumper stickers, including:

Let the Lord be Magnified, Jesus Christ
I (heart) Skating at Dells Skating Center
Mine Safety
We Have it Made for life
Get Bear [University mascot] Proud
Praise the Lord! JESUS CHRIST
FAITH WORKETH BY LOVE, JESUS CHRIST. (Field Notes GCA 5/87)

Another locker has hand-made signs saying:

This is a new lock!!!!
Hands Off!!!!
I've got a lock so don't try anything!
P.S. The door is that way (arrow). (Field Notes GCA 11/6/86)

The girls are dressed in jeans, pants with suspenders, or pedal pushers topped with big shirts or sweatshirts. They are wearing hightop sneakers or flats with white lacy anklets. Nearly all have pierced ears; some are wearing a different earring in each ear. Two sisters are wearing lavender and gray culottes and yellow and pink kneesocks because the Holiness church they attend does not allow pants for girls and women. Boys are wearing jeans, casual shirts, and some version of running shoes. Nearly everyone is wearing at least one Swatch wristwatch. One boy sports a three-inch-wide digital watch on a big black leather strap. The students hang their jeans jackets in a closet which also serves as the hallway between two classrooms. The jackets are laden with message buttons that proclaim:

Have a Nice Day—Somewhere Else
Don't tell me what kind of day to have
I refuse to have a battle of wits with an unarmed person
Of all the things I've lost, it's my mind I miss the most
Go Bears [local University team mascot]
I sell Girl Scout cookies
The new Peach Bowl
Miami Vice
I like you just the way you are
Benson's Chapel Winnipeg '88 Youth
Is there life after Happy Hour?
(Field Notes GCA 10/3/86, 5/13/87, 3/2/87, 3/10/87)

Mrs. Mitchell was not enamored of the buttons, and in fact said, "I hate those" when she noticed that I was noticing them. She said that in the previous year they had asked parents not to let the children wear them—not so much for what they said, but because they became a hazard when the students passed one another in the tight hallways of the school. Although she, personally, didn't like them, she didn't think she could or should ban them unilaterally, because the students' parents had differing opinions about them. (The same was true about belief in Santa Claus and about what students could and couldn't listen to and watch outside of school.) (Field Notes GCA 5/13/87).

At 8:30 the home room teacher, Mrs. Halsey, comes into the classroom. Young Mrs. Halsey, in her twenties, looks small and trim in black slacks, a white long-sleeved shirt with embroidery at the collar, black flats, and nail polish. Mrs. Halsey is close to having a bachelor's degree from the local secular university. She has not decided whether she will return to school for the several semesters it takes to finish the required sequence of courses, having switched majors from mathematics to statistics. Mrs. Halsey is one of two black teachers at GCA.[1]

Mrs. H: Good morning boys and girls.
Students: Good morning, Ms. Halsey.[2]

She calls the roll, calling one of the girls "Dawn Darling," and another "Foxy Mamma."

Mrs. H: Read Psalms chapter 6, Samuel.
Samuel: Oh no, I've got a stuffy nose, I can't. (He pauses.)
            Psalms what? (He reads.)

At 8:36 Mrs. Halsey assigns three students to stand at the front of the room and hold the Christian flag, the Bible, and the American flag. The class recites the three pledges. Some of the seventh graders try not to recite, and others try to substitute words, while others play it straight.

There may be an underlying disagreement concerning the advisability of wearing message buttons on jackets, but there is no disagreement about the basic conservative Christian message the Bible teacher should teach the seventh graders in the first period every morning. Today their Bible teacher, Mrs. Gibson, taking her lesson plan from the A Beka curriculum for Bible 7, gives this lecture:

Mrs. G: We are conceived in sin. We are born in sin. A little
            infant has a sinful nature. . . . Where did the sin nature
            come from? How did we get the sin nature?
Dawn: Adam and Eve.
Mrs. G: Adam and Eve. The first sin, OK. . . . But, God made a
            way of escape for us—paid the price through Jesus
            Christ. OK, we've all learned that; we've all accepted
            Jesus and asked him to forgive us of our sins and give
            us a *new* nature. And then we stop; now I'm saved. . . .
            But we have to go on. . . .
            We can have what's called, in Romans 6, the mechanics
            of a victorious Christian life. . . . There are five of
            them. . . . (Romans Chapter 6, 7, 8). It helps you to
            understand what you have in Christ Jesus—that you've
            come from the old sin nature to the new man, and the
            new man is in Christ Jesus. . . . We'll just go over these
            five points today. . . . Beth, would you read Romans
            6:6.

Beth: For we know that our old self was crucified with him
           so that the body of sin might be done away with, that
           we should no longer be slaves to sin (Romans 6:6
           NIV).

Mrs. G: OK. Number one, the self is crucified. It would do you
           good to write this down. We are no longer—no longer
           what? What are we talkin' about here today?

Marcia: Slaves in sin.

Mrs. G: Slaves in sin. If you're in bondage, then you're a slave.
           OK. Number one, the old self—the old sin nature—is
           crucified. You know, our self wants to be pleased. You
           know I want to be pleased. I wanna take care of me.
           This is the old humanist thing that they are teaching
           you today. "Take care of yourself. I respect what *you*
           think. If you think that's right, then do it. OK? That's
           right for you." That's the old self. We don't need to
           satisfy self because satisfying self is a sin. In verse 6, it
           makes us a slave to sin, meaning we have to sin. We
           have no power against it; we're powerless. What does
           sin bring? Death. Well, I don't want death; I want life.
           So we have to allow our self, the old sin nature, to be
           crucified with Christ. . . . So that means I am no longer
           a slave to that sin. . . .
           But Number two is Verse 11. Would you read that
           loudly please, James, verse 11.

James: And that is what some of you were. But—

Marcia: You're in Corinthians, James!

James: Uh! (He rifles through his Bible.) In the same way,
           count yourselves dead to sin but alive to God in Christ
           Jesus (Romans 6:11 NIV).

Mrs. G: The self is dead to sin. . . . I'm crucified and resurrected
           with Christ. . . . I'm dead to self, but I'm alive to
           God. . . . I'm a new self. I'm a new creation.
           OK, number three is verse 12. Verse 12 loudly, please,
           Marcia.

Marcia: Therefore do not let sin reign in your mortal body so
           that you obey its evil desires (Romans 6:12 NIV).

Mrs. G: What's it saying there? Don't let sin reign in your body,
           so you will not obey its evil desires. . . . You and I, even
           though we're a new creation in Christ Jesus . . . we still
           allow sin to reign in our lives at times. Well, maybe I
           have sinful desires or lust—to eat. . . . Overeating is sin,

too, if that's your God—if you allow it to be your God. . . . If we don't take charge over that, then it's gonna cause our evil desires, OK, to allow sin to reign in our mortal bodies. This is my mortal body; this is my earth suit. God's given me a soul that lives forever but he's only given me this earth suit to last a short portion of time. So if I allow sin in—say selfishness—I want everything myself; I wanna be first in line all the time; I wanna make the best grades all the time; I wanna be the first in my family; I want everybody to cater to me. Well see, that's selfishness—and that's sin. . . .

So next, we have number four—verse 16. Dawn, would you read that please.

Dawn: Don't you know that when you offer yourselves to someone to obey him as slaves, you are slaves to the one whom you obey—whether you are slaves to sin, which leads to death, or to obedience, which leads to righteousness? (Romans 6:16 NIV).

Mrs. G: Well we were just talking about being a slave. . . . This is telling you to be a slave. Why would you want to be a slave? What does it lead to?

Dawn: Righteousness.

Mrs. G: That's right. Not all slavery's bad. Offer yourself as a slave to obedience, which leads to righteousness. OK. We're a slave to something; we're gonna serve something, right? We're in servitude—each one of us. So, as verse 16 says, you're a slave to whoever you obey. If you obey God, you're a slave to God. If you're a slave to self then you're a slave to sin. You're a slave to sin which leads to death; no one wants to die. Or you're a slave to obedience, which leads to righteousness. I stand justified, complete, right before God, in righteousness. OK, it's not my righteousness. My righteousness is as filthy rags, the word of God tells us. No matter what I do; if I give every one of you a new set of clothes; if I make sure everybody in the whole world has something to eat; if I make sure all the little puppy dogs have a warm place to sleep tonight; no matter what I do, I *cannot* attain righteousness that makes me right before God. There's only one righteousness that makes me complete and right before God's eyes, and what is that? Where do I get that?

Lynn: From God.

Mrs. G: That's right—from God, through Christ Jesus. From Jesus, whom God sent. . . .

And then in verse 17 it says, "But thanks be to God that, though you used to be slaves to sin, you wholeheartedly obeyed the form of teaching to which you were entrusted. You have been set free from sin and have become slaves to righteousness" (Romans 6:17,18 NIV).

In verse 19, this is point number five. "Just as you used to offer the parts of your body to slavery to impurity and to ever-increasing wickedness, so now offer them in slavery to righteousness leading to holiness" (Romans 6:19 NIV). . . .

That's the last part. Offer parts of your body to righteousness. Give it to the Lord. You say, "I use my hands to do good." I'm going to offer my hands to God. My hands, to do something right to bring glory to God, and not to bring it to me. I'm going to use my head—my mind—to think good thoughts, to think how can I glorify Him?

What can I do to take care of my family, to take care of my brothers and sisters, to take care of mankind, to bring good to them instead of evil, instead of bringing it to my self? So in turn, when we do help others or when we do seek God and become a slave to Him, we bring life to ourselves. . . .

So let us do that, you and I. Don't think, "Well, I'll do it when I'm twenty-five." Do it *now*. Because if you begin to sow to self—the desires of your self—that is sin, and believe me, you're old enough to be able to do that. God forbid, I don't want any of you to. Begin to sow to righteousness and Christ Jesus, to obedience to the Lord.

Obedience. You think, "Oh my parents and my teachers are so tough on me. They discipline me for doing the littlest things; this and that; this and that." You know what they're teaching you. Obedience. If you can't learn obedience to your parents, to the laws of

our land, or to your teachers, then you do *not* know
obedience. You won't even *know how* to obey God. So
that's why—because your parents and your teachers
love you—that we teach you obedience, at a young
age, so that you can be able to serve him, to obey him.
So we don't do this to be mean to you; we do it because we love you.
You all have a wonderful day. I love you. See you.
(Field Notes GCA 1/6/87)

The Bible teacher leaves the room.

Marcia:	You know she likes him; she talks about him all the time.
Sharla:	I like him as a friend.
Marcia:	"Hi, Honey!"
Sharla:	He said that! And I have two witnesses!
Samuel:	I wonder why he said that.
Sharla:	Because of what his dad said.
Samuel:	His dad told him to tell you that? (Field Notes GCA 10/20/86)
Sharla:	My mother would ground me 'till Jesus came. (Field Notes GCA 10/29/86)
Dawn:	And so then Andrea said, "Do you wanna go mess up the salad bar?" (Field Notes GCA 10/2/86)
Lynn:	How do you make a tissue dance? (pause) Put a little boogie in it.
Craig:	(groans) Ooooh.
Lynn:	I got that from Dawn and Andrea. (Field Notes GCA 1/13/87)

The students continue to talk, growing louder and louder. Sharla, Marcia, Beth, Dawn and Andrea begin to sing:

The Lord told Noah there's gonna be a floody floody.
Get those children out of the muddy, muddy.
Oh, children of the Lord.
The Lord told Noah build an arky, arky
built it of barky, barky.
It rained for forty daysies, daysies
Animals came on by twosies
Elphants and Kangaroosies, roosies.

54

At 9:10 their homeroom teacher, Mrs. Halsey, comes into the room, and they continue to sing.

Dawn: We're not finished.

Marcia: Are we going to do prayer requests and praise reports?

Their teacher says, "You sang through your praise reports." Nevertheless, she lets the students begin prayer requests, which ask God for aid, and praise reports, which thank God for help received.

Dawn: I have a major praise report. My aunt had her baby.

Mrs. H: Did she?! What did she have?

Dawn: It's a little girl. Five pounds eight ounces, twenty inches long. (Field Notes GCA 1/5/87)

Marcia: I want to pray for my mom—her kneecap is scraping something—I don't know what. She has to have a knee operation. (Field Notes GCA 2/24/87)

Andrea: My cat—she's acting real weird. I want to pray for my cat that she won't tear the house down. (Field Notes GCA 2/2/87)

Craig: My sister got kicked by a horse. She was trying to teach it how to jump barrels. (Field Notes GCA 2/2/87)

Sharla: My dad was working on a roof. My dad fell on my dog. He was slobbering and his legs were locked. But he's fine now. (Field Notes GCA 1/12/87)

Mrs. H: Hmmmm. He might have had a concussion. (Field Notes GCA 1/12/87)

Sharla: I wanna pray that my wrist would get better. (Field Notes GCA 4/20/87)

Samuel: I praise God that I'm growing. (Field Notes GCA 10/20/86)

Andrea: I'm going to get my hair cut on Saturday. (Field Notes GCA 4/7/87)

Marcia: We got to go shopping on Saturday. (Field Notes GCA 4/20/87)

Marcia: Loretta [an adult friend] asked me to go skating—my mom won't let me because she doesn't believe that Loretta asked me. So I pray that Loretta will talk to my mom. (Field Notes GCA 1/20/87)

Beth: I want to pray that we get to go to the beach. (Field Notes GCA 11/6/86)

Marcia: I praise God that Candace gets to stay with me. Sunday we're going to The Rock [Church]. Sunday from 3 to 6 to Riley City Park and an Explorers meeting. It's a picnic. (Field Notes GCA 10/17/86)

Marcia: I want to praise God that we won a basketball game. We played Riley. We won 22 to 18. (Field Notes GCA 3/3/87)

Dawn: My dad is finishing the last few chapters in his textbook that he is writing. (Field Notes GCA 2/2/87)

Marcia: I want to pray for this little boy on the Dells van. His name is John. I want to pray for him that God will just tell him to stay up front and not bother us. (Field Notes GCA 1/13/87)

Sharla: I want to pray for my sister because she's not quite all there. She doesn't play with a full deck. I have one sister who's really a brother.

Marcia: She is crazy. (Field Notes GCA 3/10/87)

Dawn: I want to pray because tonight, I have to go to the dentist, then piano, then a Girl Scouts' banquet. (Field Notes GCA 3/10/87)

Mrs. H: Let's bring all these things to the Lord. Rhonda, will you pray? (Field Notes GCA 4/7/87)

Rhonda: Father, we thank you for what you have given us, and we pray that all the prayer requests may come back as praise reports. In Jesus' name we pray, Amen.

The subject matter of this set of praise reports and prayer requests is representative of the topics discussed each day in homeroom. Overall in the seventh-grade homeroom, nearly half (47 percent) of the reports or requests concerned physical ailments; about one-fifth (18 percent) concerned experiences. Concerns for material things, competition, academic work, and jobs accounted for about 5 percent apiece. Emotional, spiritual, and environmental considerations made up about 1 percent each of the reports (9 percent had missing data; total was 139 praise reports and prayer requests for GCA's seventh graders).

After their Bible class, which takes up forty minutes—a little less than their remaining seven class periods, which are fifty minutes long—some of the seventh graders go to Math 7 class, others to algebra class. There is very little religious content in these classes, where the students learn and practice mathematical and algebraic concepts. (See chapter 9 for an analysis of the sacred and secular content of various classes.)

History 7, on the other hand, on many days can sound very similar to

Bible 7, as acknowledged by a student, who reported to her teacher that her mother "likes the history book because it goes along with what we're learning in church and what we're learning in Bible" (Field Notes GCA 10/28/86). History 7 in the A Beka curriculum is world history. Unit 1 is "The Beginning of World History and the Ancient Middle East," sub-headed "From Eden to Israel." Unit 2 is subheaded "Preparation for Christ," and unit 3 "Response to Christ, (The Middle Ages and Distortion of Christianity)" (Combee 1979).

At 10:50, the students pick up their book bags and clatter down the stairs to Mrs. Mitchell's classroom for Science 7. There is more opportunity in this class to remind the students of the conservative Christian ideology of creation and orderliness. Some class days are heavily sacred in content, and some not at all, as the students learn about "classification systems" (and "biblical Creationism"), "life processes of organisms" (and that "each organism was designed by God to live in a certain environment"), the "reproduction of organisms" (and that "the ability to reproduce is part of God's design for living things"), as well as "ecology" and "the human body" (Pinkston 1984, 99, 186).

At 11:40 they bound up the stairs and down again to the kitchen on the other side of the building. They grab lunch bags and boxes out of the refrigerator and jockey for position at the microwave. The fifth and sixth graders have lunch boxes emblazoned with Snoopy and other Peanuts characters, Return of the Jedi, the Cabbage Patch Kids, Munchie Tunes with Brunchie Bear, Garfield, Donald Duck, and Ghostbusters. The food inside is all-American fast food. The lunchroom at GCA smells like a pizza parlor every day, as small pizzas are zapped in the microwave. Microwaved French fries are also popular, and occasionally someone has microwaved fish sticks. They eat in their seats in their homerooms, while they talk loudly, the decibel level depending on the degree of supervision at the time.

After lunch, the seventh graders spend two of their fifty-minute class periods in Language 7 and Reading/Spelling 7. Mrs. Nichols has taught language arts as well as history. She has a bachelor's degree and has taught English in public schools and Catholic parochial schools. Her three children attended GCA. She said she was attracted to GCA because of Mrs. Mitchell's strong stand on "the free market society." She began by helping out at GCA, and later taught, receiving various teaching assignments, from fall 1984 through December 1986.

On this day Mrs. Nichols calls two students to the board to write a spelling word which she calls out. The first to finish wins and stays at the blackboard to take on a new challenger. Two others are called to the board simultaneously to make a sentence out of any of their vocabulary words. Then they compete at spelling and alphabetizing three spelling words (Field Notes GCA 11/25/86).

During a Language 7 class, they may diagram sentences, marking direct objects, indirect objects, and objects of prepositions, for example. They may rewrite a dialogue from their workbook, inserting quotation marks correctly; learn to use apostrophes to make possessives and contractions; learn capitalization rules; or study vocabulary words and definitions. They read stories that they have written, all competing to be the first to read. They take turns reading aloud stories from their reading book. The teacher might read, with a dramatic flair, a Sherlock Holmes story. They take quizzes on a story's content, have spelling and vocabulary tests. They grade one another's tests and are asked to recite their grades orally, while the teacher records them in her gradebook.

Some days they go to the public library, Mrs. Nichols driving the van. They choose books to read for book reports, or work on gathering information for history assignments. Once Mrs. Nichols threatened not to take them to the library anymore, because she didn't like the books that they were choosing. Rushing out of the van and into the library, the girls flocked to the YA (Young Adult) stand, and came away with books titled *Sorority Girls, Kathy Hamm Needs a Date, Ten Boy Summer* (a "Sweet Dreams Romance"), *It's No Crush, I'm In Love!, Sweet Valley High, Kidnapped!,* and *Sixty Silly Jokes You Can Play on Your Friends* (Field Notes GCA 10/3/86; 10/29/86; 3/24/87; 4/28/87).

Ms. Palmer joined the faculty as language arts teacher second semester, after Mrs. Nichols left the school. She has a bachelor's degree, a master's degree in special education, and another certification in educational testing. Her long curled blond hair, big eyes, and long dark eyelashes, which she sets off with eye makeup and rouge, make her every seventh-grade boy's dream of a teacher. Today she wears a purple blouse with a necklace shaped like a star, black slacks, and black high heels. In her class, between the various curricular activities, the students talk and giggle, and are chastised again and again by their new teacher, who usually calls them "honey," unless she is reminding them that their behavior is reminiscent of kindergarteners or second graders, and worse than the students in the public schools where she has taught.

Ms. P: There are some extremely rude people here. I'm going to bring this up to you every time you do it until you learn to act right. That does not go, kids, no matter where you are. You are in for a rude awakening. If you have school in public school next year, you're going to have to learn discipline. I know you're a tight little group, and I like that. There are a lot of positive things. But I want you to be polite to each other. (Field Notes GCA 2/2/87)

Language class is not overwhelmingly Christian or biblical in content, by any means. Some of the poems and stories are biblically oriented, as are some of the sentences and vocabulary words, which can lead to an exchange like this, when the sentence to be diagrammed is "Have you yielded your life to Christ?"

Ms. P: Good question. Have you? I haven't forgotten what I asked you to do [for Bible class]. Remember to think about "what has the Lord shown you" or "how has the Lord blessed you—yesterday or last week." (Field Notes GCA 2/3/87)

Some of the seventh graders have opted to take choral music from 12:50 to 1:30 on Tuesdays and Thursdays. Mrs. Ramsey, the music teacher, has one son in the school and a daughter who is an alumna, now attending public high school. Her husband serves as the treasurer of the school. Mrs. Ramsey has a bachelor's degree in business and a lifelong interest and talent in music, which she brings to bear in music classes for students in kindergarten through seventh grade two days a week. She supports Mrs. Mitchell as her best friend.

Physical education (PE) time is 1:30. PE is sometimes "free play" supervised by one of the teachers, who take turns. On Tuesdays and Wednesdays, it is games supervised by one of two male volunteer PE teachers. Mr. Farrell was PE teacher for just one year at GCA. You met him in chapter 1 on the playground. He was a graduate student at a local university and also held a computer class for grades five through seven twice a week at the school. (Two personal computers were borrowed for the school by a parent from his place of work.) In 1987–88, Mr. Farrell had received a graduate degree in computer education and took a full-time teaching position in a Christian school in another state.

From 2:20 to 3:00 is study hall, supervised by their homeroom teacher, except for the girls who have opted to take home economics from Mrs. Anderson on Mondays, Wednesdays, and Fridays. Mrs. Anderson has two young daughters at the school, and her husband is on the board of directors. Having earned a bachelor's degree in home economics, she teaches the subject at the school, where she strives valiantly to communicate her sense of a precisely correct way to do things to the adolescent girls. She volunteers as the yearbook photographer and is available when-ever parents are needed as drivers and helpers.

As 3:00 nears, the students load up their book bags and are allowed to go into the locker rooms and coat closets to get ready to leave. At 3:00, their parents come to pick them up. Students who live in Dells, ten miles away, ride in a van which parents take turns driving; they drop the children at a central location in the town, where other parents are waiting.

Hamlin Christian Academy (HCA) is housed in a large building which was once a car dealership. Now it is the home of the "nondenominational (independent, Pentecostal)" church and school run by Rev. and Mrs. Howell.

Founded in 1977, HCA is the only pure Accelerated Christian Educa-tion (ACE) school in the Southeastern Valley. Three others are hybrids. Maranatha Christian Academy uses A Beka in grades kindergarten through four, and teaches math in the traditional classroom way, while using ACE for other subjects in grades five through twelve. Porter Chris-tian Academy and Calvary Cross Christian Academy use BASIC materi-als which are written by ACE, but they do not use the whole ACE system of wearing uniforms, using flags to gain the attention of "monitors," and so on. Instead they house students at students' desks in age-graded class-rooms with teachers. (See also Rose 1988 for a description and analysis of a school using the ACE system.)

With forty-five students, HCA is the median school in enrollment in Southeastern Valley. At $850 for tuition, it is among the most expensive schools, but according to Mrs. Howell, they have a variety of work-for-tuition plans, and they try not to turn a student away for financial reasons.

Students wait in their cars or stand along the outside of the building, waiting for Rev. and Sister Howell to arrive. When they do, all come into the building, and Sister Howell, dressed in a bright red blouse with a bow and navy skirt (ACE's colors are red, white, and blue) greets the children. Noticing a little girl draped over an older girl's shoulder, she asks, "Is she feeling all right?" and reaches out to pat the little one (Field Notes HCA 11/7/86). One little girl is crying and hanging onto her older sister. Mrs. Howell asks about her.

Sister: I don't know. She's been crying a lot.
Mrs. H:,   Well if she needs to go home, we'll call your mother.

This is the only school where the students wear uniforms. Even the tiniest girls wear navy suits with straight skirts and jackets softened by sleeves puffed at the shoulders. The older girls accessorize these stylish stewardess-like uniforms with patterned hose—fishnet, or black with tex-tured zigzags up the back—and the highest of high heels. Some of the teenage girls have modish swept-back Farrah Fawcett hairdos. But not everyone is wearing a uniform. Some of the boys have on ACE ties; most don't. Some wear navy pants, some cords, some jeans.

At 9:15 Rev. Howell mounts the podium and speaks into a microphone.

Rev. H: OK, in your seats everybody. It's time for our day to begin.

It takes a little while for the students to settle into the folding chairs set up in rows facing Rev. Howell's high podium. They recite the pledges to the Christian flag, the American flag, and the Bible, standing with hands over hearts.

Rev. H: Well what a [rainy] day. What is that going to do to your field trip? Well, it will mean a real long recess.
Students: Yay!
Rev. H: We have several out with the flu. The flu has hit the state and the school. When I call your name tell me you are here. We have our jet engine [heater] on, so it's hard to hear, so call out loudly.

He lists the forty-five names. Several students share the same last names.

Rev. H: Let's hear it for Mary Finley and for Frank Ferguson and for Pauline Dillon who [receive ACE certificates for passing tests] today.

Three smiling students come forward and everyone applauds.

Rev. H: God Bless America—let's sing it.

Son Nicholas Howell plays the electric keyboard; a bit into the song another student climbs up to the podium and plays drums. Rev. Howell sings in a clear, strong baritone voice, with students singing and clapping along. It is a rousing version.

Rev. H: (In speaking voice) God bless America. Go to your of-fices and open your Bibles to Psalms 100. Then we'll pray and you can start your work.

The kindergarteners stay downstairs; the other children go up the stairs to their carrel-like "offices." Above the offices are colorful calendar-style pictures of flowers, birds, animals, and trees; published by ACE, they contain scripture verses that characterize Christ's qualities. Once all the children are in front of offices, at Rev. Howell's signal, they recite Psalms 100. A few have memorized it; the rest still read it. This is their memory work for the month.

Barry, a high-school-age boy, comes up a bit late and stands with his hand slung over his desk. Rev. Howell turns to him.

Rev. H: Barry, would you pray for us today?

Barry prays very quietly, ending with "in Jesus' name we pray, Amen."

Some of the students are called to the testing table in another room by Rev. Howell. Students open their PACE workbooks, published by Accelerated Christian Education, and begin to work. Some ask to go to the scoring table.

High-school-age Philip puts the Christian flag up into the hole above his desk which serves as its stand. Mrs. Howell sees it and goes over to him. He needs the "supervisor's initials" on the proper line, to show that he has finished this part of his workbook and has checked his work. Mrs. Howell takes his book and checks to see whether all the blanks are filled. She finds one which he has marked wrong with a red X, but not subsequently filled in. The blank reads: "A round muscle is called a __ ." She hands the book back to Philip, who says "OOOh" when he sees that he has overlooked this blank. Mrs. Howell later tells me that he was embarrassed to find this omission. He fills in the blank. Even though Mrs. Howell and I are still standing right next to Philip's desk, in a moment he puts up his American flag. Mrs. Howell leans over to him and he asks to go to the scoring table. She tells him he can and he does. He checks the one blank and then circles his red X, with a red pen which is kept on the scoring table and nowhere else. He goes back to his office carrel, which is a few steps directly behind the scoring table. He puts up his Christian flag. Mrs. Howell, who is still standing just a few steps way, comes over. She checks that one blank to see that it is filled in, and puts her initials in the blank.

Philip obviously knows the procedures, and seems not at all disturbed by following them. Mrs. Howell remarks, "That teaches them orderliness." Rev. Howell notes that "the ACE school is the quietest school you'll ever be in" (Field Notes HCA 10/28/86).

The students take a five-minute break every hour. Rev. Howell (and ACE) say they need it for their eyes—after an hour of close work, they need to let the eyes focus on distance. And, Rev. Howell says, "they like to talk and other things with their friends. Boyfriends and girlfriends get together" (Field Notes HCA 10/28/86). But there are other ways of taking a break. Some of the older boys help organize fund-raising paperwork and trophies. A little girl hangs around Mrs. Howell with her glasses in her hand. Mrs. Howell asks her, "May I help you?" and sends her back to her room. A little while later the same girl is standing beside the office door, and Mrs. Howell asks if she can help her. She asks again to clean her glasses, and Mrs. Howell gives her permission.

At noon, they have lunch. On good weather days, they go outside to play volleyball over the net in the front yard of the school.

At 2:55, the students are to clean their offices, mark goals made today, set goals for the next day, and tell their monitor whether they are supposed to take a test tomorrow morning so that these can be readied by the staff after the school day is over.

At 3:00, school's out.

It is graduation night for the Springfield City Christian School (SCCS) seniors. Sponsored by a large independent Baptist church in City since 1973, SCCS has 530 students in grades kindergarten through twelve, 30 teachers, and a tuition of $1495 for high school. The school also sponsors a large day-care facility. As we enter the sanctuary, we are handed a light-brown program, emblazoned with the school's logo (I Timothy 4:12: "Let no man despise thy youth; but be thou an example of the believers, inward, in conversation, in charity, in spirit, in faith, in purity") and the words "truth, honor, loyalty." The Class Verse listed on the front is II Timothy 3:14: "But continue thou in the things which thou has learned and hast been assured of, knowing of whom thou has learned them."

The huge cream-colored sanctuary is carpeted in smoke blue with cloth pew covers to match. The auditorium floor is canted so that all can see the pulpit. The organ is played loudly and triumphantly by the administrator's wife, so that it stays above the buzz of the large audience. The organist, accompanied by a five-piece brass ensemble, switches to the graduation march, "Pomp and Circumstance," as the thirty-three graduates (twelve of whom are honor students, graduating with a 3.0 [90 percent] grade point average or higher), enter. In the procession is Mr. Bradley, Associate Pastor for School Ministries, and administrator of the school. He and the others on the dais are wearing robes, master's or Ph.D. hoods, and mortar boards. The dais and lectern are white, flanked by green plants. There is a huge movie screen in the center of the stage.

An invocation is given by the Chairman of the School Operations Committee, followed by a welcome by the Pastor of Redwood Baptist

Church. Two parents come forward to give preplanned "parent testimonies."

Tall, slender Mrs. Kirk steps up to the podium. She has short blond hair and glasses. She is dressed in a navy dress under a long silver sparkly coat, with a silver necklace and earrings, and navy high heels. Amid coughs in the audience, Mrs. Kirk tells the history of her three children's sojourn in Christian school.

There were a lot of things that we started feeling in the public schools with our children. For example, when Louis was in first grade I went to school for the routine teacher's conference and when it was over she said, "I'd like to ask you a question," and I said, "Sure." She said, "Are you and your husband Christians?" And I said, "Well yes we are, but why did you ask?" And she said, "Well we have a snack time every day and Louis always bows his head and prays when he eats." So he couldn't do that anymore.

Another time was in the third grade, and he brought a test paper home. A teacher had marked his answers wrong on questions about evolution and creation. He'd marked creation, and she had marked it wrong. So I took the paper in to the teacher and I wanted her to change it. And she said, "Well, we don't teach that here; we teach the theory of evolution." And I said, "Well, that's just it; it's just a theory; it's not proven, and my son is *not* wrong." . . . And so I said, "I want it changed." And she said, "It's not going to change his grade, so it doesn't make any difference." I said "That's not the point; I don't care about the grade." So she finally agreed with me and she changed it. . . .

The children would come home and say, "We have to mark certain things on our test papers because the teachers want those as the answers, even though we know it's not right." It's not right for children to have that kind of conflict. At school they have to mark something knowing it's wrong, just to get the grade the teachers want. So it wasn't too hard, really, to choose to send the children to the Christian school.

When Mr. Bradley called me a few weeks ago and asked me to do this I asked God to give me a verse from the Bible to help express why I wanted my children here. And He gave me II Timothy Chapter 3 Verse 14 and 15. I didn't know until Sunday night that 14 is the verse the class had chosen as their class verse. But I'd like to read it to you from the Living Bible.

"But you must keep on believing the things you have been taught. You know they are true for you know that you can trust those of us who have taught you. You know how, when you were a small child, you were taught the holy Scriptures; and it is these that make you wise to accept God's salvation by trusting in Christ Jesus."

I can trust these teachers to teach my children. They don't have the conflict of what's right and wrong—one version for home and church, and another in school. I can trust the teachers to tell them what is right. . . .

I have to fully trust God to help my children make decisions because I'm not always going to be here.

She ends her testimony by making it clear that the extra time and money spent on Christian education is worth it.

Mr. Hammond, a father with mustache and sideburns and wearing a gray three-piece suit and aqua tie takes the dais to present another parent testimony. Explaining how he came to send his children to Christian school, he said that he felt "influenced from God."

This school is blessed by God. . . . The teachers here and the administrators have yielded to God's direction in teaching our children and administering the school. And God has provided the funds for the school to grow, and prosper and stay on financially sound ground. . . . I think the school also has been a tool for us to shield our children from the world we have around us, that tends to lead children into alcohol, drugs, abusive language, rock music, and even into the humanistic approach to learning, instead of using God's Word as the basis of learning. . . .

I send them to Christian school because that is preparing them to live in the real world. It is preparing them to set priorities in their lives. It is preparing them—teaching them that there is a right, and there is a wrong. I think the world today has a problem with things being right and wrong and things being in gray areas. So, with the principles that are taught here, as far as I'm concerned, our children are ready for that real world, because of what they've experienced here. . . . Graduates from here will be ready to face the future.

Like Mrs. Kirk, he agrees that the extra money spent on Christian school is worth it.

The senior class president rises to give recognitions to their sponsors. Some of his thank-yous have a humorous touch, and the audience whoops and applauds. Administrator Mr. Bradley has a big smile on his face throughout the festivities.

Following "Faith of Our Fathers" sung by the audience with the accompaniment of the organ, and a "contemporary Christian" song sung by two young girls, the salutatorian, with a large gold ribbon around his neck, gives his address, followed by speeches from the two valedictorians (one girl and one boy). They extol the virtues of a life centered on a personal relationship with Christ, characterized by integrity, diligence, self-control, and patience. This is the way to ward off the attacks of Satan. What is the answer to a wounded world—characterized by nuclear weapons, AIDS, terrorists, communism, humanists, attacks on the family, abortion? The answer is Jesus Christ.

From this moment on, any decorum or reserve is shattered by the whoops and hollers of the graduates, as now the huge movie screen comes to life with pictures of the seniors as babies and children. There are informal shots of them at school, and lots of pictures of cars. Slides of the parking lot and the lunchroom flicker by. Then come their senior pictures, the girls with black drapes across their bare shoulders, pearl necklaces, and earrings, the boys sporting bow ties.

Contemporary Christian music is played as the reflections glide across the screen. As some of the faces flash by, the seniors and the students in the audience break into loud "oohs," "yays," and laughter. The screen images of others are met with chilly silence. The show ends with pictures of class trips and a facsimile of the announcement for their graduation ceremonies.

Now the diplomas are awarded by the pastor and the school administrator, as each student comes to the middle of the dais to accept a diploma, pausing for quite some time for a professional photographer to take a picture. Just as happened with their screen images, some of the real graduates are recognized with yells; others aren't. Each of the girls accepts a red rose. Graduates meet their parents in front of the dais; the girls present them with the rose they have just received. They turn the tassels on their mortar boards to signify that they have changed status from SCCS seniors to SCCS graduates.

The senior class sponsor gives a prayer of dedication. The assembled audience sings "How Great Thou Art," and the graduates loudly move out of the auditorium, throwing off their mortar boards and robes and whooping as the organ majestically plays the recessional "Crown Him with Many Crowns" (Field Notes SCCS 6/12/87).

This brief introduction to life inside the Christian schools, coupled with the vignettes in the introduction, displays the conservative Christian parents' formal rationale for sending their children to Christian schools, and reveals the ideology the children are taught in Bible classes. It illustrates a culture which is made up of this Christian ideology, with the vocabulary and maxims of the education profession added in, and commingled with the forms and symbols of American popular culture. We will explore this mélange by first examining the conservative Christians' goal culture, which interacts with traits drawn from the existing cultures—American popular culture and the culture of the education profession—to produce Christian school cultures.

4

Christian Culture: The Christian Walk

When Springfield City Christian School parents Mrs. Kirk and Mr. Hammond were called upon to give testimony as to why they had enrolled their graduating children in Christian school years ago, their rationale was based on a comparison of the American culture versus the life they envisioned for their children. In Wallace's (1966) words, Christian schools are engaged in a "revitalization" process, endeavoring to create a "goal culture" that is different from the "existing culture." An exploration of the traits the conservative Christians would include in their goal culture in effect operationalizes their ideal culture.

The "Christian life-style" is to some degree "mythical," because no one claims to have achieved it, although all conservative Christians have an idea of what it should be. While some of the conservative Christians with whom I talked warned that their own ideal culture might be different from those of other conservative Christians, actually there were very few differences in the words they used to describe them to me. Christians of independent Baptist, charismatic, Holiness, Pentecostal, Presbyterian Church in America, and Wesleyan persuasions all painted a similar picture. One thing that differed was the version of the Bible most often used: King James for Baptist, Pentecostal, and Holiness churches; New International Version for charismatics. I have quoted from the particular version used by my various sources, noting in the citation versions other than King James.

Although the conservative Christians often advocated "walking the Christian walk" and "living the Christian life-style," all commiserated that it was impossible to create a truly Christian culture on this earth. "That would be heaven," said several. But, to approximate such an ideal, they said it would be necessary for people to be "Christlike." To learn what that would entail, "all we can do is look at the Scriptures for examples (of Christ's qualities)." They would include "love and compassion, and all the fruits of the spirit mentioned in Galatians" (Field Notes SCCS 3/11/87; GCA 11/13/86).

68

That would be heaven. Joy. Perfection. Pure Christianity? Pure Christianity is complete joy. There would be no competition. No one is judged; there is no judgment going on. You only see the fruits of the Spirit. . . . Fruits that are good and excellent. So therefore the only things that would be there, would be positive. . . .

Peace—peace that surpasses all understanding—whatever that means. We can't understand that, because we live in a chaotic world. . . .

Number one—of highest importance—would be love, the love commandment. . . . ("A new commandment I give unto you, That ye love one another; as I have loved you, that ye also love one another" [John 13:34–35]). Most things, like showing love, are done in secret anyway. You don't have to flaunt it for it to be a show of love. Jesus showed love many times quietly. . . . He didn't say "I'm going to the house of the Pharisees!" He just went. . . . For Jesus, the greatest commandment was love (Field Notes GCA 11/13/86).

The foundation of all meaningful Christian interaction is love. . . . The specific attributes that serve as the basis for [Christian] relationships are *humility, longsuffering, patience,* and *gentleness* (Ephesians 4:2). (LWCC 1984, emphasis theirs)

Thus, the conservative Christians often relied on love and the fruits of the spirit to describe the Christian ideal. They also hearkened to the beatitudes, as recited from memory by the capped and gowned graduating kindergarteners at Porter Christian Academy, sponsored by a Holiness church.

Blessed are the poor in spirit: for theirs is the kingdom of heaven.
Blessed are they that mourn: for they shall be comforted.
Blessed are the meek: for they shall inherit the earth.
Blessed are they which do hunger and thirst after righteousness: for they shall be filled.
Blessed are the merciful: for they shall obtain mercy.
Blessed are the pure in heart: for they shall see God.
Blessed are the peacemakers: for they shall be called the children of God.
Blessed are they which are persecuted for righteousness' sake: for theirs is the kingdom of heaven. (Matthew 5:3–10)

A bulletin board on Grace Christian Academy's wall spelled out the desirable qualities of a Christian. They were printed in green ink on six white paper hearts that were mounted on silver foil beside a picture of a man in armor. "Therefore, as God's chosen people, holy and dearly loved, clothe yourself with compassion, kindness, humility, gentleness, patience, be gentle and forebearing with one another (Colossians 3:12–13). Armed for VICTORY" (Field Notes GCA 9/23/88).

The golden rule had a prominent place at GCA. Mrs. Mitchell had written it on a six-foot-long piece of computer paper and posted it above the door of her science classroom. She suggested it to the math teacher for the ruler she was making on the wall in her room; "That will be the golden ruler" (Field Notes GCA 8/86). The seventh-grade homeroom teacher at GCA told her charges: "Christianity is giving to others and keeping your eyes—your heart—on the Lord" (Field Notes GCA 3/2/87).

Alongside the love, the fruits of the spirit, the golden rule, and the qualities described in the beatitudes was a desire to be separate from the world. "In our Christian walk, we are told to refrain from the works of the flesh" (Field Notes SCCS 3/11/87). "Now the works of the flesh are manifest, which are these; Adultery, fornication, uncleanness, lasciviousness, idolatry, witchcraft, hatred, variance, emulations, wrath, strife, seditions, heresies, envyings, murders, drunkenness, revellings, and such like . . ." (Galatians 5:19–21). "Be not conformed to this world" (Romans 12:2), and "Be ye not yoked together with unbelievers" (II Corinthians 6:14) were often repeated within the Christian schools, reiterating the desire to be "separate."

> We are in the world, but not of the world. . . . The Bible says it, in First Corinthians 13: "If I speak in the tongues of men and of angels, but have not love, I am a noisy gong or a clanging cymbal. And if I have prophetic powers, and understand all mysteries and all knowledge, and if I have all faith, so as to remove mountains, but have not love, I am nothing. If I give away all I have, and if I deliver my body to be burned, but have not love, I gain nothing." (I Corinthians 13:1–3 RSV) (Field Notes SCCS 3/11/87)

Christian attributes are operationalized on the report card of Springfield City Christian Schools, a large school sponsored by an independent Baptist church. The elementary report card is divided into two sides, one for scholarship, and the other for character development, which is subdivided into spiritual development, social development, and work habits. Under the spiritual aspect of character development are listed these four traits, with a box for each of the four grading periods alongside.

Shows a good attitude regardless of circumstances
Displays kindness to others
Obeys promptly and cheerfully
Displays honesty
(SCCS)

The Association of Christian Schools International markets three-by-five-inch cards with pictures of small children manifesting Christian character traits, which include:

Creativity—Doing Something in a New Way: Genesis 1:31
Joyfulness—Being Happy Inside and Out: Psalms 35:9
Tolerance—Accepting Others Even if they are Different: James 2:1
Forgiveness—Treating Someone as Though He Never Hurt Me: Colossians 3:13
Generosity—Sharing What I have with a Happy Spirit: II Corinthians 9:7
Loyalty—Supporting Someone Even When the Going Gets Tough: Hebrews 3:14
Discernment—Able to See Things as They Really Are: Hebrews 5:14
Fairness—Treating Others Equally: I Timothy 5:21b
Self-Control—Doing Something Even When I Don't Feel Like It: I Corinthians 9:25
Orderliness—Everything in Its Place: I Corinthians 14:40
Diligence—Working Hard to Accomplish a Task: Proverbs 22:29
Patience—Waiting with a Happy Spirit: James 5:11.

Likewise, ACE sells "inspiring character posters featuring forty of the Character Traits of Jesus." With scenes of nature in the background, each one lists a desirable attribute of the Christian, with an excerpt from scripture. A person should strive, besides manifesting some of the character traits noted by ACSI, to be honest, truthful, sincere, gentle, humble, peaceful, merciful, courageous, fearless, virtuous, sincere, friendly, committed, equitable, optimistic, appreciative, responsible, observant, flexible, resourceful, perseverant, consistent, decisive, determined, purposeful, confident, prudent, thorough, efficient, available, cooperative, submissive, punctual, and attentive.

And so, the picture emerges—not surprising to anyone familiar with Christian ideology—of Christians whose ideal goal culture would be one where everyone is Christlike, loving, compassionate, not competitive, unconcerned with the things of this world, and separated from wrongdoing and unbelievers. A final mark of the Christ-like person would be humility.

Scripture is also clear that God wants us to be characterized by humility; He promises that "he who humbles himself will be exalted" (Luke 18:14). Humility is accepting our creaturely status and our dependence on God. It is the recognition that apart from God we can do nothing, that outside of Christ we are lost sinners. Humility is . . . resisting our sinful desire to be number one and gratefully subordinating ourselves to God's will. Humility is knowing our rightful place (Joosse 1987, 27).

Although most of the Christ-like attributes to which the Christians aspire are considered admirable by the rest of America, this emphasis on humility points the way to a major point of difference between the American existing culture and the Christian goal culture.

Ideological Boundaries: The Christian Sense of Self

When people are engaged in the revitalization process of creating a new culture, they must make decisions about what to approve and what to shun. How do the conservative Christian administrators and teachers decide what to keep and what to eschew from the cultural surround? What informs the decisions made within the Christian schools? Ideas at the highest level of their hierarchy of values draw a boundary line that separates acceptable traits from unacceptable ones. The most basic of these premises—those regarding the eternal life of the human being— were delineated in the statement of faith. A more subtle idea is the particular view of the self valued by the conservative Christians, which is a key to understanding the choices made within Christian schools. To explore this ideological bedrock, we will make comparisons to other cultures, for this is the way anthropology shines a light onto cultural form; a look at alternatives—at what might be—throws into relief what is. We will be comparing what have been called "indigenous psychologies" and "implicit personality theories"—alternative views of the self.

THE SENSE OF SELF: ALTERNATIVE
CULTURAL POSSIBILITIES

Let us start with a dichotomy between societies which have an "individualistic" or a "collective" sense of self;[1] later we will expand this to a trichotomy by including the conservative Christians' view of self.[2] The categories should be seen as ideal types that serve to broadly characterize various cultural forms.

American society is said to be an individualistic one (Bellah, et al. 1985; Hsu 1972; Luckmann 1967; Marsella 1985; Tocqueville 1969). Our society has reified the self.[3] The manifestations of an individualistic sense of self are numerous. Take competition, for example, which begins with Vic Braden's Tennis for Two-Year-Olds, continues to T-Ball, Little League, and on into the adult corporate world. Individual achievement is prized and is cause for pride and reward from early on. A visit to the house of a friend who has a child is likely to be an exercise in watching the child performing—doing whatever it is the child is doing at a particular developmental stage. Our legendary movie lines, repeated over and over, reflect individualism: "Frankly, my dear, I don't give a damn," says Rhett Butler egotistically (in response to Scarlett O'Hara's own egotism).

Self-actualization is a way to find meaning in life. Problems in self-actualization are considered mental illness. We Americans are quite familiar with this individualism, which characterizes modern Western societies but which is said to be exceptional among the world's cultures (Dumont 1985, 1986; Marsella 1985; Wikse 1977).

A less familiar alternative sense of self is found in collective cultures. Some examples are: some Native American groups; peoples of the Pacific; and the Hutterites, the Amish, and subcultures within Appalachia. A look at various aspects of these two ways of being serves to clarify the dichotomy.

In individualistic societies, there is a task orientation, as opposed to the person orientation which is common in collective societies, where there is an overriding concern with making things go smoothly within the group. What this means is, if you are confronted with the choice between accomplishing a task *and* hurting someone's feelings, versus *not* accomplishing a task *and not* hurting someone, you will tend to choose the former if you are a member of an individualistic society.

The latter choice is exemplified by anecdotes from the Appalachian mountain region of the United States. For example, a Presbyterian minister tells of wanting to fix the road to his newly assigned church. With the elders of the church, he discusses getting slag, a byproduct of coal mining, from the coal companies free of charge. Subsequently he has the slag laid onto the road, and on the first rainy day, it turns to a slimy, slippery mess which eventually has to be bulldozed away. He asks the elders, "Why didn't you tell me this would happen?" They reply, "Well, Reverend Weller, you seemed to want to do it, and we didn't want to hurt your feelings" (Weller 1965; see also Dumont 1986, 106, 160, 260 for discussion of the primacy of relations between human and human in collective societies, versus the primacy of relations between human and objects in individualistic societies.)

The modes of identity associated with these two orientations differ, as well. Middle America, especially in recent years, has been noted for its expressions of selfhood.

The common sense of conscious reason which has its loci in individual organisms, proposes a sense of separation. Consciousness separates men from each other, each man in solitude behind his own eyes,
each one imprisoned by his own skin, each enclosed alone between
the dates of his birth and of his death. The common sense of separation endorses the common sense of self-sufficiency and autonomy,
notions that are sanctified virtually to the point of apotheosis in
Western capitalist society. (Rappaport 1976, 33)

Political theorist John Wikse (1977, 1, 2, 6, 9), describes the American
ideology as viewing "the self as private property." "We can think of ourselves as self-sufficient, self-reliant, self-actualized, and self-possessed." It
is a "a mode of self-consciousness" which celebrates the "freedom of the
solitary, private man," and which "emphasizes extreme individuality as
the genuine foundation for being oneself."[4] "In the extreme it is the fantasy
of the self-sufficiency of the individual, the project to complete and contain
all meaning within the separate self."[5]

In collective societies, on the other hand, one's identity is ultimately
bound up with the community; the self is a product of the collectivity. Kai
Erikson (1976, 86) discusses the embeddedness of the self in the collectivity in Appalachia. "One's stature in the community as well as one's inner
sense of well-being is derived largely from the position one occupies in a
family network [and in peer groups] and to step out of that embracing
surround would be like separating from one's own flesh." People invest
much of themselves in the commonality, and become "absorbed by it."
"The larger collectivity around you becomes an extension of your own
personality, an extension of your own flesh."[6] (See also Hostetler and
Huntington 1967 re the Hutterites.)

Dorothy Lee (1986, 12) would label this the "open self." "In such
societies, though the self and the other are differentiated, they are not
mutually exclusive. The self contains some of the other, participates in the
other, and is in part contained within the other." The difference between
the individualistic and collective identities has been likened to the difference between two eggs hard-boiled together in a pan, and two eggs fried
together sunny-side up. The egg whites (identity) stay separate in the first
case, and merge(s) in the second. (Although, just as the egg yolks remain
separate in both cases, so do both kinds of societies recognize each person
as a separate entity.)[7]

A whole passel of traits goes with a society's mode of identity. For
example, an indirect style of communication, which anthropologist
George Hicks (1976) calls the "ethic of neutrality," accompanies the
collective orientation. In parts of Appalachia, a person may not directly

ask, "How much did that new car cost?" Instead, he might say, "I bet a car like that cost a right smart," or "You can't get a car like that for $200." And the owner of the car can answer "Yep," or "Nope," or "It cost __ dollars," or not answer at all. The same ethic applies to controversial subjects and to verbal confrontation in general. It is a " 'round Robin Hood's barn" circumlocutory way of communicating, letting the person questioned have his head, leaving the reply up to him. (See also Briggs 1970 concerning the Inuit [Eskimo] use of this form of communication.)

Within the collective mode, it is not desirable to step out, to be recognized, to set yourself apart as different from—perhaps better than—your group. Philosophy professors have noted that it is difficult to teach philosophy in the traditional way to Appalachian students, because causing them to criticize one another's thinking is like searching for the philosopher's stone (Acquaviva 1980; Bogert 1980; Humphrey 1980). The same trait is noted for the !Kung San, hunters and gatherers of southern Africa, among whom arrogance and pride are denigrated (Lee 1984; Thomas 1959).

Competition among individuals is hardly compatible with the collective mode. The inhabitants of the Trobriand Islands, near New Guinea in the Pacific Ocean, were so noncompetitive that although missionaries easily taught youngsters to play basketball, they could not teach them to keep score. The children had no reason for wanting to learn; they did not care who won (Lee 1959). When I relate this example to my middle-American students, they ask, "Then why did they want to play?"

Mental illness in cultures such as these is not likely to be defined as a lack of self-actualization. More common is separation anxiety, which can occur when members of the collective are separated for some reason, or running amok, which sometimes occurred in Inuit cultures when closeness to people and repression of hostile feelings seemed to combine to produce a type of short-lived hysteria.

Obviously, cultures with these differing views of the self manifest different goals in their child-rearing. Hence, it is not surprising that American children meet with challenges, competition, and rewards for individual achievement early on.

It is probably necessary to convince the American reader that it is possible to have children who are *not* individualistic and competitive. Taking a cross-cultural perspective, we see that examples abound. Edward T. Hall (1976) says that "culture has always dictated where to draw the line separating one thing from another." The cultures we are labeling individualistic "cut the apron strings" from the child's nurturing group.

The collective cultures do not; people grow away from childhood, but not away from the group. Hall's examples are China, Japan, traditional Jewish families of central Europe, Arab villagers, the Spanish of North and South America, and Pueblo Indians of New Mexico. (See also Johnson 1985 concerning Japan.)

How are children raised to have a collective consciousness? They are rarely alone; often they can find refuge with any adult in the group as a momentary surrogate mother or father. They do not have things of their own. It is only in modern Western or westernizing cultures that newborn babies are brought home in their own car seats, in their own clothes, and put to sleep in their own beds, in their own rooms, surrounded by their own toys. A !Kung mother does give her baby some beads; when the baby grows to a toddler, she is encouraged and caused to give them away, setting her in her culture's lifelong pattern of sharing and reciprocity.

Child-rearing styles which produce or encourage the rugged individualist as opposed to the collective adult are well depicted in Margaret Mead's film series "Four Families," portraying farm families in India, Canada, Japan, and France. Each of the families has a one-year-old baby with one or two older siblings. At the time, in the 1950s, only one of the four families' babies, the Canadian, had her own bed in her own bedroom, with her own toys.

Scenes of the mothers bathing baby showed that the Indian mother washed her baby as if he were a rag doll or an extension of herself. The baby was not expected to resist his mother's motions with his own little arms and legs, and he did not. The Canadian baby, on the other hand, had to be persuaded to leave her toys in the care of her two older brothers and come away to take her bath. While she was in her little plastic tub, she grasped the washcloth. Her mother entreated her, "Give me your washcloth; please give it to me. Now give me your washcloth." She finally relinquished the washcloth when asked nicely by her mother, and as her mother tugged on it. The Canadian baby was not perceived as being bad; she was asserting her individuality and ownership, as she was expected by her culture to do. The Canadian mother recognized a legitimacy to the baby's actions, and her entreaties reflect that the washcloth (and many other things) belong to, and are under the control of, the baby. (I am reminded of mothers who tell of impatiently waiting while their toddlers decide what to wear to day care.)

At the risk of oversimplifying the world's diversity, alternative cultural possibilities may be understood by delineating this dichotomy of the sense of self and the way it is connected to other cultural traits (see table 5.1).

Table 5.1 Alternative Cultural Orientations

	COLLECTIVISM	INDIVIDUALISM	CHRISTOCENTRISM
Identity:	"Embedded" in the collective	Self: independent, autonomous, atomistic "Do your own thing" Self-reliant Self (and others)	Bent to God "I can do nothing myself" (without God/Christ/Holy Spirit)
Locus of loyalty:	Family and community		God/Christ/Holy Spirit (Jesus–Others–You = JOY)
Relations with others:	Person-orientation Relation to people important	Task-orientation Relation to tasks and things important; "In" the world	Separate from the world (but some are apologists for materialism)
	Recognition not desirable Competition not desirable	Recognition desirable Competition desirable—a motivator	Can be anointed by God to do his will Competition not desirable; fruits of the spirit desirable
Communication:	Indirect: "ethic of neutrality"	Direct	Direct
Celebrations:	Of the history of the community	Of personal life passages and achievements	Of Christians' relationship to God/Christ/Holy Spirit
Child-rearing:	Don't "cut the apron strings"	Cut the apron strings	Cut the apron strings from people; tied to God/Christ/Holy Spirit
View of human nature:	Dependent upon culture's particular ideology	A product of inheritance and environment	Sin nature

THE CHRISTIAN SENSE OF SELF:
CHRISTOCENTRISM

One way to deny the individualistic self is to "submerge" it in favor of a collectivity. But the conservative Christian sense of self is neither a collective one, nor is it one sharing the characteristics of the middle American individualism described above.[8] This is an arena, in fact, in which the conservative Christians see themselves on a collision course with American mainstream culture. They label what we have called individualism as *humanism,* and find it antithetical to their ideology. The conservative Christians sometimes refer to their desired state of being as *Christocentric*—centered on Christ. Let us compare Christocentrism to modern American individualism in the same way that we have just compared individualism to collectivism.

The successfully Christocentric person is not embedded in a collective. Neither is he autonomous and independent; he will say, in fact, "I can do nothing myself." He recognizes the existence of his own will and self, but wishes this self to be "bent to God." The conservative Christian educators specifically object to public schools' emphasis on "make[ing] your own choice" and "values clarification" (Field Notes GCA 9/29/87).

The desired place of the self is expressed in an illustration from a school handbook (see figure 5.1), which is accompanied by this poem:

When I am led by the Holy Spirit,
I am mighty in spirit.
Every person must come
to the place where he
submits his mind as
the servant of his spirit.
(DCS, 13, from Schindler
and Pyle 1979, 49)

Doing God's will was expressed every morning in the faculty prayer at Grace Christian Academy in words like these: "We would die to our will, Father, and just let you work through us" (Field Notes GCA 4/20/87).

The Bible lesson described in chapter 3 exhorts the seventh graders not to "obey self and sin," but to "obey God; be a slave to God" (Field Notes GCA 1/6/87). " 'I hope to see my children grow up to surrender their lives to the Lord,' " says a parent (quoted in Ammerman 1987, 167). The GCA administrator often exhorted parents to come see how their children were "growing in the admonition of the Lord." In a more vernacular

MY SPIRIT

HOLY SPIRIT

WILL
MIND
EMOTION

BODY

Figure 5.1 When I Am Led by the Holy Spirit (Reprinted, by permission from Claude E. Schindler, Jr. and Pacheco Pyle. *Educating for Eternity.* © 1979, by Association of Christian Schools International.)

idiom, a teacher who was praising two graduating seniors said, "They have really sold out to the Lord" (Field Notes MCA 6/19/87).

"Dying to self" is an expression often heard within the conservative Christian realm. Tracts explaining "The Key to a Victorious Christian Life" give as the number one stricture "Die daily. I Corinthians 15:31 (I protest by your rejoicing which I have in Christ Jesus our Lord, I die daily), and II Corinthians 4:10 (Always bearing about in the body the dying of the Lord Jesus, that the life also of Jesus might be made manifest in our body)." Letters to the editors of Christian magazines make clear that "the central teaching of Jesus Christ and His Word is that the self must be crucified. . . ." (Focus on the Family 1987a, 24).

The locus of loyalty for the Christocentric person is to be Christ himself, not his own self, and not a community. "The individual soul receives eternal value from its filial relationship to God, in which relationship is also found human fellowship" (Dumont 1986, 30). The modern-day cliché for this was given to me by a parent from GCA. "J-O-Y sums it up," she said. "Jesus—Others—You, and you can't have JOY unless you have the letters in that order—with Jesus first" (Interview PC, 8/3/87).

When we are at ACE conventions we sing the song "The Family of God." It is printed onto the convention program for those who don't know it by heart.

> I'm so glad I'm a part of the family of God,
> I've been washed in the fountain, cleansed by His blood!
> Joint heirs with Jesus as we travel this sod,
> For I'm part of the fam'ly, the fam'ly of God. . . .
> (Field Notes ACE 11/10–11/11/86, from Gaither and
> Gaither 1970)

The song points up the fundamental difference between Christianity, and, for example, the Confucianism of traditional China and Japan, where the real family is the object of piety. For conservative Christians it is not the real family to which loyalty and filial piety is owed, but the Family of God, and ultimately only to the triune God himself. The weight of authority granted to anyone else is derived authority; family status granted to anyone else is derived family. (See also Bellah 1970.)[9]

Indeed, today's conservative Christians say that you can depend on no human being; you must depend on God (Jesus) alone. Even the Body of Christ—saved Christians who "will be raptured out when Jesus comes"—cannot be depended upon, because all have a sin nature. Jesus, because he was the Son of God, is the only mortal ever to live on earth who had no sin nature. The conservative Christians find support in the scriptures for the belief that God, Jesus, and the Holy Spirit are the only ones on whom you can depend.

> He that loveth father or mother more than me is not worthy of me; and he that loveth son or daughter more than me is not worthy of me. (Matthew 10:37; see also Luke 14:26)

Students at GCA are told that they cannot depend on *themselves,* or on *any other person.* They cannot depend on their brothers and sisters, on their fathers, on their mothers, or even on their peers in the church. They must come to depend, ultimately, on God alone. This was reiterated in Bible 7 class.

We don't cling to man—man will always fail us. We are like a ball of clay, or like jello. . . . We must be *totally* dependent on the Lord. (Field Notes GCA 5/5/87)

The seventh grade homeroom and Bible teacher recalled the story of Job to her students. Job had lost home and family.

Do you remember Job? The guy who had everything taken away from him—and how he still loved the Lord?

What if your mother and father were killed, and everybody in your family was killed, you had no money, you had no house, everything in your house was destroyed—and there you are. OK? You're homeless, there's no income, you don't have your family to fall back on. Would you wonder where God was? . . .

I don't know if I could say—"the Lord giveth and the Lord taketh away; and if that's what you want, you can have it, Father"—that would be real hard. . . . But the Lord says that's where we have to come—we should be able to give everything away—and only cling to him. . . . (Field Notes GCA 3/3/87)

A substitute Bible teacher told a group of high-school students at Baptist-sponsored Abundant Life Christian Academy, "Your mother is your best friend outside of Jesus" (Field Notes ALCA 3/18/87). The titles of the children's books sold at Christmastime by Willie George, a popular charismatic Christian figure for children, included *God Is my Best Friend* and *God Is Never Too Busy to Listen.*

Of course, this Christocentrism is not new for the conservative Christians. St. Augustine said in *The Confessions:* "You have made us for Yourself, and our hearts are restless until they find peace in You." In this, the conservative Christians are also descendents of Calvin, who maintained "with iron consistency the complete impotence of man in the face of the omnipotence of God" (Dumont 1985, 115; Calvin 1989).[10]

In fact, in the history of the Judeo-Christian tradition we find the seeds of *both* Christocentrism and modern Western culture's individualism.

Origins of Individualism and Christocentrism

Thinkers who have pondered the evolution of the sense of self have posited that the collective orientation came first, and have found in Christianity the wellspring of the individualistic mode (Dumont 1985, following Mauss; Mauss 1985; Niebuhr 1960; Schlossman 1906; see also Beteille 1983; LaFontaine 1985; MacFarlane 1978). Some locate the birth of the worth of the individual (as opposed to the "community") in Jeremiah's suggestion that, after the destruction of the temple of Jerusalem, "Jahweh might not be confined to his sacred abode but might visit the individual in exile" (Smith 1968, 253; see also Skinner 1922). Before that time, the individual was "related to God only insofar as he [was] a member of the covenant community" of Israel (Smith 1968, 253). In his time, Jesus is said to have addressed "a dual emphasis on the individual at one pole, and the community of individuals, at the other." This duality is carried forward by the teachings of Paul, and "all later Christian thought has shown the results of [this] tension" (Smith 1968, 255). But individuality ultimately holds sway. Notwithstanding that individuals are members of "the family of God," it is thought that "each individual remains known as such to God; there is no melting or blending of individuals into each other. In this sense, for Christianity, individuality remains an ultimate trait" (Smith 1968, 262). The importance of the *individual's* relationship to God continued in the works of Augustine and Thomas Aquinas.

Luther "placed a new emphasis upon the individual's confrontation with God through the Bible rather than through an authoritative institution" (Smith 1968, 260).[11] Luther thus furthered the cause of privatization by breaking from the necessity for the priestly link between God and humans (Dumont 1985; Troeltsch 1960; Wikse 1977).

Calvin took a sidestep from the self-orientation which had accompanied the individualization of Christianity.[12] "To Calvin the chief point is not the self-centered personal salvation of the creature, . . . but it is the Glory of God" (Troeltsch 1960, 583). For Calvin "the sin of pride is the central obstacle to human organization" (Wikse 1977, 87–88). In Calvin's idea of the soul's predestination for heaven or hell, even an elect "individual has no value of his own; but as an instrument, to be used for the tasks of the Kingdom of God, his value is immense" (Troeltsch 1960, 589).

During the Enlightenment, Immanuel Kant moved farther toward positing the autonomy of the individual will than the Reformers (and today's conservative Christians) would have liked, by declaring, "Dare to use your own reason" (Smith 1968, 261). The evolution of individualism and Christocentrism continued side by side, so that today, as the conservative Christians see it, the battle lines are drawn between "Do your own thing" and "I can do nothing myself (without Christ)."

We have seen that "man-in-relationship-to-God" is the very basis of the Christian's identity and view of human nature (Dumont 1985); this is especially true for the conservative Christians, who define a Christian as having a personal relationship with Christ. How is this relationship attained? Several metaphorical relationships with the divine lie at the base of the identity gained in conservative Christianity.

Metaphors to Describe (and Bring About) the Desired Relationship with God

Metaphors embody a process by which humans can take on a "new self." "Metaphorical thinking is constitutive of our selfhood," M. Brewster Smith (1985) asserts, because, following Lakoff and Johnson (1980), he sees that human thinking as a whole is metaphorical. Perhaps the use of language itself pushed humans along this track, for language separates the thinker, who is the subject, from the object of his thought. The use of metaphor ameliorates the separation; the subject takes the point of view of the other at the object end of the copula. The process of identification involves moving "from the preoccupation with the predicate back across the copula to an understanding of the subject." Metaphors can provide identity to "inchoate (i.e., inadequately identified) subjects" (Fernandez 1974, 122, 129; see also Ricoeur 1979).

I heard several metaphors and similes used to explain the nature of humans and the desired relationship between God and humankind: "Man is a worm"; "Become like little children"; "I am a puppet of the Lord"; "We are like sheep"; "I am a bondslave for God."

"MAN IS A WORM." The Christian view of the self begins with a lowly sinner. He is "wretched, and miserable, and poor, and blind, and naked" (Revelation 3:17). He is a worm. "How much less man, that is a worm, and the son of man, which is a worm?" (Job 25:6). This verse is accompanied by the following "teaching" in the Institute for Creation Research's (1987) *Days of Praise* magazine:

> First, the worm teaches us that man is insignificant in comparison to God. . . . What is man in comparison to God? It is no wonder that Bildad exclaims, "How then can man be justifed with God?" (Job 25:4)

How indeed, can man be justified with God? How can the desired relationship between a human and the deity be accomplished?

The worm also teaches us that Christ was willing to become as lowly as we in order to save us. . . . [In Psalm 22:6 David exclaims:] "But I am a worm, and no man, a reproach of men, and despised of the people." David compared Christ to a helpless, powerless, down-trodden worm; unnoticed and despised! What a contrast between the "I AM" and "I am a worm." On the cross, Christ became lower than the lowest man. He took our place, became our substitute and sacrifice. Christ is God's answer to Bildad's question about justification and holiness. (ICR 1987)

To come into what the conservative Christians take to be the right relationship with God, then, it is necessary to accept one's status as a "worm," or at least, as a "child."

"BECOME LIKE LITTLE CHILDREN."

"Who is the greatest in the kingdom of heaven?" He called a little child and had him stand among them. And he said: "I tell you the truth, unless you change and become like little children, you will never enter the kingdom of heaven. Therefore, whoever humbles himself like this child is the greatest in the kingdom of heaven." (Matthew 18:1–4)

Quoting this scripture at several faculty meetings, Mrs. Mitchell said, "We should become trusting, lowly, loving, forgiving," like a child. These were the qualities a Christian school should teach, she continued. She ended with this plea: ". . . I praise God for allowing us to work with these children. If we can become daily more like them . . ."(GCA Faculty Meeting 12/2/86).

We have all heard the commonplace metaphor "I am a child of God," but the conservative Christians add a new dimension to it. For before people are saved, they are the devil's children.

There are a lot of good people who are lost. But that doesn't change the fact that the devil is their father. The devil was our father, until we got saved. . . .

Jesus is the son of God, but we are, too, just as much. We are the children of God. We are the sons and daughters of God. We are the legitimate sons and daughter of God. (Field Notes MCA 2/6/87)

"I AM A PUPPET/SHEEP OF THE LORD." In a concert presented at Grace Christian Academy, two Christian singers, who sang in Christian coffee-houses as well as in schools, sang an original song:

> Once I was a rambler
> in this world of woe
> Never knowing, which way I should go.
> Satan was my master, and
> I was his slave
> 'til the day when I heard my Savior's call.
>
> Christ is the greatest puppeteer
> I'm not ashamed to say
> He pulls my every string
> He guides my every way.
> Yes I'm a puppet of the Lord
> But it's totally my choice
> He bore my sin
> Now I'm born again
> That's why I can rejoice.
> (Field Notes GCA 4/14/87, from
> Amason 1990)

"Obey the shepherd" was the message of the Musical Graduation Program at GCA entitled "We Like Sheep." "We are like sheep; we follow our leader, our savior" (Field Notes GCA 5/13/88, from Hill 1987).

Many conservative Christians believe that to truly come into the right relationship with God, it is necessary to become a "bondslave for God."

"I AM A BONDSLAVE FOR GOD." The crux of the Christian message (as put forward in Romans), and this frequently used metaphor—"bondslave for God"—were explained in the Bible 7 class described in chapter 3. The teacher joined old ways of phrasing the message—old metaphors from the Bible—with newer, more colloquial idioms.[13] The metaphors she used to exhort the students into the desired relationship with God included:

> You're a slave to self;
> We should no longer be slaves to sin;
> You are slaves to the one whom you obey;
> You're a slave to God;
> Offer yourself as a slave to obedience;

You have been set free from sin and have become slaves to righteous-
ness (Romans 6:17–18 NIV);
I'm a new self;
I'm a new creation.

It is no accident that self and sin are equated—"You are a slave to self;
you are a slave to sin"—for self-concern is sin to the conservative Christians. Concern with self is, in effect, idolatry (Carter 1986). Dr. James
Dobson, a psychologist with broad appeal throughout the conservative
Christian movement, discusses the "tyranny of the self."[14] He says that
the Christian faith

> offers the only way of life which can free us from the tyranny of the
> self. Make no mistake about it. The human ego is a cold-blooded
> dictator. When it is unsatisfied, it can paralyze its victim, destroying
> every vestige of confidence and initiative. When it is pampered, on the
> other hand, its thirst and greed merely become ever more insatiable.
> Unlike the appetite for food, water, sex, and other physiological re-
> quirements of the body, the need for self-esteem becomes more de-
> manding as it is gratified. The principles of Christianity can free us
> from this egotistical tyranny. (Dobson nd)

> Bondage to God is voluntary on our part. As His bondservants, we are
> to walk in His will and be used by Him in the carrying out of His
> Divine plan for mankind. In doing so, we are made free, and His desire
> for joy, peace, and happiness in our lives is fulfilled. (LWCC ndb)

Conservative Christians believe that humans are free to choose their
master, and to reap the subsequent rewards or punishments. (They are
free to do so after the "age of accountability" has been reached, that is.
Most believe that before that, children, even though they are born with
"sin natures," will go to heaven if they die "unsaved.")
James McKeever (1986), editor of *End-Times News Digest (END)*,
writes what it means to be a bondslave of God. He uses as the basis of his
discussion scriptures from Deuteronomy 15:12–18, Exodus 21:1–6,
Luke 2:25–35, Revelation 7:1–3, 9:2–4 and Philippians 2:5–11.

> An even better name for "bondslave" would probably be "God's
> Volunteer Permanent Slave." . . .

> It would be almost impossible for most people to conceive of a free
> person walking up to a slave master and volunteering to become a
> permanent slave. . . . that is precisely what God asks us to do . . .

those who know God well realize that it is the only path to victory and an overcoming life. . . .

For a person to voluntarily become a slave, he was voluntarily making a commitment to die for his master, if his master wanted him to die, to have no possessions except what the master gave him, to have no discretionary spending money of his own, to have no time of his own and no rights at all. (McKeever 1986; see also ICR's *Days of Praise* 4/9/88)

Thus the conservative Christians' path to the right relationship to God (and rewards in this life and salvation in the next), is paved with voluntary submission of human will to the will of God. Then, by God's grace, a person is saved.

After the saving, some of the same metaphors, and some different ones, are used to describe the relationship with God. There is a before-and-after quality to the metaphors. Aristotle said, "To adorn, borrow metaphor from things superior; to disparage, borrow from things inferior" (Fernandez 1977, 104). The reader might then expect that the "before" metaphors would be of the disparaging variety, and the "after" of the superior variety, as is the case, for example, in the African Fang cult of Bwiti. Here, the supplicants end a ritual with the metaphor *bi ne banzie*—we are angels (Fernandez 1977). But in Christianity, things are not that simple; the disparaging tone remains. For humanity does not become an angel or like a god—it remains a worm. But at the same time, the saved individual becomes one of the "King's Kids" (Field Notes 1/28/87). "Daniel was God's vessel," noted the seventh-grade history teacher, as the class read a chapter about Assyria, Babylonia, and Persia; the teacher noted that "Daniel was God's vessel. Each of you and me, . . . will be a vessel of God, used by God, even if we don't realize it. But Daniel was blessed because he knew" (Field Notes GCA 11/25/86).

To summarize, the process of being saved could be glossed by several metaphors conservative Christians use to describe their relationship with the divine.

Before Salvation	*After Salvation*
I am a worm	I am a worm
I am wretched, miserable, poor, blind and naked	I am wretched, miserable, poor, blind, and naked
	I am like a child
I am a slave to sin	I am a slave to obedience
	I am a slave to righteousness
I am a slave to self	I am a bondslave for God

I am the devil's child

I am a child of God
I am a King's kid
I am God's vessel
I am a new self
I am a new creation

The Paradox: Bondage versus Freedom

My own expression for what we have here discussed under the rubric of Christocentrism was *no self,* for that is how I perceived it—a denial or negation of self. But just as people who have grown up in collective cultures do not see themselves as denying an individualistic self, neither do the Christians see their denial of self as a loss of freedom. "The eternal purpose of God is also holy and wise and does not deprive man of freedom (Luke 22:22; Acts 2:23; 4:27, 28; John 1:12, 13; Philippians 2:12, 13)" (HCS). The conservative Christians themselves see their view of the self as a paradox.[15] "By submission we are made free. . . . Our "old man" dies, and we are set free from the jurisdiction and power of sin. "We are to reckon ourselves as dead to sin and alive to God in Christ Jesus." (LWCC ndb)

While it is easy to see Christocentrism and the rules that accompany it as *limiting* freedom, the conservative Christians see it as freeing. (See also Ammerman 1987, 195ff). A perhaps more practical or down-to-earth view of the freedom that comes from dying to self and becoming a bondslave for God is "our freedom comes from having these decisions made" (Cumbey 1983). Or, as kindergartener Sandra said, "I never have to think about it; I know" (Field Notes GCA 3/5/87).

> Preacher: You see sin is the opposite of a slave. The sin nature is rebellion. The slave nature is "Hey, I wanna do something. Tell me what it is you want me to do. I am a useful instrument." You may not know it, but you enjoy being told what to do. We in America have that humanistic mentality of being able to do what you want, when you want, so long as you don't hurt anybody else. And it's pandemonium; it's chaos. Your human nature *loves* to be in control and under submission. And to be under control, you gotta be a slave, and to be a slave you gotta know that you're owned.
>
> Audience: Isn't that because God has everything in order, and we by nature wanna be orderly?
>
> Preacher: Exactly. Well put. (Ault and Camerini 1988)

Why Become a Bondslave for God?

Why would anyone want to become a bondslave for God, especially when surrounded by the "free-spirit" selves of American society? (This is unlike primitive cultures with collective selves, where there is but one choice.) "It's the Lord's will" worked well in times when nature seemed more nearly omnipotent and inexplicable. But in today's America, technology and the cultural bent toward individualism combine to make it something the conservative Christians must constantly look to, and teach their children well. What are Christians gaining from this relationship with their God?

In the Christian ideology, the most important gain, of course, is salvation to a life of eternity in heaven. The alternative is eternal damnation in the lake of fire of hell. But the modern brand of conservative Christianity is not all "pie in the sky." For if you walk the Christian walk, and bend your self to God's will, then you may ask God for what you need on this earth. All of the Christians I heard, whether Baptist or charismatic, taught this to their students. We will note, too, in chapters to come, that while all glory is to go to God, some glory inevitably adheres to the saved human.

Manifestations of Christocentrism

Being a bondslave for God is supposed to be played out in many ways within the walls of the Christian schools. It means that the individual's will should be bent to God's will; thus it serves to denigrate "going by your own conscience or feelings." It means that all should "give God the Glory," and let God "lead, guide, and direct" every action in their own lives, and in the life of the school.

Being Christocentric

The Christian idea of the self and its relationship to God is in conflict with American mainstream individualism. To continue to compare the two modes of thought, table 6.1 summarizes differences with regard to where the two locate the source of power, how they explain events, and the grounds they use for making decisions.

"TO GOD BE THE GLORY"

For the conservative Christians, glorifying the self is a short definition of the despised humanism. "What was the main concern of the Assyrian kings?" asked one of the questions devised by seventh graders to quiz one another in history class. "To glorify themselves," came the answer. "That's a good question," noted the teacher. "The roots of humanism were back then" (Field Notes GCA 11/6/86).

For the conservative Christians, "I can do nothing myself," and its converse, "all things are possible in Christ," express the desired relationship between their own egos and God. The illustration in figure 6.1 depicts the desired conservative Christian "death of the self" based on Galatians 2:20: "I am crucified with Christ: nevertheless I live; yet not I, but Christ liveth in me: and the life which I now live in the flesh I live by the faith of the Son of God, who loved me, and gave himself for me." (See Ammerman 1987, 193ff. concerning "powerlessness and power among believers.")

Since God is the locus of power, and God's will is the explanation for events, it is necessary to "give God the glory" for all things, great and small. A school handbook says: "All of the activities of the Christian must be subordinated to the glory of God who indwells us (I Corinthians 8:9, 12–13, 10:31)" (Ebenezer Christian School). It is an ideal which finds expression often in conservative Christian conversation. At an Accelerated Christian Education convention, founder Donald Howard periodically proclaimed "to God be the Glory." Workshop leaders prayed that the sessions would be "to the glory of God" (Field Notes ACE 11/10–11/86).

Table 6.1 Alternative Cultural Means for Making Decisions

	INDIVIDUALISM	CHRISTOCENTRISM
Locus of power:	Human action	God/Christ/Holy Spirit working within you
Explanation for events:	The result of human action, or coincidence/chance	God's will
Grounds for making decisions:	Self: "Rationally analyze information" and/or follow intuition	God's leading

The same phrase was the theme of the American Association of Christian Schools' Mid-East Regional meeting for teachers and administrators. In nearly every prayer, the Grace Christian Academy administrator said, "We just praise and magnify You" (Field Notes GCA 12/02/86). "Praise God" was a profusely used expression.

Among the adults, at least, this ideal of giving God the glory is manifested. While arranging her classroom bulletin board, a teacher noted the source of her ideas: "The Lord gave me this one about 2:00 in the morning. I guess He thought if He gave me this I would go to bed" (Field Notes GCA 8/86). The administrator "had a vision" for the school and others "felt led" to follow her in creating it. The Lord led her to the curriculum the school uses. Later she had a vision of the school logo. Along the way the Lord gave her ways to teach mathematics to children. The Lord prepared her for a set-to with parents about homework, and readied her to compromise and require less homework (so that students could spend more time with their families) (Field Notes GCA).

Unlike individualistic America, to the conservative Christian way of thinking, humans are not to take credit for their positive qualities. If a mainstream American music director were interviewed about a successful musical program, the underlying assumption would be that her creative abilities, talents, and hard work, and those of her coworkers, had caused the program's success. Compare this to an interview with a Christian crusade's music director. She had just finished singing beautifully when she was interviewed about the music program.

> I didn't know what to do—it was flat. I asked the Lord in the car. He gave it to us little by little—not as fast as we would have liked. He said He had raised us up to do something special. . . .
>
> The dancers . . . orchestra . . . choir . . . just came together the week before. As I look back on it, I think all of the promises He made have been fulfilled. (Robison 1986)

NOT

Lord, bend that proud and stiffnecked "I,"
Help me to bow the neck and die,

HRIST

Galatians 2:20

Beholding Him on Calvary.
Who bowed His Head for me.

Figure 6.1 Not I, But Christ (Anonymous)

A Baptist principal's prayer to open a school Christmas program said:

And Father we're so pleased to have an opportunity tonight to display—not talents—but an ability to remember what we do have in the Lord Jesus Christ. (Field Notes MCA 12/16/87)

If a fourth-grade teacher told a mother, "Your daughter has such a sweet spirit; she is so sensitive," we would expect the mother to thank the

93

teacher, by way of acknowledging her part in instilling this quality in her child. Instead, when this occurred at GCA, the mother replied, "I know it's not her—it's Jesus working through her" (Field Notes GCA 10/17/86). A pastor and administrator, and his teacher wife, told me that "when [the students] are being uneasy to love, and we are being patient, it's not because we're made that way. It's because the spirit of Jesus is in us, and is coming out" (Field Notes ACE 11/11/86).

If it is not thought to be human effort which makes the world go 'round or the school open from day to day, then humans would not be expected to be thanked for their efforts. I wondered about this as I did little odd jobs to help at Grace Christian Academy and the other schools. I emptied wastebaskets, moved folding chairs, vacuumed, made photocopies. One teacher always thanked me profusely; others less so. Compliments tended to be put in the idiom of giving God the credit. For example, the most compliment-prone of the teachers, admiring the GCA administrator's abilities for finding a scripture or a teaching appropriate to the issue at hand and presenting it nicely, said, "Kathleen, I can see why God put you here to lead us" (Field Notes GCA 1/13/87). And she would say to new teachers, and to me, "You have been such a blessing to our school this year." Although this could be construed as meaning "You have been nice to have around because of your own qualities," it is also meant as "You have been a blessing from God." In prayers, the administrator called for the Lord to help each teacher to remember to lift up the others with encouraging words. This is an interesting network of selflessness. That is, in true selflessness the teachers would not expect encouraging words. The administrator feels that encouraging words are called for; but, it is the Lord who is to initiate the saying of those words, and to counsel what they should be.

For the students, "giving God the glory" is much less prevalent, and consists of uttering the phrase "Praise God" (also used profusely by some of the teachers), when handed a piece of school work with a good grade attached, or when giving their praise reports which begin, "I wanna praise God for . . ." and continue as reports on all manner of positive happenings.

The Rewards of Giving God the Glory

It is thought that the human does gain something for his efforts in glorifying God, as he does when he becomes a bondslave for God. What that something is was stated in a church's lessons:

> As the congregation works together to both seek and do His will, they should at all times express their confidence in both the desire

and power of God to care for them . . . Finally, when that which He has ordained has been fully manifested, then the joy of the congregation should be expressed first by direct praise to Him, and then through open declarations that give Him all the credit and the glory for both His power and providence. By this means, His name will be magnified to the world, and the congregation will experience a greater measure of His lasting peace. (LWCC ndb)

So, the peace so often associated with walking the Christian walk will be enhanced for those who give God the glory. But it is inevitable that the human givers will themselves be the recipients of some reflected glory.

Reflected Glory

The conservative Christians, no matter how hard they try to constantly give God the glory, will at times bask in it themselves, especially when looking backward toward creation, or forward toward the millennium, or when comparing themselves to the unsaved.

The concept of creation which the conservative Christians hold is based on a "great Chain of Being," which constructs a hierarchical taxonomy. God, the creator, is at the top. Angels are a special kind of being under God—not like God, but not like humans either. At the low end of the hierarchy are animals and plants. In the middle come humans, who could be divided, as we shall see, into the saved and the lost.

If the saved Christians are to be "raptured out" when the millennium comes and the rest spend eternity in the hellish lake of fire, then that must surely impart a sense of special status.[1] Troeltsch (1960, 590) says of Calvinism: "The value of the individual depends wholly upon the merciful grace of election, and it may give honor to none save God alone. This leads to the result that against a background of the severest self-condemnation there stands out in clear relief in Calvinism the sense of being a spiritual aristocracy."

Even without Calvin's predestination, the doctrines of God's grace (as opposed to man's "works") and the "security of salvation" (salvation, once gained, cannot be lost) adhered to by most conservative Christians gives believers "standing and privilege . . . as a result of His doing" (ICR 1988).

Thus, it could be argued that the conservative Christians' insistence on the difference (now and eternally) between the saved and the lost implies the propagation of a special status for themselves. Yet it is certainly not a status they wish to *reserve* for themselves or for their progeny. Rather, they work to see that the whole world has "the choice" in front of it. This has been so since the beginnings of Christianity.[2]

In addition to the status a person gains by being a member of the saved group, an individual can gain status by being anointed by God to do a certain task or to hold a certain position. It is similar to being called by God, except that not just people, but Christmas programs, songs, and so on, can be called *anointed*.

The concept of being anointed adds a rightness to a person's actions. And yet, in circular fashion, the very feeling of rightness is what is used to signify that something is indeed anointed. "How do you tell if something is anointed?" was a question I asked frequently. If the music program went badly—if it didn't seem to come together, if it was a struggle for the music director and "nothing came to me"—then it was not anointed. The director of music at GCA explained that when "things (words and music to a song, or the theme for a program) just come to me—from God—God gives them to me" then her efforts, and the music program itself, were anointed (Field Notes ACSI 1/30/87; see also Field Notes GCA 10/24/86).

A person's anointed status lends legitimacy to his position and activities, both for himself and for those around him. For example, at faculty meetings, issues where teachers were at odds with parents would most often be settled in favor of the teachers' view, with these words prevailing: "We are anointed to teach these children" (Field Notes 9/30/86). At another school, the administrator told me, "The pastor is God's man, and God has chosen the teachers" (Field Notes DCS 12/10/86).

When the board of directors wanted to express their confidence in the school administrator to the assembled crowd of parents at a Parent-Teacher Fellowship meeting, they did so with these words: "We believe that Kathleen is called to be the administrator" (Field Notes GCA 10/17/86). At another PTF meeting, the first for a new teacher who had been hired after another teacher had left the school, the chairman of the board of directors said to her, in front of the assembled parents, "We believe you're supposed to be here" (Field Notes GCA 1/12/87). The administrator herself was careful not to take possession of the school in her manner of speaking (even though she was the school's primary [human] advocate). She said, "I don't want the parents to think it's my school," and often stated, "It's God's school."[3] This thought was reiterated at every faculty morning prayer.

The administrator said of the board of directors: "God brought those men together to be the board of directors" (Field Notes GCA 1/13/87). Her statement was prompted by the facts that board members' various areas of expertise meshed nicely, and that they were able to deal harmoniously with problems that arose during the year. They did a good job harmoniously *because* they were called by God, and the fact that they did a good job harmoniously was *proof* that they were called by God.

The children may not be as impressed with the status of being saved individuals—with a special role in a coming millennium and a potentially anointed status here on earth—but they have their own ways of gaining status vis-à-vis their peers. Public schools are ridiculed.[4] Some of the children talk about a "before" when they went to public school, and say they didn't like it as much, or they didn't learn as much, as now at Christian school. Donald Howard, ACE's president, says Christian school pupils should feel sorry for students in public schools, and sometimes the students pray for their peers in public schools (Field Notes ACE 11/10–11/86).

As we have seen, the adults, at least, hold to the principle of giving God the glory for all things. They take credit for nothing—not for creating a school, for administering a school, for writing a curriculum, or for building an international organization to market a curriculum. To the conservative Christian way of thinking, the schools were not created by human beings; God raised them up. The parents did not make their own decisions to place their children in the schools; God told them to, rather directly, or made a way—cleared a path—which made it obvious that it was the right thing to do.

If God's hand is the explanation for all events, then it is not surprising that the grounds for making decisions would be *God's leading.*

"GOD LEADS, GUIDES, AND DIRECTS"

Giving God the glory is a necessity for the conservative Christians. But giving God the glory is not sufficient. It is necessary for the conservative Christians to look to God's will as the explanation for events and to seek God's leading in all things.

If a person has put the Holy Spirit and one's own self into the desirable relationship—with the Holy Spirit in control, and one's own self in a lesser position,—then this person will have little difficulty doing God's will. During chapel at a Baptist-sponsored school, the principal, who was also the assistant pastor, exhorted the students to get into the right relationship with the Holy Spirit, so that they would not be tempted to go to places where they should not.

> *You* want the Holy Spirit to be a *backseat driver,* and you want to drive the car wherever you want to go. But that's not the way it

is.... *You* get in the back seat and the Holy Spirit drives the car. And you won't go to those places, because He won't take you there! (Field Notes MCA 3/6/87; the same metaphor was used during chapel at SCCS [Field Notes SCCS 3/11/87]).

So God, Christ, the Holy Spirit is the driver of the Christian's life, while the Christian is to sit in the backseat. Every morning prayer at GCA exhorted God to "lead, guide and direct" the life of the school and its inhabitants. Sometimes the administrator reminded God that "You are the potter; we are the clay" (Field Notes GCA 10/15/86). The desire to instill the willingness to do the Lord's will is reflected in the hymns chosen for the baccalaureate and commencement services at Calvary Cross Christian Academy, supported by a Holiness church. The assembled group sang "Take My Life, and Let it Be," and "Have Thine Own Way, Lord" (Field Notes CCCA 5/24/87, 5/25/87).

Explaining Events

If God is thought to lead, guide, and direct the minutiae of everyday life, then "nothing happens by accident." The middle-American individualist explains events by hearkening to human action, or concedes that they are due to chance, or coincidence. But the conservative Christians' point of view allows for no coincidence. It is reminiscent of the explanatory mode used by the Azande of Eastern Africa. British anthropologist Evans-Pritchard (1937) found that the Azande made the same links that he did when explaining something like a grain bin on stilts falling over and killing a man who was sleeping in its shade. That is, they might inspect the bin's ruins and conclude, as he would, that termite or ant damage to its supporting stilts caused it to fall over. The difference between the Azande and the British or American individualist is that the individualist stops at that; the Azande asks a further question: How is it that the grain bin fell over just at the time this particular man was sleeping under it? Coincidence, the individualist would say; witchcraft, say the Azande; God's will, say the conservative Christians.

In a similar vein, how did the science teacher at a school learn about a new (secular) science curriculum? Here are the links in the explanatory chain, recognized by the conservative Christians: The teacher knew about the curriculum because she visited a school that used it; she visited the school because she met a teacher who taught there at an Institute for Creation Research (ICR) seminar; she went to the ICR seminar because someone had given her husband a promotional brochure to give to her. So far, the middle-American individualist and the conservative Christian share the same explanation. But the brochure was given to the teacher because God led the person who had it to think that she would be interested in it. God led the teacher from the other school to the ICR seminar, as well. God "led [the teacher's] footsteps" when she was looking over information solicited from the curriculum purveyor. God led another teacher to see her doing this and to think to tell her that a professor at a nearby university had knowledge of this curriculum, thereby leading her to yet another source of information.[5]

It is necessary, then, to ask for, and to listen to, God's leading in all things (and not to just "follow your self"). This is, again, at odds with American individualism.

The Grounds for Making Decisions

In modern American society, the grounds for choosing among a variety of options are found, at base, within the self. Bellah et al. (1985, 152) declare that an emphasis on self-reliance is the very essence of our sense of self "the notion of pure, undetermined choice, free of tradition, obligation, or commitment."[6] And so,

> If the self is defined by its ability to choose its own values, on what grounds are those choices themselves based? For . . . many, . . . there is simply no objectifiable criterion for choosing one value or course of action over another. One's own idiosyncratic preferences are their own justification, because they define the true self. . . . The right act is simply the one that yields the agent the most exciting challenge or the most good feeling about himself (Bellah et al. 1985, 76).

This constitutes a textbook statement of what the conservative Christians abhor. This is what they label as humanism, or as humans aspiring to be as Gods; it is what they wish to protect their children against.

An assistant principal told his charges, during chapel:

> You cannot rely on your self. . . . That's what I've been telling some of you, that you should ask the Lord where you should go to college. But we don't—we just say "OK self, what do you want to do?"

> I remember, some years ago, when the Lord dealt with me . . . over at College. And I said Lord, where do you want me to be? And—

you've heard this—I got down on my knees between the plumbing and the building materials, and I said, "Lord, where do you want me to be?"

Using the colloquial style of his students, the teacher continued:

So—it's not just what your self wants to do, but *ask*.
Ask
Uh, Lord, where should I go to college?
Uh, Lord, should I go to Bible college?
Uh, Lord, which Bible college should I go to?
Uh, Lord, what girl should I date?
Uh, Lord, should I date? Am I old enough?
Is she the one?
Uh, Lord, should I follow Jesus?

It's funny—the answer will always be there.
If you follow Jesus, you'll never be sorry.
He says I will provide for you; I will protect you; I will
solve your problems. (Field Notes MCA 3/13/87)

That God's will is to be followed in *all* things results in and supports the conservative Christians' contention that "to the Christian, all things are sacred"—again a point of difference between Christocentrism and individualism.

"TO THE CHRISTIAN ALL THINGS ARE SACRED"

"To the Christian all things are sacred," says the handbook of a school sponsored by a Baptist church; one of the objectives of the school is "to help students realize that there is not any difference between the secular and sacred" (Ebenezer Christian School). The handbook of a school sponsored by a Presbyterian Church in America congregation agrees, including in its statement of faith: "We believe that the eternal purpose of God includes all events (Ephesians 1:11; Daniel 4:35; Psalms 115:3; Acts 15:18; Proverbs 16:4; II Timothy 1:9); therefore, a Christian should look at all of life from God's perspective and not treat part of his life as sacred and part as secular" (HCS).

The kindergarten teacher tells a student who is frustrated by learning to tie her shoes, "You can do all things in Jesus" (Field Notes GCA 3/5/ 87). A story read to kindergarteners at GCA at naptime says: "I find it comforting to think that God cares about everything his children do. There's nothing too small to pray about" (Field Notes GCA 5/19/87, from *Tales from Grandma*).

And indeed, the teachers' prayers do assume God's concern with quotidian matters. Prayers are offered every morning before school begins, before some classes in the schools, sometimes before taking tests, when someone needs to be healed, before any eating, before or during field trips, before ball games, at the end of faculty meetings, during Parent-Teacher Fellowship meetings, at board meetings, before and after most main sessions at Christian educators' conferences, and before most workshops, and sometimes before interviews with anthropologists (Field Notes SCCS 3/11/87; see also Peshkin 1986).

The content of the prayers shows that the conservative Christians are living their belief that God cares about all things great and small. The kindergarten teacher hurries down the hallway praying softly—explaining to me, "I have a lot to do when I get home"—she is asking God to help her. She asks God to intensify the sleep she gets when she has to work late (Field Notes GCA 10/30/86. The teacher in charge of photography for the year book requests that the faculty pray to "bless the camera to take clear pictures" (Field Notes GCA 11/25/86). The kindergarten teacher says to a not-quite-settled youngster at naptime, "I'm going to pray over you, Sandra, [I'm going to ask Jesus] for calm" (Field Notes GCA 3/5/87). Any decision concerning the school is submitted to prayer. For example, at faculty meetings teachers were asked to pray for zoning permits for a school building (Field Notes GCA 3/17/87). When one of the toilets at a school was out of order a few days before school opened, a teacher gave it a risky flush and said, "In the name of Jesus, go down." She also called a plumber (Field Notes GCA 8/86).

Prayers ask that God supernaturally provide for the weather, for personal things needed by teachers (summer jobs, for example), and for the schools' finanacial needs. "We know You are supernaturally paying these bills" (Field Notes GCA 11/3/86). Prayer is invoked during time-outs at ball games. The battle cry goes up when a girls' volleyball team and their coach clasp hands in the middle of a circle: "The battle is the Lord's!" (Field Notes 1/16/87 MCA, from I Samuel 17:47).

Another manifestation of the principle that all things are sacred is use of scripture. The Bible is used to explain and legitimize school policies, and as a mode of discipline (for example, finding and copying scriptures which deal with the miscreant's behavior). Verses of scripture are often (but not always) used on school letterheads and brochures, on report cards, and on notes to the janitor about what needs to be cleaned, and are written by some teachers on student papers.

The archaic language of the Bible is used in prayer. But language and characters from the Bible are also used in everyday contexts. "The angels camp 'round and about you. . . . Is your garment soiled? . . . Is that pleasing to the Lord?" When a student brings in a colorful carry-all, the administrator says, "Denise, that looks like something Joseph would wear," referring to Joseph's coat of many colors (Field Notes GCA). Persons from the Bible are sometimes discussed as if they were contemporaries. A high-school Bible class reads about Samson, and the students, on their own, ponder his motives—"Why did he do that?" They get excited about this man, and one says, "I don't like him" (Field Notes ALCA 3/18/87).

At a science fair sponsored by the American Association of Christian Schools, projects judged best included both a "Biblical Abstract" and a "Scientific Abstract" (as well as descriptions of "Hypothesis," "Procedure," and "Results and Conclusions"). "Biblical Abstracts" illustrate the desire to find the sacred in all things:

Project: What Factors Make a Stronger Electromagnet?

When a material becomes magnetized, the atoms become lined up. This shows God's order in the universe. The electromagnet is a model of winning souls to Christ. The electromagnet needs electricity to attract pieces of metal. A Christian needs the power of God to win people to Christ. In Acts 1:8, the Bible says, "But ye shall receive power, after that the Holy Ghost is come upon you: and ye shall be witnesses unto me both in Jerusalem and in all Judea, and in Samaria, and unto the uttermost part of the earth."

Project: What is the Effect of Acids on Real Teeth and False Teeth?

The Lord tells us to take care of our bodies and this applies to our teeth as well. Just as the teeth were destroyed, so will our lives be if they are not cleaned out daily. I Corinthians 3:17 "If any man defile the temple of God, him shall God destroy: for the temple of God is holy, which temple ye are." According to this verse, temple means body. If we allow any abuse in any way that is wrong, God will judge us. God made us for His own glory and we should want to serve Him in any way He wants. We should care for our bodies the same way we care for our hair. Lastly, I Corinthians 6:20 says "For ye are bought with a price: therefore glorify God in your body, and in your spirit, which are God's." We should want to serve the Lord with our bodies. We should care for our bodies enough to want to glorify Him with them because of what He did for us in Calvary. He sent His only son to die for us. We should take care of our teeth *every day*!

An Association of Christian Schools International Art Festival showed the same desire to see all things as sacred. Beside the titles of some of the artwork were scripture verses. The one which seemed to reach the farthest to find a connection was an entry in "Painting—grades 1–3." Rendered in crayons and turpentine, it was a graphic portrayal of a box of Cascade dishwasher detergent and drinking glasses. The caption was "Wash me as white as snow" (from Psalms 51:7 "Purge me with hyssop, and I shall be clean: wash me, and I shall be whiter than snow").

In nonindustrialized societies, there are no cleavages between the various parts of life that we now label work and play, sacred and secular. But modern society is characterized by a myriad of unifunctional institutions that have burgeoned into fragmented pieces. The conservative Christians want to tie some of these parts back together. The desire to coalesce the sacred and the secular renders the conservative Christians reminiscent of Weber's "traditional" religion, common to nonindustrialized traditional societies.

Weber's typology of religion into traditional and rationalized types distinguishes the two with regard to the degree of separation of various aspects of life, and the structure of the religious realm itself. The *traditional* religion was inextricably, and naïvely, bound up with secular custom. Naïvely, because there was no myriad of choices to be made with regard to gods to honor, or roles to play, or life-styles to follow. Modern society's *rationalized* religion, on the other hand, is "apart, . . . above, . . . outside" of ordinary life.[7]

In traditional religion, the sacred is found everywhere—in the "rooftrees, graveyards, and road-crossings of everyday life." In rationalized religions, sacredness was removed from these commonplace items, gathered up and placed in a concept of the divine. Thus, the rationalized religion brought with it an increase in distance between humans and the sacred (Geertz 1973, 171–175; Parsons 1949; Weber 1948, 1963).[8]

As an example of traditional religion, Geertz (1973, 176) describes Bali, where there is an absence of "doubt or dogmatisms," a "metaphysical nonchalance," because the people are practicing their religion all the time. Ties between humans and the sacred are maintained through "numberless concrete, almost reflexive gestures done in the general round of life."

We can picture, on the one hand, a mainline American Christian, practicing a rationalized religion which is outside ordinary life, abstract, with the divine located in God. This person goes to church on Sunday, hears an exposition of an abstract point, perhaps reads from the Bible, perhaps prays, but is not in the habit of saying grace or performing other personal religious rituals.

The conservative Christians, on the other hand, seem to want to push the clock back to a more traditional form of religion. They do not wish for their religion to be above, apart, or outside of ordinary life. In fact, school handbooks admonish that "to the Christian, there is no separation of sacred and secular." The unembarrassed saying of grace in restaurants, the "praise Gods" scattered throughout conversation, even the stickers on car bumpers, exemplify the conservative Christians' desire to sacralize the secular and to mark them as traditional religionists, in Weber's terms. All things are sacred, so the sacred, awesome quality of otherness is gone. Their Bibles are used every day, highlighted, written in, hearts drawn and stickers stuck all over them. They are thrown on the table as students come in from PE before chapel. They are taken into the bathroom to read.

The structure of the religious realm itself is different in these two forms of religion. In traditional religion, there is a "cluttered arsenal of myth and magic" to be used whenever disaster strikes, or when humans need help (and to answer the great questions of life and death, as well). The approach to answering such questions is on an ad hoc basis—a "discrete and irregular approach to fundamental spiritual issues." The rationalized religion is "more abstract, more logically coherent, more generally phrased" (Geertz 1973, 172). To use an oft-quoted example from Evans-Pritchard (1937), the traditional Azande would be likely to ask: "Why has the granary fallen on my brother and not on someone else's brother?" The rationalized British would be more likely to ask: "Why do the good die young and the evil flourish as the green bay tree?"

As we shall see in the chapters to come, to the outsider the mode of decision-making the conservative Christians have used when building their schools would seem to be of the discrete and ad hoc type. If an "abstract, logically coherent, more generally phrased" mode were used, the outsider would expect to find a clear playing-out of the Christocentric ideology within the school walls. This ideology *is* manifested in the schools to some degree, but it is subject to much compromise.

Walking the Christian Walk the American Way: The Fruits of the Spirit versus Competition

The Christian walk and the American way are at odds on many points. The conservative Christians maintain that they want to be separate and different from the world; the rest of America perceives their difference as a threat. As we have seen, the conservative Christians envision a goal culture where separation from wordly things, the compassionate and non-competitive fruits of the spirit, and the humility borne of Christo-centrism are found. But an administrator said:

> I don't know that any—very many—people actually live that Christian life like we're supposed to. We can't, because like I told you, it's not heaven.

> There *should* be a difference. But I would like for someone to come in and be able to see a difference. If we were in a goldfish bowl, they could say, "Look at the behavior of that fish, it's different from the behavior of that fish over there."

> I mean we can say, "Well look, we don't smoke, we don't drink, we don't carouse." But there's supposed to be more to it than that. There are some [who do follow the Christian life] but—and pastors will tell you this, too—not as many as there should be. (Field Notes GCA 2/14/87)

The administrator at SCCS explained that

> different doesn't mean odd or harebrained. But we know we belong to God. He has a claim on our lives. . . . It should be obvious—observable. We had a visitor one day, sitting on the couch waiting for me. When I came for our appointment she said, "There's something

different about this place." Different is the way it ought to be. . . . Education for eternity. Education with eternal perspectives in mind. Not teaching how to make a living, but teaching how to live. If you know how to live, then making a living will come.

And yet the difference is equivocal. Christian schools are neither all separated Christian culture nor all American popular culture; they are a mixture of both. Compromises have been made. There is recognition that the Christian school is not 100 percent Christian because, as Mrs. Mitchell said, "It's not heaven." Administrators told me that "the world is affecting us more than church is," and "the Christian school is not the savior of the world" (Field Notes GCA 2/14/87; SCCS 3/11/87).

The conservative Christian sense of self, as we have seen, conflicts with the American sense of self. One negates and denies the self; the other glorifies the self. For the conservative Christians, to glorify self is sin.[1] In his famous study of the American character, Tocqueville saw religion as a brake—a mitigating influence—to strong individualism. He regarded religions "as an expression of the benevolence and self-sacrifice that are antithetical to competitive individualism" (Bellah et al. 1985, 223). Certainly, the Christocentrism desired by the conservative Christians is antithetical to a self-oriented individualism and competition. If the total institution model of Christian education is correct, then the church, the home, and the school should all be teaching the same values (as Christian educators say is their goal); they should be sufficiently isolated from contrary values, and we should see the Christian culture manifested in the faculty and the students at Christian schools.

Yet walking the Christian walk in America means that the Christian path—where selves are bent to God's will—will be situated within an environment of American concern with self. The tension between Christocentrism and individualism was evident in the Christian schools, where children who were, after all, American kids, were exhorted to bend their wills to God's.

On the one hand, love, which was considered to be the most important of the Christian attributes, was shown in the schools, especially between teachers and students. At Grace Christian Academy, Mrs. Turner said to her charges as they left for the day: "Good-bye, David. I love you, David." Sometimes she kissed them as they went out the door. At Hamlin Christian Academy, when the pastor and his administrator wife arrived in the morning, she moved among the children, greeting them. The administrator at GCA stood at the top of the stairs near her office and informally talked with teachers. As the students arrived and trudged up the stairs, she greeted each one cheerily. The hug quotient was high. At Dells Christian School, students surrounded their young administrator and hugged her whenever she walked into the room. At Porter Christian Academy, the kindergarteners, ready to leave for the day, walked from their chairs to their teacher and gave her a hug; then, filing by my chair, each one spontaneously hugged me, too. Charmed, I mentioned it to the administrator, who said, "I hope you don't mind, but they're the lovin'est things" (Field Notes PCA 5/20/87).

These are small schools, and the familiarity of the teachers with the students and their parents gives the schools a family atmosphere. (In fact, at PCA, many of the students *are* related to one another and to the teachers.) At Springfield City Christian School, a larger school, the kindergarten teacher was more formal, but certainly kindly to her young charges. At Abundant Life Christian Academy, another large school, the high-school students felt free to joke with their English teacher, teasing her about her haircut and disparaging her love of poetry. Other researchers have found that when students are asked what they like about Christian School, they list the palpable concern that the teachers have for them as an advantage (Parsons 1987; Peshkin 1986; Rose 1988).

On the other hand, much of the behavior in the schools looked like walking the Christian walk the American way.

HUMILITY VERSUS RECOGNITION

Recall that the Christian walk included doing things out of love, quietly; a desire for recognition was not to be the motivating factor. From this Christian emphasis on being humble and not exalting yourself, the total institution model would anticipate a Christian school culture which would be manifested in children who did not wish to push themselves forward, who were shy about presenting their work, modest about telling their grades, and reticent to correct others. As we saw in our earlier discussion of the self, in many cultures which are collectively oriented, these traits are found in adults and taught to children. But in the Christian schools we instead find attributes of individualism: desire for attention and recognition for individual achievement.

Students are not reticent to put themselves and their work forward. "This would like nice right *here,*" says a fourth grader, holding her art work up to the wall behind the teacher's desk. "Read mine! Read mine!" say the seventh graders as the teacher selects history papers to read aloud; when she reads the students' assignments, the authors beam with pride (Field Notes GCA). Likewise, in language class, the students clamor to

read their writings out loud (Field Notes GCA 10/15/86). As I was reading Science 7's critiques of evolution—posted on the classroom wall—
Samuel asked proudly, "Did you read mine yet?" (Field Notes GCA 11/6/
86). In kindergarten at Dells Christian School, the teacher selects the best
of the pictures the young students have colored and hangs them on the
blackboard railing. The kindergarteners want their work to be recognized
and displayed. As the youngsters finish their work, a chorus goes up: "Is
my picture good, Miss Webb?" "Is my coloring good?" (Field Notes DCS
12/10/86, 2/12/87). When report cards come out, each student tells what
he or she got. In fact, they tell it more than once—to the different teachers
(and the same student colleagues) in the various classes they go to that
day (Field Notes GCA 11/6/87; see also Field Notes ALCA).

For the students in kindergarten through seventh grade at GCA, listening to others was certainly not automatic. It was a behavior the teachers
wished to instill. A bone of contention for the seventh-grade homeroom
teacher was that the students seemed more concerned with reciting their
own prayer requests and praise reports than they were with listening to
others' (Field Notes GCA 11/13/86). The teacher constantly reprimanded
them about being polite and listening to one another. Trying to do her
part early on, the kindergarten teacher attempted to instill courteous
listening behavior; to accustom the students to reading aloud and listening to one another, she asked students to read from their first reading
book, which they did, haltingly, of course. But it was a lost cause to try to
get the other twelve four- and five-year-olds to listen to their peers.

Not only are the students not shy about putting their own work and
concerns forward; they also are not necessarily supportive of one another. In kindergarten, Gena spontaneously wanted to show the class the
picture that she had colored. The teacher allowed her to bring it to the
front of the classroom for viewing, but she got no rave reviews from her
classmates. They were even less kind to the four-year-olds, exclaiming
"Eeeew" to show their disgust at the way they colored their pictures. At
the Thanksgiving Feast for the kindergarten through second graders, the
students dressed in costume, and, much to the teacher's chagrin, dispar-
aged each others' clothes (Field Notes GCA 11/26/86). Although the
teachers tried to encourage the students to share, sharing was not a
behavior that came easy to American Christian school students, unlike
those trained in a less individualistic society. Kindergarteners would build
a corral around their pile of crayons with their arms in order to protect
their horde (Field Notes DCS 12/10/86, 12/12/86, 1/7/87).

The Christian school is not necessarily a place where all students accept
one another in Christian love so that cliques do not form. In kindergarten, the students leave one another out of their play and are vocally

adamant about who can and can't come to their parties. From kindergarten through senior year the presence of cliques was obvious from the seating arrangements on the vans, and from students' comments about one another. Getting ready to go on a long field trip, a high-school girl begged to move to a different van, "because I'm sitting next to Susan." "There are only three uncool people in our class, __ , __ , and __ ," pronounced a seventh-grade boy (Field Notes ALCA, DCS, GCA). At graduation time, the popularity of some students is obvious, as their peers cheer and sometimes laugh for them when they cross the stage at the church to receive their diplomas. For the less popular, there is silence (Field Notes SCCS 6/12/87).[2]

Unlike collectively oriented cultures (and Jehovah's Witnesses), Christian schools most certainly celebrate birthdays. At some schools lists of birth dates are published or put on school calendars. Posters are hung that show each child's birthday, and birthday parties are frequent.

An analysis of the prayer requests and praise reports (864 requests from twelve grades plus faculty in four schools—ALCA, DCS, GCA, SCCS) offers a measure of selflessness. Praise reports and prayer requests are solicited at particular times, such as homeroom or Bible class, and at chapel and faculty meetings. This is the time the students and faculty share what is on their minds.

For whom is concern expressed in prayer requests and praise reports? The subject of the requests and reports combined was most often oneself, then one's family, then the school. The church and its communicants accounted for a very small proportion of all the prayers and praises. But there were some differences between faculty and students, and there were some differences between the prayer requests, asking God to provide, and the praise reports, thanking God for providing.

For whom are these prayer requests made and praise reports given? The faculty most often makes requests for the school at large or for the people in it, then themselves and their families. The younger students pray for family members, then themselves; older students for family, then friends. The younger students in kindergarten through seventh grade make requests for themselves more than twice as often as the faculty. The faculty's praise reports follow the same pattern as their prayers—first the school, then themselves and their families. The students' praise reports, however, are overwhelmingly concerned with themselves (43 percent) or themselves and other family and friends (18 percent).

For neither students nor faculty is the church or the people in it of great concern when making prayer requests and praise reports (1 percent; 5 percent for the ALCA students, who were concerned about a church official who was hospitalized).

Table 7.1 Subjects of Prayer Requests and Praise Reports

	PRAYER REQUESTS FOR WHOM? MADE BY				PRAISE REPORTS FOR WHOM? MADE BY			
FOR WHOM	TOTAL	GCA FACULTY	GCA & DCS STUDENTS (K–7)	ALCA & SCCS STUDENTS (9–12)	TOTAL	GCA FACULTY	GCA & DCS STUDENTS (K–7)	ALCA & SCCS STUDENTS (9–12)
Family	30%	11%	36%	33%	18%	23%	18%	33%[2]
Self	25	14	29	7	42	23	43	0
School	17	58	6	7	5	31	4	0
Friends	8	4	8	20	4	0	4	0
Self & others	3	5	3	3	18	8	18	0
Others	3	3	3	0[1]	1	0	1	0
Church	1	1	1	7	1	0	1	0
Environment	1	0	1	0	1	15	0	0
No data	11	5	13	23	12	0	11	67
Total	100%[3]	100%	100%	100%	100%	100%	100%	100%
No. of prayer requests / No. of praise reports	533	112	391	30	331	13	315	3

[1] "0" signifies less than .5%
[2] Note the small number of cases in this column.
[3] Figures may not sum to exactly 100% due to rounding.

It is interesting to note that among the high-school students (although the number of prayer requests is small), there is more selflessness in the requests than for the children in kindergarten through seventh grade (7 percent as compared to 29 percent requests for self). Perhaps the Christian teachers are right that, over the long haul, students will come to reflect the concerns that teachers wish them to have. "If we prefer others at the microwave, then they will. If we prefer others going in and out of doors, then they will. They may not right away. But I guarantee, eventually they will. They will. By faith I know they will" (Field Notes GCA 11/18/86). Perhaps the socialization process stands incomplete.

THE FRUITS OF THE SPIRIT VERSUS COMPETITION

The goal Christian culture revolved around the fruits of the spirit: "love, joy, peace, longsuffering, gentleness, goodness, faith, meekness, temperance." One of the attributes of Christian culture was that "there would be no competition. There wouldn't be any judging going on" (Field Notes GCA 2/14/87). In the Christian schools there is ambivalence about competition. Students are competitive, but are troubled by competition among their peers; teachers sometimes foster competition, and sometimes despair of it.

Students Displaying Competition

At Grace Christian Academy, the third and fourth graders behaved the most competitively. They competed in every possible setting: on the playing field, in the lunchroom, and in the classroom. They competed to see who could get work done the fastest, who would get the best grade, who would finish speed drills first (and second, and third, until who was last was determined and known to all), who could drink his juice the fastest, and whose house was visited by one of the cute kindergarten boys more often. In short, "who won?" was important to them.

The younger children were also concerned about who got what grades, but were somewhat more supportive of one another. The first and second graders knew which child always got the lowest grades, and when the report cards were handed out, they said, with hope rather than sarcasm in their voices, "Marcus got an A, didn't he?" Alas, the teacher had to answer "No" (Field Notes GCA 10/31/86). The teachers tried to lessen the competition over grades by not allowing students to open their report cards until they got home. The effect, however, was simply to delay the comparing until the next day.

But even the kindergarteners, who could sometimes encourage one another, showed the roots of competitiveness that would most likely be honed rather than hindered in later years. So that the children would not compete ("Me," "me," "choose me") for the various tasks to be done each day—holding the Bible and the flags for the pledges, passing out juices and milks, being the line leader, saying prayers—the kindergarten teacher had worked out a system for passing these jobs around (using an octopus on the wall with names at the ends of the arms as a signal for who was to do what). But, once that was settled, they found other ways to compete, for example, by seeing who could roll up the flag held for the pledges the faster (Field Notes GCA 5/19/87). They competed at finishing their numbers, with the winner saying "Nyah, nyah, nyah," and the teacher repeating, "That doesn't matter" (Field Notes GCA 3/5/87).

The first and second graders competed, too. The teacher drilled the students on their "math facts" with flash cards. She held up a card and called on a child to give the answer to the problem on it, in around-the-room fashion. A child who answered correctly was handed the card. At the end of the session, the teacher scooped the cards off the students' desks, whereupon the students became very upset because they wanted to count everybody's horde to determine who won. She told them it didn't matter, and not to be concerned about it, but because of their strenuous insistence, she couldn't go on with the rest of the lesson until she figured out the scores and announced them (Field Notes GCA 2/13/87). On the same day one of the first-grade girls, admonished by the teacher not to get too far ahead in her work before she learned what was to be done, said "Oh, I want to get ahead of everybody!" (Field Notes GCA 2/13/87). On the last day of class, the teacher gave each child bean plants that she had carefully potted from the class seed-growing experiment. She had one for each child, and they drew lots to see who got which numbered plant. After the drawing, the students rushed to compare plants and see who got the "biggest plant" (Field Notes GCA 5/27/87).

Competition in material acquisition is not unknown. The young boys keep track of each others' GI Joe men and accoutrements; the girls do likewise for Pound Puppies and My Little Ponies. A first grader and a second grader had this conversation at lunchtime:

Wendy: I'm the culotte girl. I always wear culottes.
            I have nine pairs—more than anybody.

Corinne: I have ten pairs.
Wendy: I have eleven.
Corinne: I have nineteen.

Even cheating to get ahead is not unknown at Christian school. During the crab race at Field Day, the PE teacher calls out, "Andrew, don't cheat like that," as the second grader, noticing that he is behind his best friends, turns over and crawls frontward for a few steps before flipping over to continue being a "crab." The boy's mother said, "He is so competitive; he *has* to win" (Field Notes GCA 5/22/87).

If any of the schools would be thought to show a lack of competition, it would be those sponsored by Holiness churches, which make the most effort to maintain separation from the world with regard to appearance. But even here, the first- and second-grade teacher calls the children to her desk one by one to show them their achievement test scores, and says, "But where they were low, you were high average; does that make you feel good?" "I was higher than everybody else?" the youngster wants to know (Field Notes PCA 5/20/87).

Teachers Fostering Competition

Although sometimes the teachers despaired about competition among the students, at other times they fostered it. Thus, competition is not necessarily deviant behavior among the students; it is a part of the Christian school culture. The first- and second-grade teacher at a Holiness-sponsored school, following the conventional wisdom of educational professionals, implied that competition among students enhanced the learning environment. "I like it better with more than one student to a grade. There's more competition, more discussion" (Field Notes PCA 4/8/87). The A Beka Arithmetic 6 book says that arithmetic is, among other things, "participating in healthy competition" (Howe 1981).

GCA's kindergarten teacher used competition to try to enthuse her charges when she asked, "Are you five-year-olds going to let the four-year-olds beat you again?" (Field Notes GCA 11/18/86). The third- and fourth-grade teacher tried to turn her class's competitiveness to her advantage by setting up a point system for good and bad behavior. They did compete for these points, keeping track of who was ahead. The teacher gave prizes every six weeks to the child with the most points (Field Notes GCA 3/17/87).

The seventh-grade history teacher devised a group project, in order to help the students learn to work in groups. They immediately saw an opportunity for competition—and named themselves after professional football teams (Field Notes GCA 11/25/86).

The teachers fostered competition by playing games such as "Error." This game was a ploy to be sure all the students were paying attention when one was reading aloud. If the person reading made a mistake, the one who first caught it was to say "Error" and take over the reading. Reading aloud became a matter of a few words and then a cacophony of "Error! Error!" as the reader stumbled over a word. Once in a while, one of the students provided a mitigating influence, as one day when sixth grader Brandon said petulantly after a chorus of "Error" directed to Patricia's reading, "She *corrected* it!"

Other competitive teaching tools included having two people at the blackboard doing a math problem or spelling a word. The winner stays at the board to challenge a new comer, while the loser has to sit down. The older students grade one another's work. The language teacher asks: "Who missed a lot?" The students call out the names of the students whose papers they graded.

Awards were given for student work. The spring programs and graduation ceremonies are replete with awards, and although some schools try to give everybody an award for *something,* for example, "for the greatest improvement in spelling in one six-week period," some of the awards are obviously more equal than others. Some, for example, have trophies attached to them (Field Notes GCA 5/11/88; ALCA 6/2/87; CCCA 5/19/87; DCS 5/28/87; PCA 5/25/87; SCCS 7/12/87).

The ACE schools claim not to be competitive, since they are based on individualized instruction. One administrator told me: "We don't do a lot of comparing of students. Each one has to be treated individually. In Matthew 25:25, the man with two talents wasn't criticized for not having five, and the man with one wasn't criticized for not having two, but the man with one was criticized for not using it. Encourage them to do *their* best. I think it's scriptural and I think it's fair" (Field Notes MCA 12/15/86).

Another ACE school administrator said the students only compete "with themselves" (Field Notes HCA 10/28/86). Yet, at both schools (and all schools that actually follow the ACE program), the students receive certificates when they pass a test at the end of each booklet of programmed instruction or PACE. The certificates are given out in front of the class or the school (Field Notes HCA 11/7/86). At Maranatha Christian Academy there are honor roll trips, and a plaque in the hallway naming the students who are "Most like Christ in the Learning Center."

The state and national support organizations for Christian schools sponsor student competitions, patterned after statewide competitions held for public-school students. The Association for Christian Schools International sponsors judged art shows. The American Association of Christian Schools organizes competitions in art, music, science, speech and drama, writing, Bible, and testing in English, mathematics, science, geography and history, Spanish, home economics, political science, secretarial science, and spelling. The Executive Director of an AACS state branch said that the most important function of his organization was promoting and running student competitions (Field Notes AACS Competition 4/9/87).

Teachers Despairing of Competition

Although the teaching and disciplinary measures they used fostered competition, the teacher often despaired of the competition their charges displayed. From five-year-olds on, the question "Who won?" and the claim "We won!" filled the air after any kind of game. With the little ones who did not yet have a grasp on the intricacies of the rules, both sides would claim to have won and finally ask the teacher to intervene to tell them who *had* won.

The Grace Christian teachers were especially concerned about the third and fourth graders; their competitiveness was blamed on the experiences they had before coming to GCA. "They have always been very competitive. They came to us after kindergarten—in an open classroom situation" (Field Notes GCA). The first- and second-grade teacher researched noncompetitive games, but she despaired of convincing the children actually to be noncompetitive.

The volunteer PE teacher was bothered by the cutthroat competition on the playing field (Field Notes GCA 10/21–11/4/86). Mr. Farrell followed a curriculum, suggested by the administrator, that evaluated the students on the degree to which they displayed the fruits of the spirit each time they were on the playground. It included a "Fruit of the Spirit Daily Assessment" sheet, with a column for each student's name, and columns headed "LOVE, JOY, PEACE, PATIENCE, LONGSUFFERING, GENTLE, MEEK, TEMPERANCE, and FAITH." The instructions said to "Mark each fruit with a ' + ', meaning 'fruit was exhibited,' or a ' − ', meaning 'fruit was lacking' in this area" (Ward 1985; GCA 8/29/86 Handout). The teacher took this to mean that competition should be at a minimum, and worked hard to discourage it. After a trying day, he described a class with the third and fourth graders, playing football.

I got the teams wrong. One was real strong and one real weak. One boy from the weak team was really upset—to the point of tears—saying "the teams aren't right, the teams aren't right." I said to him, "I know I haven't done it right; but could I just watch you for a while and then I'll make some adjustments?"

I asked one boy from the good team to go to the other one. He said, "No! No! That's not fair!" He wanted to beat them 50–0. I asked another guy—. Some of these kids have been—win, win, win!

Then I asked one boy who has a good attitude to move over to the weak team—and he did. And the game was 2–0 and it ended up 2–2. That's what I like to see.

Those two guys—I kept them after class—and talked to them. One was saying I shouldn't have changed the teams. I said—you could win 50–0, but where is the sportsmanship in that? His attitude.

It's my challenge for the year. My challenge. I'll need the Lord. (Field Notes GCA 10/21/86; see also 11/4/86)

The students' grumbling didn't stop with Mr. Farrell's heart-to-heart talk with the boys, however. They complained among themselves about how Mr. Farrell didn't know anything about football—and especially about making up teams. Mr. Farrell tried to meet his challenge by bringing his Bible to PE class and beginning the class with prayer and allusions to scripture.

Father God, we ask You to be with us. To control our attitudes and our actions. We give this time to You. Scripture tells us . . . that we are temples of the Living God. We belong to God and He loves us. So we are going to give ourselves to Him—do Him honor, even as we do whatever we're going to do today. . . . Help us with our attitude—to have the same attitude Jesus would have if He were here. We also know that You are a God of protection—so protect us from injury. In Jesus' name, Amen. (Field Notes GCA 11/4/86; 9/16/86)

This earned him the disapprobation of students, who muttered, "This class is just . . . *talking*" as they trudged back to their classrooms (Field Notes GCA 9/16/86).

At another school, the assistant pastor, who was also the principal and coach, reported that his school made an effort to lessen this kind of competition in PE: "When we have PE we pick fair teams. And then when we play football we do what we call ones and twos. Where the ones throw the ball and then . . . the twos throw the ball and . . . that way you make sure that you throw to every kid—not just the best players" (Field Notes MCA 12/15/86). But he also said that the school was "real good" in athletics, and in fact had won two state tournaments. "We have a pretty good record. . . . This is our seventh year, and we're 120 and 20 [in basketball]." The school plays only basketball and softball because it is too small to field a team for football, soccer, or baseball, where "you can't have an eighth grader up against a senior." Basketball can be played with its eleven high-school boys, nine of whom play ball (Field Notes MCA 12/15/86).

Students Despairing of Competition

Sometimes even the students despair of competition. During one of the football games on the playgrounds at GCA, fifth grader Carl ran from the playing field to the swing set, where his best friend Warren, a small fifth-grade boy, was swinging. "I escaped," sighed Carl (Field Notes GCA 5/87).

Late in the year the sixth-grade girls had a discussion about sportsmanship, prompted by a story about a hockey game in reading class. The teacher, trying to draw a moral from the story about cheating, says:

Teacher: Like maybe in your PE—you see somebody not following the rules.
Emily: Marvin and Gary's little mouths.
Rachel: I'm not trying to be cruel, but I think they should work on that. Because it makes everybody—
Emily: That's what gets me fired up [to play well].
Patricia: That's what gets me fired up, too.

(The girls have internalized the American idea that competition is a motivator.)

Rachel: But sometimes it's not that great a sportsmanship to say, "We're going to beat ya'll's butts."
Teacher: Who does that?
Rachel: Emily mostly.
Emily: That *one* day.
Rachel: But you kept saying it.
Patricia: Trying to get some team spirit!
Rachel: I don't think we should take the game that seriously. It's just PE—it's not like the teams are enemies.

Emily:	You know how Gary and Marvin used to cry because they weren't on Samuel's team? Well now they're on Craig's team and they're just—Yaaay!
Rachel:	Just don't say to the other team—"We're beatin' you! We're beatin' you!"
Patricia:	We don't say that.
Rachel:	I know but—

It was time for the class to end, so the three sixth graders filed out. The teacher turned to me: "Have you been watching PE? It's frustrating when you're in charge" (Field Notes GCA 4/28/87).

Walking the Christian Walk
the American Way:
Separation versus Worldliness

The American cultural traits which emerged from the Christian classroom and playground, even though they sit in opposition to the Christian walk, include recognition of individual achievement, competition, and materialism. Their presence signals compromise between Christian separatism and the world of American popular culture.

SEPARATISM VERSUS MATERIALISM

The conservative Christians' desire to be "separate from the world" led me to anticipate that this separation would be manifested in the material realm. I had associated strong religious conviction with simplicity; I recalled scriptural admonitions such as: "It is easier for a camel to go through the eye of a needle, than for a rich man to enter into the kingdom of God" (Matthew 19:24). I was following Tocqueville who thought that "the main business of religion . . . 'is to purify, control, and restrain that excessive and exclusive taste for well-being' so common among Americans" (Bellah et al. 1985, 223, quoting Tocqueville 1969). But it seems that many of today's conservative Christians have the taste Tocqueville decried, and the apologetics to support it. Eschewing material goods is not one of the traits today's conservative Christians share with the earliest Christians. Discussing the "austere morals of the first Christians," Gibbon (1960, 166) relates that:

> Gay apparel, magnificent houses, and elegant furniture, were supposed to unite the double guilt of pride and of sensuality: a simple and mortified appearance was more suitable to the Christian who was certain of his sins and doubtful of his salvation. In their censures of luxury the fathers are extremely minute and circumstantial; and

among the various articles which excite their pious indignation we may enumerate false hair, garments of any color except white, instruments of music, vases of gold or silver, downy pillows (as Jacob reposed his head on a stone), white bread, foreign wines, public salutations, the use of warm baths, and the practice of shaving the beard, which, according to the expression of Tertullian, is a lie against our own faces, and an impious attempt to improve the works of the Creator.

The acceptance of material goods was, in fact, one of the things which first gave me a mild case of culture shock. Expecting to find a protest against American excesses manifested in simplicity, I packed my suitcase accordingly for the first fieldwork experience—an Institute for Creation Research seminar. I spent quite a while searching out my plainest attire. When I arrived I found that the participants at the seminar were the "beautiful people" of today's society, and that I was quite underdressed. They wore colorful flowered skirts and even pants. They wore jewelry—pierced earrings (sometimes more than one per ear).

The convictions of the conservative Christians regarding eschewing wordly things line up along a continuum, with the Holiness churches at the most separate end (and even Holiness congregations differ from church to church with regard to proper dress, and so on), and the evangelicals and charismatics, more accepting of worldly goods, at the other end of the continuum.

Thus, the schools sponsored by Holiness churches go the farthest to try to maintain the separation from the world that all the conservative Christians say they want. At Calvary Cross Christian Academy there is no attempt to control the lives of the students off the school grounds, but at school no jewelry of any kind (other than a watch) is allowed, and there is a strict and modest dress code. Those who actually follow the strictures of the sponsoring church do not own televisions. But even the Holiness-sponsored schools' graduation ceremonies buzz and hum with the sounds of expensive cameras autofocusing. And K-Mart and its treasures are sufficiently salient to the first and second graders to make this story meaningful to them. The teacher devised it and put it on the blackboard to teach her students to notice details. In perfect script she had written:

May received five dollars for her birthday. She took the money to the K-Mart store. She saw a pretty doll that cost three dollars. She liked an animal game that cost four dollars. A big, stuffed, pink turtle was five dollars. What should she buy? She thought and thought. Then she bought the turtle, and went home. (Field Notes CCCA 5/6/87)

At the far, far other end of the continuum are proponents of Kingdom Now theology, which prophesies that when the end times heralding the millennium come, saved Christians will be able to lay claim to the material goods of the unsaved. This prophecy is reminiscent of the time in history when the ancient Christians discussed the New Jerusalem—coming with Jesus' return at the millennium—and painted it in the colors of their day:

A felicity consisting only of pure and spiritual pleasure would have appeared too refined for its inhabitants, who were still supposed to possess their human nature and senses. A garden of Eden, with the amusements of the pastoral life, was no longer suited to the advanced state of society which prevailed under the Roman empire. A city was therefore erected of gold and precious stones, and a supernatural plenty of corn and wine was bestowed on the adjacent territory; in the free enjoyment of whose spontaneous productions the happy and benevolent people was never to be restrained by any jealous laws of exclusive property. (Gibbon 1960, 158)

Likewise, this branch of today's conservative Christians have repainted the New Jerusalem, predicting that when Christ returns to earth, the saved person will be able to claim the house, garage, and BMW of his lost (unsaved) neighbor. To other conservative Christians, this idea is abhorrent; they see it, in fact, as a false teaching arising from the confusion and deception of the last days themselves. One school administrator could foresee the non-Christian attributes such a situation might engender. She said, "Let me ask you—Isn't it true that whenever you have [private] property, greed comes in?" (Field Notes GCA 2/14/87). In this, she was reading her anthropology of the coevolution of private property and social stratification correctly. But, although Kingdom Now theology and its variants are going too far for many conservative Christians, sackcloth is not required. (See Hunter 1983 for an analysis of what has been called the "health and wealth" gospel in evangelical literature.)

God Doesn't Mean for Us to Be Poor

A teacher told me: "God doesn't mean for us to be poor" (Field Notes 6/23/86). Jim Bakker wanted to build his PTL (Praise the Lord and People that Love) ministry's Heritage USA resort park because the church camps he attended when he was young were rundown and shabby, and he thought, "Why can't everything be nice?" (*Time* 1987b, 62). He justified his large clothes closet by saying, "God doesn't like junk" ("Frontline" 1988). In Bible 7 at GCA, the teacher discussed money, reiterating what she had heard at church service the previous evening:

> But you see, the love of money is the root of all evil. Now *money* is not evil; but it's the *love* of money that's the root of all evil. . . .
>
> Now God does bless us with money, OK? Don't get me wrong. He does bless us; He wants his children to be blessed. But he doesn't want us to seek after that, you see. That's just another by-product of serving God—is being blessed, financially, spiritually, physically, every way. (Field Notes GCA 10/2/87)

At GCA, the administrator said that God can't change the numbers on a check, but he can make it go farther (Field Notes GCA 10/15/86). This was echoed by a Baptist administrator:

> I've found that 90 percent after you've given the Lord 10 percent goes farther than 100 percent. And I've found that 85 percent goes even farther than that, and 80 percent goes even farther than that.
>
> I've known the Lord eleven years next week, and I could tell you all kinds of things [that have happened to me]. I'd rather have less with His blessing, than more without Him.
>
> Last year I wanted a swimming pool for my kids real bad. The one I wanted cost $1200. I prayed that it would go to half price. It did, but that was still too much. Two days later I had a fellow give me one. It's not a big pool—just eighteen feet and four feet deep. I fenced it in; the Lord took care of all that. But we've had all kinds of fun with it and really enjoyed it last summer.
>
> . . . . My truck . . . was $5000 and I got it for $2000.
>
> How much more do you have to make to save that much? The Lord controls everything. The Lord controls health and cars and houses. . . .
>
> The staff has seen the same thing. Saved people have problems, too, but it's nice to have a problem-solver. (MCA 12/15/86)

In the alumnae newspaper of a Christian college, a columnist writes of praying for a new dress, and of getting it, with the Lord as her partner (Green 1987, 7). In a story in Willie George's (1987) *Deputy* magazine for kids, a boy prayed for a bicycle, and bought it, but it was stolen. He prayed for another one, and was able to buy it, too, with the Lord's help. At the Maranatha Christian Academy Christmas program, through a series of events a poor little girl is given a doll and exclaims, "This is the doll I prayed for!" Her benefactor, an older girl, reminds her, "Remember, God answers prayers" (MCA 12/16/87).

These stories are not told to impress the listener with what the teller has accumulated. The Baptist principal and assistant pastor made it clear that his priorities are with spiritual, not material, things: "The Bible is clear; a man can gain the whole world and lose his soul. The world's goods are fading at best. The clothes I have on, in two years won't be worth throwing in the rag bag. My car won't be worth leaving on a mountain and burying. The world's goods last at best a hundred years. And eternity is significantly longer than that. So that's the most important" (Field Notes MCA 12/15/86).

The stories are provided as testimony of God's power to provide for those who are saved and "walking the Christian walk." A skeptic might say that the conservative Christians' insistence that God ordained their material well-being is a way to avoid interpreting their capitulation to materialism as an accommodation to their cultural surroundings. But the stories are the testimony of people who live by faith, on low salaries, and yet are taken care of, as they see it, by the Lord's largess. As a parent at GCA told the school at chapel, you have to be good, and then you may ask. "If your heart is pure before God; if you have been keeping his commandments, then we can ask what we will. . . . Then we can come boldly into the throne room" (Field Notes GCA 10/14/86). "We just pray in what we need—I guess that that's the best way of putting it. But I feel if the Lord calls you to do something, he's obligated to supply the means" (Field Notes MCA 12/15/86).

Student Material Culture

The students' material culture—the artifacts they wore and carried to school—displayed a familiarity with American popular culture. The students' clothing, within whatever limits were set by the school, reflected today's teenage fashions. All of the schools had some sort of dress code, but only one had uniforms. (Some public schools in Maryland and Washington, D.C., are using uniforms that are more uniform than any I saw.) The dress codes of the schools are an attempt to maintain standards of decency, to forestall competition and materialistic fads among the students, and, in some cases, to affirm the difference between the sexes. Several of the schools do not allow T-shirts with writing or pictures on them, so as not to have students wearing a statement with which the school would not agree, and to avoid advertising. However, all of the schools had T-shirts or jackets with their *own* logos on them, and of course students were permitted to wear those. One Handbook even states, "Tops with writing or advertising are not acceptable except when writing is related to Redwood Baptist Church" (SCCS Handbook).

Students, to the degree that they could, wore today's teen fashions. I was often the only female above the age of five without pierced earrings, at all but the schools sponsored by Holiness churches. (I never saw a boy with pierced earrings at any of the schools, but I did see little boys and fathers with long ducktail haircuts.) Swatches wristwatches were nearly universal, except at the one Holiness school which had the strictest dress code. But even there, the students were fashionable within their limits, with silver barrettes, glasses with lowered temples and initials, and faddish anklets with high-top shoes, some silvery. Since longer skirts were "in" at the time, these girls were not, by their attire, separated from their public-school sisters. If miniskirts become popular, the Holiness school girls will be left behind in the fashion world. For undoubtedly, their skirts will have to stay at or below the knees. But just as undoubtedly, their skirt lengths will also creep up to split the difference. Their teacher said she had had difficulty causing the students to adhere to the code—problems with jewelry, nail polish, tight skirts, and skirts slit too high. She reported threatening one boy with a loose shirt tail, "You tuck it in, or I will!" (whereupon he did). "Picture shirts" are not taboo here, so one boy wore a T-shirt and camouflage trousers (Field Notes CCCA 5/11/87). At a Baptist church school—which was considered quite conservative (the school made headlines when it refused to play basketball with another Christian school's team because it included girls) a girl sat in the back of English 11 with a leather-look outfit and a big Madonna-like bow in her hair. Another girl sported high-heeled high tops (ALCA 3/19/87).

Uniforms were worn at Hamlin Christian Academy, the ACE school sponsored by a nondenominational charismatic church. For the girls, from kindergarteners to seniors, they were navy blue suits on the order of crisp stewardesses' uniforms. With the uniforms, the older girls wore textured and seamed hose, and extraordinarily high heels. For the boys, the anticipated spit-polished black shoes and good trousers were nowhere to be found, even here. Running shoes and blue jeans were ubiquitous.

As we learned in chapter 3, the buttons the students at GCA wore on their jeans jackets reflected the mixture of popular and Christian culture. On the seventh graders' jackets, "Benson's Chapel Winnipeg '88 Youth" coexisted with "Is there life after Happy Hour?" "I sell Girl Scout cookies" and "Miami Vice." (Field Notes GCA 3/2/–3/10/87). One of the boys sported a big button which said "Super Terrific Person" (Field Notes GCA 3/10/87). Their locker doors were personalized (on the inside) with bumper stickers, mixing "Let the Lord be Magnified, Jesus Christ" with "I (heart) skating at Dells Skating Center" and "Get Bear [local University mascot] Proud."

The students' lunchboxes and backpacks were covered with Popples, Muppets and Muppet Babies, Strawberry Shortcake, Ronald McDonald, Snoopy, Donald Duck, SnackTime Munchie Tunes with Brunchie Bear, Pound Puppies, Cabbage Patch Kids, Garfield, Popeye, Knight Rider, Darth Vader, Return of the Jedi, and Ghostbusters (Field Notes GCA 10/2/–10/6/86, 10/9/86, 3/17/87; see also Field Notes CCCA). The toys they brought to school to play with at recess were GI "Joe men" and Pound Puppies. Show 'n Tell day looked like a stroll through a mini Toys R Us.

When the pastor of the Wesleyan church drew the church's school together for chapel to discuss Easter, he asked the students in kindergarten through third grade, "When you think of Easter, how do you remember it? What does it mean?" "Baskets and eggs," the pastor's first-grade daughter replied (Field Notes DCS 4/16/87). The second-grade boys at GCA spent several recesses building their castle out of paper, tape, and glue; it had a hot tub, a shower room, and a garage for the "limo" (Field Notes GCA 10/14/86). The fifth and sixth graders discussed the cars they wanted on the way to the public library in the van. "My first car is going to be a Mazda RX-7—and I'm going to buy it." "I want a van with a refrigerator and a TV and everything" (Field Notes GCA 11/6/86).

The switch from Christian to popular cultural idioms was often lightning fast. During class, second grader Eric asked, "Can I pray, Mrs. Sherwood? There just went a rescue squad." Immediately afterward, Eric had some difficulty with a toy GI Joe man and said, "dirty, stinkin' rotten thing; I'm gonna blow its head off," whereupon Mrs. Sherwood reprimanded him about his attitude (Field Notes GCA 2/13/87). Christian and pop symbols came together face-to-face on a table one day when GCA was about to be dismissed for Christmas vacation. A crèche sat on the table, and second grader Andrew held his GI Joe man up to it. The GI Joe man and Mary and Joseph were just the same size. The Joe man barked at Joseph, "What do you mean telling me to halt?" and then "blew him away" in a burst of "gunfire" (Field Notes GCA 12/19/86).

There are limits, of course, to the inclusion or intrusion of pop culture. The schools are neither all popular culture, nor all separate Christian; they reflect a syncretized mélange of the two. Kindergarteners at Springfield City Christian School's recess were looking at cards one little boy had. When the teacher investigated she found Garbage Pail Kids depicting, for example, "Art Apart" whose limbs are separated from his head and torso, "Cindy Looper" who is "draped over a guillotine waiting for her head to be lopped off," "Soft-Boiled Sam" with cracked eggshell skin, and "Brainy Brian" who holds his brain in his hand (Castillo 1986; Katzman 1986; Chaplin 1986). She asked the little boy not to bring them to school anymore. As she showed them to me, one little boy peered over her shoulder and said "Oh I *hate* those!" (Field Notes SCCS 3/11/87). (Of course, conservative Christian parents aren't the only ones who find the Garbage Pail Kids repulsive and forbid their children to collect them. Ann Landers and her readers, for example, have spoken out against them.) The things the children could play with included the chalkboard, Tinkertoys, dolls, play food and armored tanks ("I'll blow you up," said one little boy to another) (Field Notes SCCS 3/11/87).

Some of the students, even the youngest ones, know what it is of the world that they are supposed to eschew. Kindergartener Gena won a poster depicting Jem, a Barbie type doll who has an all-girl rock band. She brought it to school, and when it was unveiled, fellow kindergartener Sandra and second grader Wendy said, "Yech, it's rock 'n' roll stuff!" (Field Notes GCA 3/5/87). The kindergarteners asked each other, "Did you know She-Ra and He-Man were coming to the City? Ycch!" (Field Notes GCA 1/9/87). (Note that they know who She-Ra and He-Man *are*.) Sandra often led these campaigns. If she continues in this vein into a Christian high school, she is liable to be labeled a "Miss God" by her peers (Peshkin 1986).

Parents gathered for a field day picnic discussed the problems they were having with neighborhood birthday parties. If favors such as Smurfs are given out, sometimes their children would say, "I don't want those" (because Smurfs do things "by magic") (Field Notes GCA 5/22/87). On the other hand, a child-care worker at a Wesleyan day-care center, herself the daughter of a Holiness pastor, had covered the walls with Care Bear Posters and said, "I love Care bears," notwithstanding, it seems, the magical "Care Bear Stare" they use against threatening things (Field Notes DCS 1/7/87).

In the index of the yearbook of Springfield City Christian School, the large school sponsored by an independent Baptist church, one would be hard-pressed to tell from the senior alphabet that these students went to Christian school. In their alphabet, B is not for Bible, nor C for Christian, nor G for God, nor J for Jesus. Rather:

Algebra, Annex, Awesome,
Books, Braces, Buttons,
Classrings, Cokes, College,
Dates, Decisions, D-halls,

Eagles, Enthusiasm, Exams,
Fads, Friends, Fun,
Geometry, Golf, Grades,
High School, Homework, Honor Roll,
Jams, Juniors, Junk food,
Keepsakes, Knowledge, Knapsacks,
Laughs, Lockers, Lunch,
Memories, Math, Mondays,
New York, Notes, News,
Originality, Opportunity, Ocean,
Pacific, Parties, People,
Reeboks, Report cards,
Secrets, Swatches, Smiles,
Teamwork, Tests, Term papers,
Unique, Ultimate, Unforgettable,
Victory, Volleyball, Vocabulary,
Wins, Walkmans, Weekends,
Yearbook, Young, Yesterday,
Zat's all folks!!

At the same time, these students wrote "senior papers" detailing their personal philosophies of life, with titles such as "One Purpose" and " . . . About Life, and Other Vital Things . . ." The prescribed topics included discussions of God, the Trinity, God's Word, Truth and Reality, Knowledge and Wisdom, Man, Sin, Life after Death, and their own personal Life View, including opinions on Dating, Marriage, Education, and Humanism. In writing their personal philosophy papers, they created thesis statements such as:

Because the purpose of life is to glorify God, it is necessary for each person to have a philosophy of life which will direct the individual to the accomplishment of this aim.

and

An understanding and application of basic biblical doctrines will form a biblically correct philosophy of life. (Field Notes SCCS 5/87)

The Christian school culture is, rather than a total institution, a mixture of Christian and popular culture, and each is present to a certain degree. The salience of a variety of concerns can be measured by an analysis of student prayer requests and praise reports. At many schools, there is a time set aside every day for the students to "share" the things they wish to pray for, and to praise God for answering prayers and bestowing blessings. These shared prayer requests and praise reports tell us what conservative Christians believe they can legitimately ask God to provide, and for what gifts they believe God deserves praise. They show what students and faculty had on their minds; this was the time that they shared what had happened to them—what they were excited about.

In general, the analysis of 864 prayer requests and praise reports from four schools—ALCA, DCS, GCA, SCCS—shows that they most often concern physical, experiential, and material desires (see table 8.1). *Physical* cares included a variety of ailments, and included requests for "travel safety" (or "travel mercies") whenever anyone took a trip. *Experiences* included parties and sleepovers, birthdays, visits from grandparents, trips (restaurants, bowling, fishing, skating, and so on), and holiday vacations. *Spiritual* concerns—such as that someone be saved—were voiced in this way, but not nearly as frequently as more quotidian needs.

Faculty were much more likely than students to ask for God's help for *academic* or school considerations, including discipline and parent-teacher conferences, as well as school programs, trips, and parties. For students, academic concerns were expressed in words like these: "I wanna praise God that it's a review lesson; and pray that I get a 100."

Other concerns each accounted for 5 percent or less of the total prayer requests. *Mental* or emotional requests were for God's direction or wisdom, or for aid in getting along with a sibling or with juggling all the extracurricular activities of a busy teenager's life. Help with nonacademic *work* was requested generally for a parent, but sometimes for oneself: "I want to pray because I have to babysit on Saturday." Sometimes students asked God to favor their side in *competitions:* "I pray that today will be beautiful and we'll get to go outside for PE and Samuel will be on my team and our team will win." They also asked for advantageous weather or other *environmental* help: "I want to pray that the bees will not come back to our house." Two percent of the prayer requests are coded under a general *Pray For* category; they were requests simply to pray for a person, which asked God to "lift up" or "be with" someone, with no indication of the specific problem.

Looking at the praise reports, which thank God for his provision, we see that the students showed a popular culture bent. They talked about experiences like going to Disney World or the beach nearly half of the time (46 percent). Another 19 percent of the praise reports thanked God for *material* things, including shopping trips: "I got a real huge kite and I got thirteen yards of string."

The fact that they ask God for his help and thank God for blessings

Table 8.1 Topics of Prayer Requests and Praise Reports

TOPIC	PRAYER REQUESTS MADE BY				PRAISE REPORTS MADE BY			
	TOTAL	GCA FACULTY	GCA & DCS STUDENTS (K–7)	ALCA & SCCS STUDENTS (9–12)	TOTAL	GCA FACULTY	GCA & DCS STUDENTS (K–7)	ALCA & SCCS STUDENTS (9–12)
Physical	54%	29%	63%	30%	17%	15%	17%	0%[2]
Academic	9	26	5	3	2	15	2	0
Material	6	14	4	0[1]	19	31	19	0
Mental	5	13	2	20	1	8	0	0
Work	5	8	4	0	1	15	0	0
Experience	5	1	6	0	44	0	46	33
Competition	2	0	3	0	3	0	3	0
Environment	1	1	2	0	1	15	0	0
Spiritual	1	2	0	3	1	0	1	33
"Pray for"	2	2	2	0	0	0	0	0
No data	11	4	10	43[3]	9	0	10	33
Total	100%[4]	100%	100%	100%	100%	100%	100%	100%
No. of prayer requests	533	112	391	30				
No. of praise reports					331	13	315	3

[1] "0" signifies less than .5%.
[2] Note the small number of cases in this column.
[3] Most of these are "special unspokens" for which the student does not share the specific nature of the request.
[4] Figures may not sum to exactly 100% due to rounding.

bestowed has as its source conservative Christian ideology. But the things they ask and thank God *for* are the things they've learned to want from American popular culture.

"You Can't Take It All Away"

An administrator told me, "You can't just take it all away—without giving anything in return." So she allows her children to listen to "Christian contemporary" music, which has a beat, but "no bad language" (Field Notes GCA). "We try not to take everything away," echoed a teacher at a school sponsored by a Holiness church, explaining that they had taken students on a trip to Heritage USA. "You can't take it all away" was also the theme of a Holiness minister when he told me that he and his wife take the seniors on a trip to Myrtle Beach, North Carolina, or to Florida—to Disney World, Daytona, Silver Springs, or Marine Land. "I don't want them to feel that they are deprived of everything by being here in Christian school" (Field Notes PCA 4/08/87). Each of the schools I visited that had a senior class (no matter how small) had a "Senior Banquet," organized in a restaurant for the seniors by the junior class. It occurred in the spring when the public schools were having proms. The boys and girls dressed in finery; but there was no dancing. There were parties afterward, but no drinking. Likewise, costume "Hallelujah parties" take the place of Halloween celebrations for those segments of the conservative Christian community that want to avoid them. For younger students—who are interested in dinosaurs, as anyone who has listened to a youngster for five minutes knows—a teacher will give a unit on the extinct reptiles, saying nothing that would interfere with the Creationist interpretation of life's beginnings.

A filmed interview of a fundamentalist pastor's teenage daughter reflected, from a teenager's point of view, that "you can't take it all away," (but "you can't have it all" either):

> [They think] when you get out in the world, you're automatically gonna do it, or you're automatically—when you have contact with unsaved people—then you're gonna automatically turn bad. It depends on how much self-control you have. If you can control yourself being around unsaved people, when they swear—that you're not gonna go home and go swear—then it's all right to be there.
>
> You know, you can't just say to all Christians, "you can't have any fun in life. You can't go shopping because they play rock music in

stores; you can't go ice skating because they play rock music." And that's the way it seems to be: "You can't do this; you can't do that."

And we get sick of hearing it—can't, can't, can't. So you have to give a little. It's whether you have self-control or not.

God can help you do it. But then if you shove God aside then He's not gonna help you do anything. If you don't want God there He's not gonna be there.

You know some people have the mentality of that they have a bell in their pocket, and if they want God there, they ring it. And at other times they say, "God, You can just go away, don't even look at me now, 'cause I'm doin' something bad, just get away." But then when they get in trouble they say, "Oh God, please help me," you know. You know, you just can't do that, you know.

You either always have God, or you don't have God at all. That's the way it is, you know. You can't have it all. (Ault and Camerini 1988)

CHRISTIAN ALTERNATIVES

What are the Christians to do about the "no fun" dilemma raised by the fundamentalist pastor's daughter or the administrators' admonitions that "you can't take it all away?" One possibility is to let the children go out into the world, where they may either actually run afoul of things which are anathema to the conservative Christians, or, as Ammerman (1987) noted, they may find that the people out there really don't seem so evil after all, and lose some of the black-and-white aspect of their faith.

A third possibility is the creation of Christian alternatives. Entrepreneurs are flocking to create these alternatives which look just like the worldly variety, but with "no bad language."[1] It's a compromise between staying separate from the world and allowing conservative Christians not to miss out on the good things in life.[2] Critics of these new Christian alternatives may say that they smack of "Christian Lite"; and conservative Christians themselves are divided on this point (although I found very few who said they hadn't been, or wouldn't go, to Heritage USA, for example). On the other hand, Christian alternatives could be seen as another example of the conservative Christians' desire to live up to the principle that "to the Christian all things are sacred"; it could be seen as a manifestation of the Weberian traditional religious aspect of conservative Christianity. In more primitive traditional religions, the sacred is found in every rock, tree, and building. In modern-day conservative Christianity, it is found in bumper stickers and T-shirts.

When the conservative Christians create Christian alternatives, they take the popular culture pattern and fashion the Christian version from cloth of Christian colors; they do not create a whole new pattern.[3] The Christian alternatives use an American popular culture template in at least three ways. One way is to fashion a Christian version of a secular institution, to be frequented by Christian families, where they can be assured that people like themselves, who do not use "bad language," will predominate. Another way is to use popular language to convey the Christian message. The third way is the use of popular mediums to carry that message, usually in jazzed-up form. All of these trends are a far cry from the high-church style of rationalized religion. Bringing God to that down-home level is reminiscent, again, of Weber's traditional religion, where everyday items and sayings reflect the meaning system, nearly unconsciously.

Examples of the Christianizing of secular institutions would be the Christian schools themselves, resorts and vacations like Heritage USA, Christian river trips, the Adventurous Christians and Covenant Wilderness Center (outfitters for trips into Minnesota's Boundary Waters Canoe Area, who along with other resorts are members of Christian Camping International). For health-conscious Christians there are aerobics programs such as "Believercise" (ad in *Focus on the Family* 1988a) and health foods by Carol Bond. And for varied entertainment, there are Christian coffeehouses and nightclubs, and Racing with Jesus Ministries, which supports "The Lord's Winning Team" (Bumper sticker at GCA 5/5/87).[4]

The use of popular idiomatic language to express the Christian message is exemplified in the musical "We Like Sheep," by Kathie Hall (1987), which contains a song lauding the praises of an "abundawonderful life," and, when all the sheep are safely in the shepherd's fold, suggests "Let's party hearty." Sports lingo is used, as when a pastor and comedian likened the New Testament to a football game where "Israel blitzed . . . to a new halfback—the church—to catch the ball and run with it and score a touchdown for the Kingdom of God" (Focus on the Family radio 1987b). The language of the business world is also tapped: "Life Insurance? Jesus Christ" (bumper sticker 6/30/88) and "Heaven went bankrupt when it gave Jesus to die for you" (Field Notes ALCA 3/18/87). It's not unusual to applaud God at school programs and PTF meetings. "Let's all give God a hand"; "Let's all give God a big hand clap that the school year is ending; we made it through another year." (Field Notes GCA 11/8/87; 5/28/87).

Using new mediums to carry the Christian message is exemplified by the ubiquitous bumper stickers, the myriad of Christian magazines, the Christian Family Video Club, and of course Christian television itself. Modern forms of advertising are used on billboards and in newspapers. (This is true not only for conservative Christian endeavors, but increasingly for the mainline churches, as well [Stern 1988].) There is the Compu Bible, and computer software for the "Bible Men Game." "Badge-A-Minit" allows you to "spread the good word" by creating badges with a paraphrase of the Christian message, such as "Use your hot-line to God" (billboard east of Terre Haute, Ind. 3/6/88), or, at Christmastime, "Jesus is the reason for the season." There are greeting cards such as Dayspring's for "When you want to share your Heart and God's Love." Hallmark's "Heaven Help Us!" line of cards contains scriptures along with a humorous message. Its logo is a smiling angel rabbit hanging from a string attached to its wings. There are checkbooks with checks inscribed "What the World Needs is Jesus," T-shirts "for kids who love Jesus" which say, "Jesus is Awesome" or "Jesus is my Forever Friend" (Willie George Ministries), and an evangelist who dresses up as Superman (called "Superchristian") (Pardue 1988). The use of cartoons and cartoon characters is common, as are games such as Bible Trivial Pursuit and games made up by teachers such as Bible Bingo (Field Notes GCA 11/21/86) and Assurance (patterned after Jeopardy) (Field Notes GCA 2/10/87). There are scratch-n-sniff stickers which proclaim "God loves me and so does my teacher," "I'm a King's Kid," "Smile God Loves You," and "God Loves You Soda I" (Field Notes ASCI 1/28–30/87, from Sword and Shield Publications).

Toys for the children to collect are very closely patterned after their secular cousins. For example, Wee Win Toys ("Leading the way to wholesome play") markets twenty-four Prince of Peace Pets, which are essentially plushy Care Bears with a patch of scripture sewn on the front, and an ear tag spelling out the verse. There is Guardian Angel Bear—Psalms 91:11 and Good Deed Bear—Matthew 5:15. But like the Care Bears' Friends, the Prince of Peace Pets go beyond the genus *Ursus,* and include Righteous Raccoon—Romans 10:9–10; Sanctified Skunk—I Corinthians 6:9–11, and Full Armor Dilla—Ephesians 6:11–17. "Heroes of the Kingdom" are the size and shape of Masters of the Universe or GI Joes, but are fashioned after biblical characters, such as David and Goliath, Jesus, and John the Baptist. "Power Ponies" are My Little Ponies, complete with saran hair mane and comb, again with Bible verses attached. A plastic costume of the "Full Armor of God," comes with helmet, breastplate, greaves, and sword. (This last was the only one of the Christian toys I saw brought to school; the children I observed were still collecting the secular versions).

The use of popular language and popular mediums is reflected in the new Christian music. Christian contemporary, Christian rock, and Bible rap are available, as are magazines devoted to Christian music. Even in this one area there is a variety of opinion among the conservative Christians. A Holiness teacher wanted to be sure that music for a program didn't have "too much of a beat"; yet, the banjo and electric guitar were played through amplifiers (Field Notes CCCA 5/25/87). A Baptist-sponsored school (MCA; also NWCA) did not allow students to listen to Christian rock inside or outside the school. Hamlin Christian Academy's singing minister records Christian music with a beat, which is played over the loudspeaker at school. Drums and an electric keyboard accompany school singing. At GCA, the teachers did not agree on what was good and bad in Christian contemporary music. They all liked some of the tamer artists, like Amy Grant, but were divided on Petra and Stryper, groups who dress "wildly" and who *do* rock. Stryper's sound is heavy metal but the words are biblical; they call it heavenly metal (CBS 1987). They throw Bibles at the audience at the end of a frenzied performance punctuated by the agonized screams of fans, reminiscent of early Beatledom. Students at one school got into trouble for buying Christian music tapes and then taping secular contemporary music over it (without changing the labels).

At school services and programs at the Holiness schools only hymns were sung, but at the schools sponsored by Baptists, evangelicals, and charismatics, "fun songs" were allowed. This turned out to be a bit of a Pandora's box in some cases. That is, there is not too much fun one can have, or make, of "Blessed Assurance," or "How Great Thou Art." But sometimes the students added even more fun to the fun songs, and stepped over a line into what the teachers thought was sacrilege. For example, they would sometimes sing "Jesus stepped on me" instead of "Jesus set me free" in voices just low enough so as not to be detected. One day GCA's grades five through seven were having Bible together, singing fun songs for kids, with body motions to go along with the words. They sang:

The Lord is the shepherd and I am the sheep.
His banner over me is love.
The Lord is the shepherd and I am the sheep.
His banner over me is love.
The Lord is the shepherd and I am the sheep.
His banner over me is love.
His banner over me is love.

He brought me to His banqueting table,
His banner over me is love.

He brought me to His banqueting table,
His banner over me is love.
He brought me to His banqueting table,
His banner over me is love.
His banner over me is love. (Reference to banqueting table from
Song of Solomon 2:4)

They got carried away with exuberance when doing their motions—
crooked hand for "the shepherd," hopping with their "paws" up under
their chins for "the sheep," and especially their motions for how they
would eat at "the banqueting table." One of their teachers asked:

Teacher:	Beth, is that how you're going to banquet with the Lord when you see Him?
Beth:	No.
Teacher:	Well then don't do it now.

Knowing that it was usually sung by younger children, they began "I'm
in the Lord's Army" with arms outstretched and loud "urrrrrrrs" when
they "fly over the enemy." The administrator burst in the classroom
door: "That sounded absolutely repulsive to me. I wonder how it
sounded to God. . . . He should spit you out of his mouth. There are
songs that we sing that are fun, but everything we do is to honor God.
Everything we do." She continued to lecture them, sending one student,
who couldn't quite quench his smile, to the office. Then they prayed, and
the administrator left.

The other two teachers read them scripture, and continued the lecture:
"I know your deeds, that you are neither cold nor hot. I wish you were
either one or the other! So, because you are lukewarm—neither hot nor
cold—I am about to spit you out of my mouth" (Revelation 3:15–16
NIV) (Field Notes GCA 4/7/87).

Still, it was easy to see how the students fell in that direction. If all
things are sacred, what is sacrilege?[5]

WHY COMPROMISE?

The compromises we are discussing here may come as a surprise to my colleagues who asked me, "Do they spend all day on Bible?" and anticipated

that the separatist and exclusivist rhetoric would be played out in hidebound schools, reflecting the total institution model. But they are no surprise to the conservative Christians who have built the schools. They are quite aware that they have made compromises, as they deal with the needs of the schools every day, calling on the Lord to help them every step of the way.

Sometimes they despair of the compromises ("The world is affecting us more than church is") and blame parents for allowing worldly things in. Rarely do they deny the compromises. The principal of a school sponsored by a Baptist church told me they were proud that over their eleven-year history, they had not changed. "We don't want to look like we're lowering our standards" (Field Notes MCA 1/8/87). In some respects, he was right. For example, the school's basketball team still wore long pants, while nearly every other Christian school team they played wore shorts. But even this school had seen change; I doubt that in 1975 the boys wore Etonics and Tigers, the girls wore barrettes with long multi-colored ribbons dangling from them, and both sported Swatches. Keeping up with the fads of the world is a relative thing, to be sure, but it was always present to some degree in all of the Christian schools I observed. Sometimes the conservative Christians acknowledge the necessity for the compromises—"You can't take it all away."

"You can't take it all away" is consistent with accepted anthropological wisdom concerning how cultures can and can't be changed. Accommodations to the surrounding culture are necessary both for the long-term survival of the conservative Christian culture within American society and for the short-term survival of the schools themselves. If the Christian walk is to endure in American society, it must be walked the American way.

The modern world affords more choice in life-styles, systems of meaning, and schooling for one's children, than did even the world of the turn of the century, when fundamentalists first dug in their heels and declared that they would not accommodate to modernity. Since then some of their choices have reflected the necessity to market the conservative Christian message in an age of "overchoice," to use the word coined by Alvin Toffler in *Future Shock*. A Christian comedian says, "You can't (evangelize) people if you go around looking bummed out" (Jenkins 1987). This marketing aspect of conservative Christianity was reflected in a skit created by GCA's seventh graders for presentation at a program for parents. The plot concerned the attempt to proselyte a Hindu. The student actors told their teacher, who played the Hindu role, that worshipping more than one god, and living many lives to work out karma, were not necessary in Christianity. The teacher, convinced, said "Sounds like a better *deal* than I'm getting now!"[6]

In Southeastern Valley, Christian schools compete for pupils with a few other private schools, with relatively problem-free public schools, with a growing home-school group, and with one another. The administrators' rationale that "You can't take it all away" when explaining why they allow teenagers to listen to Christian rock music or why they take seniors on trips to Disney World, reflect, in part, a marketing strategy. These are marketing strategies both in the sense of competing in a marketplace of ideas, and in the sense of creating new cultural forms that successfully negotiate a compromise between competing cultural traits and values.

Teachers and parents who make, or allow, the compromises with the surrounding culture want their children to grow up to go to college, be successful in careers, and be leaders in community and national affairs. They wish for them a Christian, God-led life, but they know it will be led *in* American society. If you wanted your children to go to college and be leaders in the United States, would you train them to be completely noncompetitive?

Parents and teachers know their children will live in the surrounding culture, and some feel that they will be better equipped to "handle" it if they know "what's out there." The Christian schools are often likened to a "hothouse" by both Christian advocates and Christian detractors. Advocates say the controlled hothouse environment makes the children strong, and able to withstand the slings and arrows of the world (and of the devil). But even plants in a hothouse must be hardened off before they are set out. One administrator considered introducing some secular textbooks into the curriculum because if the students had the chance to see them, in later life they would be better able to "pick and choose" (and to choose, she hopes, the conservative Christian way) (Field Notes GCA 4/20/87). For the same reason, the Institute for Creation Research touts a "two-model approach," teaching both creationism and evolution. (However, through the elementary grades, they advocate teaching only creationism.) (Field Notes ICR 8/13/86).

Still another reason for hard-and-fast rules to become diluted is the diversity found within the schools. Certainly, the Christian schools are not as diverse as American culture at large. In fact, it might be said that creating a haven of homogeneity is their reason for being. Nevertheless there is diversity among the families of the students, and, in some cases, among the teachers. (At some schools, the teachers are required to belong to the sponsoring church, but in others, the teachers come from a variety of backgrounds.) In Southeastern Valley and City, no school's student body hailed solely from the sponsoring church. Increased mixture in the student body is a national trend, according to Michael Mooers (1989), marketing manager for the Alpha Omega curriculum.

This diversity caused the students at a school sponsored by a Holiness church to question the school rules. The school made no attempt to govern the students' behavior outside the school, but did go to lengths to protect its dress code on the school grounds. The high-school students protested to their teacher that the school wanted them to be hypocritical, since their home churches didn't require these strictures, and they didn't follow them outside the school walls. They also asked whether *she* agreed with the rules, since she went to a different Holiness church, with different norms. The teacher replied that when they were at the school, she and they would follow the rules of the sponsoring church. The students, with constant supervision, followed the letter of the rules, even if letting some of the spirit slip away.

Diversity surfaced at Dells Christian School when three first- and third-grade girls planning a sleepover asked their younger hostess to "get scary (video)tapes." One suggested *Ghostbusters*. Another warned, "No, not *Ghostbusters;* that's kind of dirty." The third little girl had already seen it (Field Notes DCS 12/12/87).

An example of the diluting effect the varying home environments has on school rules happened on GCA's playground. Gena and Sandra, the two kindergarteners who had the set-to over the Jem rocker poster, had another one when Sandra accused Gena of liking rock music because she said she liked Cindy Lauper. They brought the dispute to the teacher, who had never heard of Cindy Lauper, but quickly realized that she was an alleged rock star. She said, "Sandra, you let Gena's mother tell her what she can listen to; and you let your mother tell you what to listen to." After the girls had gone back to the swings, she turned to me, and said, "That was a hard one" (Field Notes GCA). A high-school teacher at Baptist-sponsored Abundant Life Christian Academy took a young girl to task for wearing a boy's class ring (from one of City's public schools). The student objected, "My mom said I could" (Field Notes ALCA 4/10/87).

A diversity of opinion among parents on whether children should be allowed to believe in fantasy characters such as the tooth fairy, the Easter Bunny, and Santa Claus became apparent around Christmastime. The controversy started in the van with fifth and sixth graders on their way to the public library. They sang "White Christmas" and then "Santa Claus Is Coming to Town," which precipitated an argument over whether there really was a Santa Claus. A sixth-grade boy, son of teacher Mrs. Nichols, was adamant that there was not. "There is no Santa Claus. Well, there is; his name is Raymond Nichols. And there's an Easter Bunny; her name is Frances Nichols" (Field Notes GCA 11/6/86).

The argument continued the next time they went to the library. It came to a head around a table where two fifth-grade girls who were believers and three sixth-grade girls who were not were reading Christmas books, among them *The Truth About Santa Claus*. The sixth graders tried to convince the two younger girls that there was no Santa. Fifth grader Tina looked up at me with beseeching eyes. "There is a Santa Claus, isn't there, Mrs. Wagner?" I stood mute with shoulders shrugged. As they argued the fine points of seeing and hearing evidence of Santa Claus, they continued to ask me, and debated whether I would know, anyway. Sixth-grade nonbeliever Patricia said, "You know you don't believe in Santa Claus because you're a—are you a mother?" Another answered, "No, but she's married." Deciding that was sufficient, Patricia continued, "Well do you wake up and [find presents] under your tree without you gettin' up and puttin' 'em there?" I was fairly successfully skirting the issue when their teacher came up. Fifth grader Denise asked, "Mrs. Nichols, is there really a Santa Claus?" Without a moment's hesitation, the teacher answered, "No. There was, but he died—St. Nicholas." Denise protested, "My mother said there was." The teacher replied, "Did your mother tell you that? Well, maybe in your family he's real" (Field Notes GCA 12/04/86).

The conservative Christian educators should not, then, be castigated for their compromises, for they do indeed work within the context of American culture at large. How successful ("saleable") would a more "alternative" alternative be? In carrying out their revitalization process, the conservative Christians must pick and choose among cultural alternatives and must work out compromises which "synthesize a relation between [competing] cultural categories" (Sahlins 1976, 217). In so doing, the progenitors of Christian schools manifest a mode of thought discussed by Lévi-Strauss.

Lévi-Strauss (1966) made a distinction between the methods of the engineer, who plans what materials and resources are needed for a project and acquires them, and the *bricoleur,* the handyman Jack-of-all-trades, who works with what is at hand. He made the term work for the building of cultural forms as well as for technological labors. The Christian educators work in the bricoleur mode, picking and choosing from what's available, and making alterations to popular cultural themes and artifacts, rather than using an entirely new pattern to fashion alternative cultural forms out of whole cloth.

Thinking like a cultural engineer, we can imagine a process of delineating the values the conservative Christians want to see pervasive in American culture—what they wish to instill in their children—and then examining all possible ways to manifest them. Instead, like Lévi-Strauss's bricoleur, they create Christian alternatives, based on popular culture templates. Rather than abstaining from competition, Christian school organizations hold contests for finding Bible verses speedily. Rather than eschewing collecting toys, conservative Christians create My Little Ponies and Care Bears and Their Friends with Bible verses appliquéd on them. The alternatives might better be described as alterations.[7]

The bricoleur mode is carried forward by actors in the Christian school transfer culture (which lies between the existing culture and the goal culture), who have been culture-bearers in the existing culture. Teachers who have been trained in secular universities and who have taught in public schools bring with them a set of cultural traits that they put into place, modified, within the Christian school setting. When I asked a pastor and administrator why his school stayed within the state regulations for public schools (which do *not* apply to private schools) with regard to subjects to be taught, number of days in the school year, and so forth, he indicated that he and the teachers saw no reason to spend the time required to "reinvent the wheel" (Field Notes PCA 4/8/87).[8]

As the culture-bearers become actors in an attempt to create a new goal culture, they find that unless they are willing to become socially, geographically, and economically independent and isolated, they must still deal with the existing culture of the United States. As they confront the surrounding culture, compromises are made. As they discover diversity among themselves, compromises are made.

Education Culture in the Christian Classroom: Snoopy and Scripture, Phonics and Prayer

The Christian schools reflect an amalgam of cultures. Conservative Christians have not separated themselves and created a brand new culture. They have borrowed and pieced—creating a cultural quilt of pieces from various sources. One set of ingredients derives from the goal culture they are trying to revitalize, which they call the Christian walk. Mainstream middle-American popular culture is the source of other elements. Still other traits have their origin in the culture of American education and its attendant vocabulary, norms, and artifacts.

HOW ALTERNATIVE IS CHRISTIAN ALTERNATIVE SCHOOLING?

Imagine a school that is truly different—an alternative to American public school in every way. The purpose of the school would be the usual—teaching children the knowledge or basic cultural requirements they need to know to succeed (as defined by their parents)—enculturating them into their subculture. But this goal would be met by means other than the usual, traditional methods.

For example, in this alternative school, the material culture would be different from public schools. That means you wouldn't expect to see blackboards and chalk, bulletin boards and school desks. Perhaps you wouldn't expect to find traditional classrooms or even school buildings. Perhaps the length of the school day and year would be longer (or shorter) than that of the public school.[1]

The students would be taught by methods other than lecturing by the teacher and reading in the textbook. In this school, if it were a

Christian-oriented alternative school, perhaps there would be no text-books other than the Bible and tracts explaining the doctrine of the sponsoring church. Traditional subjects and perhaps grade levels would not be present. In this alternative school, evaluation, if there were evaluation, would proceed through operations other than achievement tests and be symbolized by means other than grades. Perhaps the roles of teacher and student would be modified.

You can use your imagination to create the alternatives, or hark to other cultures. Perhaps the alternative school could resemble the Jewish schools in the shtetls of Eastern Europe. Children (in these schools it was only boys) three or four years old sat in a "room with a long table flanked by hard, backless benches on which the little boys sat for ten hours a day, five and a half days a week." The children studied prayer books at first, then the Pentateuch. To not pay attention was to court severe punishment (Lee 1986, 54; Aleichem 1955; Zborowski 1955).

On the other hand, perhaps the alternative would more closely resemble the model of the traditional Oglala Sioux Indian people, where a young boy would decide to go out to explore the outdoors, and would be instructed by his father: "Look carefully at everything you see." And when the boy returned in the afternoon, he would report to his father where he had gone. His father would ask him questions: "On which side of the trees does the bark grow the thicker?" (Lee 1986, 46–47; Eastman 1902). The alternative might be training children to live communally. Or the alternative might be choosing a time in the history of American education—the one-room schoolhouse and the McGuffey reader, for example—and recreating that, unchanged.

Looked at by this measure—of how different a school could be—the alternative Christian schools aren't very alternative. This is true even though the state where Southeastern Valley is located has no requirements or regulations for private schools. All of the schools I visited, for example, had done whatever they could to approximate a school building on the traditional American model. Each of the schools longed for more space, and when they described the space they would like to have—it was the modern American public school, with "classrooms, a music room, a gymnasium and a lunchroom or cafeteria."

All of the schools used an "A-B-C-D-F grading system," with slight variations in what percentage was equivalent to each letter grade. The grade scales were the same as one of the public school systems in Southeastern Valley, and higher than the other one.

All of the schools gave "achievement tests" near the end of the school year—the Stanford Achievement Test or Metropolitan Achievement Tests. Some of the schools were proud of the fact that they used an older, "harder" version of the achievement tests than the public schools use.

The school day in these near-to-a-public-school-building-as-possible buildings begins between 8:30 and 9:00 A.M., and ends around 3:30 P.M., Monday through Friday, September to June. "Students" are placed in "grades," called kindergarten through senior. In most of the schools, the younger students spend the day in one "classroom" with one "teacher" except for "music, art, and PE." Older students make the rounds from teacher to teacher, switching classrooms to accommodate the teachers, who specialize in various "subjects." The subjects are taught from age-graded "textbooks."

For the older students, the day is broken into "periods," usually fifty minutes in length, during which they study the subjects of "history, geography, mathematics, language, spelling and reading, science, PE, and sometimes music and art," as well as Bible. The schools using self-paced materials are more different, because here children of all ages proceed through these same subjects on their own, at their own pace.

All of the schools had bulletin boards, blackboards, and chalk. No classroom contained bulletin boards with only sacred materials on them; Snoopy and Iggy and children with large round heads abound. In the church school housing a statewide competition sponsored by a chapter of the American Association of Christian Schools, a large bulletin board said "Study to Show Thyself Approved" (II Timothy 2:15). It sported Charlie Brown and his friends with scripture in the voice balloons coming out of their mouths. Lucy was quoting John 12:26: "If any man serve me, let him follow me." Charlie Brown himself continued the verse, "and where I am, there shall also my servant be." The little red-haired girl spouted James 4:7: "Submit yourselves therefore to God," and Linus continued it with: "Resist the devil and he will flee from you." Snoopy lay prone on top of his doghouse with Woodstock the bird on his stomach (Field Notes AACS Competition 4/10/87).

No musical program was completely sacred. Even Christmas programs, with their contemporary skits and ubiquitous "Jesus is the Reason for the Season," and "God's Greatest Gift—Jesus," resembled the annually televised "Boston Pops Christmas Show" rather than the "Festival of Nine Lessons and Caroles" at the King's College of Cambridge, where readers intone "Thanks be to God" after biblical passages describing the nativity.

All graduation nights contained all the trappings and symbols of public school graduation ceremonies, and the same sequence of events, with scripture and testimonials added. No school handbook was completely sacred, justifying all policies biblically and making only references to the quality of the spiritual education children would receive; none ignored the intellectual education they would obtain. A look at the mottoes of ten Christian schools shows a concern for both kinds of edcuation. Some stress "quality education":

Growth through Quality Education (GCA)
For Tradition, Values, and Excellence in Education (Springs of Life Christian School)
Quality Education in a Christian Environment (DCS)
Educating for Time and Eternity (DCS)
Quality Teaching in a Christian Atmosphere (Ebenezer Christian School)

Others concern character traits deemed desirable:

Loyalty in Study and Service (NWCA)
Christian Education—The Hope of Our Republic (NWCA)
Truth, Honor, Wisdom (ALCA)
Character before Career (Stony Brook)

while others are concerned strictly with the spiritual realm:

Learning the Mind of Christ (HCA)
. . .bringing into captivity every thought in obedience to Christ. II Corinthians 10:5 (HCS)
Open Ye the gates, that the righteous nation which keepeth the truth may enter in (Isaiah 2:2) (MCA)

According to historians, the early Christians were not enamored of knowledge.

The acquisition of knowledge, the exercise of our reason or fancy, and the cheerful flow of unguarded conversation, may employ the leisure of a liberal mind. Such amusements, however, were rejected with abhorrence, or admitted with the utmost caution, by the severity of the fathers, who despised all knowledge that was not useful to salvation, and who considered all levity of discourse as criminal abuse of the gift of speech. (Gibbon 1960, 166)

Present-day conservative Christians have also been accused, sometimes with reason, of being "anti-intellectual." But such is not the case for the modern-day Christians who send their children to these Christian schools.

Christian parents want to assure that their children can become leaders in today's world; that requires today's skills.

The Christian school administrators despaired that outsiders thought that "all we do here is Bible and prayer." The administrator at GCA began every interview with prospective parents by saying, "It's a school first." Others said, "This is not church" or "This is not Sunday school"; "It's a real school." The administrators who contended that it's "not all Bible and prayer"; and "it's not church" would add, "We just have a different value system."

The question we are continuing to address here is to what extent the different value system is expressed in the classroom. We look to see how the conservative Christian ideology is handled. Is it, as would be expected in a Weberian rationalized religion carried into the Christian school culture in a "logically coherent, generally phrased" manner? (Geertz 1973, 172). Or is it added on in an ad hoc way, as would be predicted for Weber's traditional religion? Is it a conservative Christian face painted onto forms and symbols and techniques borrowed from other cultural settings, in bricoleur fashion?

A variety of measures gauges the admixture of modern education and conservative Christian cultural attributes: the content of the vocabulary used in the schools, the professional conferences the teachers attend and the magazines they read, the textbooks, and the time spent on various topics and forms of discipline used in the classroom.

PHONICS AND PRAYER: THE VOCABULARY OF EDUCATION CULTURE

The vocabulary used in faculty meetings and at the conventions of Christian school professional organizations shows much that is derived from the culture of academic education. (As Rose 1988 notes, the vocabulary and system is different in an ACE school. She likens it to business culture rather than to education culture.) At "in-service workshops for teachers" as well as at "faculty meetings," teachers spend much time, for example, discussing "traditional classrooms," and also decrying "combination classrooms." They debate at what age students should come out of "contained classrooms" and go into "departmentalized" ones. They weigh the pros and cons of "early childhood ed" and of "labeling students as L.D." (learning disabled) through the use of "diagnostic tests." When they discuss "curriculums," they are concerned with "sequencing" and with using "horizontal materials" that are "subject oriented" and meet "SOLs" (Standards of Learning)—which is not required of private schools by the state. They discuss what "skills" should be taught to keep students "on grade level." They discuss how to "review" different "families of math facts" in order to ready students for "achievement tests." They discuss how "predictable books" can help young students learn to read and how "prewriting" might improve the writing skills of older ones. They develop "units" on various topical areas, and create "learning centers" where students can do special "seatwork." Some have had instruction in "cognitive learning" theories and techniques. They ponder ways to improve the students' "critical thinking." They give each other advice on handling parents diplomatically in "parent-teacher conferences." They even discuss the merits of several smaller Christian schools' "consolidating." Borrowing the latest addition to educational jargon (and controversy), an ad for Bob Jones University Press highlights its "accountability" (Field Notes; *Excel* 1987, 33).

The teachers spent much of their time learning teaching techniques. For the most part, the teachers—whatever their qualifications—tried to expand their knowledge. The volunteer assistant at the high school "learning center" at Calvary Cross Christian Academy, a parent who was herself a high-school graduate, took all the self-paced mathematics instruction books home and pored through them, so that she could explain to the students how to do the problems. The first- and second-grade teacher at CCCA has taken a correspondence course from the Children's Literature Institute and writes children's stories for publication in magazines. She thinks about putting her teaching aids into a book, and wants to get a college degree in education. At GCA, some of the teachers take education courses in the summer, to learn techniques that they put into practice in their classrooms, and to maintain their state teacher certifications (which are not required in this state's private schools). Others take courses with conservative Christian content, such as seminars sponsored by the Institute for Creation Research at Bible colleges. One of the teachers hoped that, as part of my research, I would devise lists of what students were learning in each grade, which she could use to clarify what she should be teaching. As the school year drew to a close, the first- and second-grade teacher at Grace Christian drew up a list of "to dos" for herself for the summer. She had listed these numbered tasks:

1. Art projects for the whole year
2. Language projects for the whole year
3. Special holidays

4. Bulletin boards
5. Math—incorporate cognitive instruction
6. Study cognitive instruction material
7. Interest centers
8. Clean out filing cabinet
9. Scientific words

Professional Conferences

The seminars and workshops presented at professional conferences for Christian school administrators and teachers show the admixture of education and Christian cultures—of phonics and prayer. The seminars and workshops are led by personnel from the sponsoring organization, by teachers from Christian schools and colleges, and by secular educational consulting agencies.

To discover what concerns are salient at these meetings, the descriptions of 319 seminars and workshops were coded by topic. The seminars and workshops took place at conventions for the Association of Christian Schools International (ACSI), and the American Association of Christian Schools (AACS) and at regional A Beka and ACE in-service conferences. Teaching techniques received by far the most attention; ideas for how to teach skills such as reading, writing, and arithmetic were presented in more than three times as many seminars as were techniques for evangelizing the child or teaching Bible.[2]

The "topics" included these:

EDUCATION: These seminars and workshops were overwhelmingly concerned with helping the teacher teach the children skills or subject matter in the areas of math, science, language arts, and foreign languages. More than 40 percent reflected this concern. Some titles were: "Creating Study Skills," "Reflective Reading: A Strategy for Building Thinking Skills," "Motivating your Students Academically," "Another L.D. Student!" and "Classroom Organization and Efficiency Now and for the Years to Come." The descriptions of these workshops included phrases currently in use in the education field today—such as "critical thinking and analysis skills" and "writing across the curriculum."

SACRED: Thirteen percent of the seminars concerned the child's spirit or Christian character, evangelizing, teaching Bible, or conducting chapel. Some titles were: "How to Weave the Gospel and Lead Boys and Girls to Christ," "Take the Pain out of Scripture Memorization," and "Evidence that the Holy Spirit is Grieved in the School."

Table 9.1 Topics of Seminars at Christian School Conventions

| | TOTAL | | | % ON TOPIC | | | | |
| | | SPIRITUAL CONTENT[1] | | | | | | |
TOPIC	% ON TOPIC	S	N-S	ACSI 1986	ACSI 1987	AACS 1987	A BEKA 1987	ACE 1986
Education	44%	11%	89%	35%	39%	66%	86%	38%
Sacred	13	100	0	12	17	0	14	6
Extracurricular	11	14	86	18	9	11	0	0
Structure	10	30	70	11	9	11	0	25
Counseling	7	35	65	12	5	6	0	0
Discipline	6	39	61	5	7	3	0	13
Material needs	6	7	93	2	10	0	0	0
Family	4	36	64	4	4	3	0	19
Total	100%[2]	(29%	71% overall)	100%	100%	100%	100%	100%
No. of seminars	319			115	132	35	21	16

[1]Percent of seminar descriptions containing *any* spiritual content (S) versus those containing *no* spiritual content (N-S).
[2]Figures may not sum to precisely 100% due to rounding.

EXTRACURRICULAR: Eleven percent of the seminars dealt with teaching such subjects as music, art, home economics, physical education, or athletics. "Providing Proper Motivation for Artistic Expression," "The Recorder Factory: A New Approach to Teaching Music!" "Drills to Develop Winning Basketball Teams," "Cheerleading," and "Motivating Young Athletes" were some of their titles.

SOCIAL STRUCTURE: One-tenth of the seminars were concerned with the social structure of the school and how to make it run smoothly, including "Lines of Cooperation and Communication," "Administrative Pitfalls to Avoid," "Teacher Self-Evaluation," and "The Christian School Secretary as a Professional."

COUNSELING: Seven percent were concerned with coping with the children's personalities and problems: "Understanding Stress in Childhood," "Helping Children through the Broken Home Experience," and "Sex Education in the Christian School."

DISCIPLINE: Six percent related to handling the children's behavior in the classroom, such as "The Classroom Teacher and Discipline: A Positive Approach," "Classroom Management and Control at the High School Level," and "Discipline: Loving Firmness."

MATERIAL NEEDS: Six percent dealt with the material needs of the school and with recruiting students: "Why aren't they Beating a Path to the Schoolhouse Door?" "Formulating a Development Program for Your School," "Peak Performances in Fundraising: Who to Ask, Why to Ask, When to Ask, How to Ask," "Improving Cash Flow by Computerizing your Billing," "First Steps in Establishing a Christian School Library," and "What you Should Know About Safety Requirements."

FAMILY: Four percent of the seminars were concerned with managing the children's families, or with keeping harmonious relationships within one's own family. They included titles such as "Picky, Picky Parents!" "Motivating Parents to be Parents," "Parental Involvement: A Real Plus for an Effective School Ministry."

Thus, the how-tos of teaching and administering were overwhelmingly represented in seminar and workshop topics, with evangelizing and teaching Bible taking a backseat. The descriptions of the seminars, written so that participants could choose among a large number of consecutive sessions, sometimes, but not always, used spiritual language. Although "all things are sacred" to the Christian, not every seminar and workshop had a spiritual face. Nearly three-quarters (71 percent) of their descriptions contained no reference to anything spiritual. Examples are these descriptions:

A New Look at the Writing Process. The teaching of writing can be an exciting, rewarding, and creative experience for both teacher and student. The ideas presented in this seminar can be adapted to fit the needs of any classroom and be a motivational tool for children at all ability levels.

Reading—Really?? We spend a lot of time teaching our children to read; unfortunately too many of them are not making it! Why? This presentation will address issues of reading, reading readiness, and perceptual skills necessary for primary reading skills.

In these descriptions of the workshops and seminars, those more likely to contain spiritual references—such as the words "Bible," "Christ-like," "Christ-centered," "God," "ministry," "scripture," or "spiritual"—were discussions of discipline, the family, counseling, and the social structure of the school. About one-third (30 to 39 percent) of the descriptions of *these* topical seminars included spiritual language. Discussions of extra-curricular activities, education (teaching techniques), or the material needs of schools were less likely to have any spiritual content; about 10 percent of these seminar descriptions contained spiritual language (14 percent, 11 percent, and 7 percent, respectively).

Some of the seminar descriptions demonstrate how spiritual language was joined with the language of the education profession. For example, the description of "Principles of Motivation" says:

Understanding motivation is an important part of teaching. These timely, biblical principles will enable you to work with your students in a fresh and exciting way.

Reducing Outstanding Debt Through Computerization: Inconsistency in follow-up can be mistaken for a weak financial policy. How to have strong collections and maintain a Christian image.

Discipline: Loving Firmness: Foundations of good classroom discipline are discussed along with several practical suggestions for achieving self-control on the part of students that leads to Spirit control.

Learning to Counsel: Counseling is primarily helping another person. While there is a place for sympathy and a listening ear, there are other occasions when it is important to probe or confront. Effective counseling must be sensitive both to Scriptural principles and good counseling techniques. This workshop will try to explore some of these areas.

Dealing with Stress: Stress is a part of life, and God's Word gives clear guidelines for dealing with it. During this session stress will be characterized, and practical direction for dealing with it will be shared.

As can be seen in these descriptions, "practical" was an often used word in descriptions of seminars and workshops. More than one-tenth of the descriptions (12 percent) contained the word "practical."[3]

The materials on display at teachers' conventions also showed the amalgam of Christian and educational concerns and motifs. The sixty-three vendors advertising their wares at a regional ACSI convention purveyed everything from play equipment to sex education materials, from Care Bear scratch-n-sniff stickers to laundry soap for fund-raising. They came from seventeen states—as far away as Arizona and New Mexico. Two-thirds of the vendors were specifically Christian in nature, such as A Beka textbook curriculum, Toccoa Falls College in Georgia, or William Jennings Bryan College in Dayton, Tennessee (the site of the Scopes trial). One-third were neutral or generic vendors such as G & L Screen Printing, the J. H. Pence Company (sellers of instructional materials, school furniture, and supplies), Recreation Environments Company, and Open Court Publishing Company. From Sword and Shield, teachers could purchase Care Bear recognition awards congratulating a student, for example, for "bear-rific work," or scratch-n-sniff stickers with "divine fragrances" that said "Smile God Loves You" (banana), "Jesus Listens when I Talk to Him" featuring a smiling telephone (lemon), or "Lettuce Rejoice!" (lemon).

Professional Resources

Magazines available for Christian teachers also reflect the mixture of Christian and educational language and subject matter. For example in *EXCEL*, "The Christian Teacher's Resource Publication," one-half to three-quarters of the articles have spiritual content, the others being strictly tips on teaching and administering borrowed from the secular realm. About 75 percent of the advertisers are Christian; the others are generic. Features such as the "Idea Bank," "Arts and Crafts," "Bulletin

Boards," "Reproducibles," "Kinder Corner," "Music Notes," and "Computers in Education" are secular in content, except around Christmastime, when the bulletin board ideas are sacred (*EXCEL* Winter 1986, Spring 1987, Fall 1987). On the other hand, *The Christian Educator*, which includes "news from home schools, Christian schools, regional, state, and city-wide organizations," is more conservative Christian–oriented, and includes articles critical of American society, such as "Violence in the Schools," "It's Hardly Hysteria to Fear this Plague" (AIDS), "'Dungeons and Dragons' Suicide," "Helping Kids Avoid Humanism," and "All Non-Christian Education is Anti-Christian!" (*The Christian Educator*, September 1987, October 1987).

Accreditation Criteria

The Association of Christian Schools International (ACSI), the largest of the Christian School support organizations, offers an accreditation program. Their accreditation evaluation criteria show that ACSI desires that "two major themes [be] obvious throughout the ACSI accreditation program. . . . "First, the program probes the spiritual aspects, the Christian aspects of the school. Second, the program is educationally sound. Those themes are intertwined in this instrument, *Evaluative Criteria for Christian Elementary and Secondary Schools" (ACSI 1983)*.

Indeed, the themes of spirituality and educational professionalism are intertwined throughout the criteria. There are sixteen broad categories of accreditation criteria, only one of which is specifically spiritual—"Philosophy and Objectives." The others concern the administration of the school, its budget, size, and facilities. The accreditors request information about the "Instructional Program," "Student Activities Program," "Guidance Services," "Media Center," and so on.

From time to time, spiritual language is introduced into (or added onto) an otherwise generic set of evaluation criteria. For example, under the section on "Statement of Guiding Principles for School, Home, Community," the school is asked to answer this question: "What demographic trends within the community are going to have an impact upon the school within the next ten years, the Lord willing?"

Staff requirements include "Character: . . . The teachers, administrators, and staff personnel shall be born again persons with clear testimonies for Christ. . . ." and "Training and Experience: . . . Teachers shall hold a bachelor's degree from a recognized college and shall be certified by ACSI."

The "Self-Study" of an ACSI Accredited School that I visited (Springfield City Christian School) shows concern with both of these attributes, expressed in the language of the conservative Christian, and in the idiom of the education profession. In answering this ACSI-proffered question: "Discuss the spiritual qualifications, the academic preparation, and the educational experience of the chief school administrator," the school personnel wrote this description:

> The spiritual qualifications of the chief administrator are as follows: he is a born again Christian, evidences a consistent life of spiritual maturity, is active in the local church ministry, serves faithfully as an associate pastor, and rules his house well.
>
> Mr. Bradley's academic preparation includes a B.S. degree in Education and an M.R.E. degree, both of which were acquired with high honors. His Masters work concentrated on Christian Day School ministry. He also holds a Professional Administrative Certificate from ACSI.
>
> Mr. Bradley's educational experience includes three years of teaching and 6.5 years in his present position as Associate Pastor for School Ministries (i.e., Chief Administrator).

The profiles of other administrators at the schools used similar language, describing each one as: "[being] a born again Christian" or "[having] a firm testimony of assurance of salvation"; "evidenc[ing] a consistent life of spiritual maturity," "evidenc[ing] a close walk with the Lord," or "demonstrat[ing] a mature Christian walk." They continued with lists of academic and professional qualifications.

A TIME TO PRAY AND A TIME TO LEARN

An administrator who had heard his school criticized by people who said "all they do is pray and have Bible over there," said that, on the contrary, "we start half an hour early so that we have all that out of the way before most schools begin their day" (Field Notes MCA 12/14/86). Indeed, the schools did not spend as much time on religious activities as one might suspect, and certainly not as much time as they could have.

The students' day began at 8:20 to 9:00 A.M., and ended at 3:00 to 3:16 P.M., making for a 360- to 400-minute day. An analysis of daily schedules showed that in twenty-eight classrooms (covering grades kindergarten through twelve) in six schools (ALCA, CCCA, DCS, GCA,

Table 9.2 How Is Time Spent in School? Daily Schedule of Activities

AMOUNT OF TIME SPENT ON:[1]		% OF DAY	MINUTES[2]	WHERE
Subjects	Minimum	20%	62	DCS kindergarten
	Maximum	80%	290	CCCA grades 8–12
Breaks	Minimum	17%	65	GCA grades 3&4
	Maximum	71%	230	DCS kindergarten
Religion	Minimum	3%	9	DCS kindergarten on non-chapel days
	Maximum	23%	90	GCA grades 5–7 on chapel days

[1]From an analysis of daily schedules for 28 classrooms, including grades kindergarten through 12, in six schools (ALCA, DCS, CCCA, GCA, MCA, SCCS).
[2]The length of the school day ranged from 360–400 minutes in the various schools.

MCA, SCCS), the presentation of explicitly religious material, or the playing out of explicitly religious rituals, took 3 percent to 13 percent of the day's time—nine to fifty minutes. During this time, the pledges to the Christian flag, the American flag, and the Bible were recited, a prayer was said, a Bible story was read, and sometimes a song was sung. In five of the schools (ALCA, DCS, GCA, MCA, SCCS), prayer requests and prayer reports from the students are heard during this time. This time also included Bible classes for older students. Chapel, with a sermon or a Bible lesson, usually presented weekly for the school as a whole, adds another thirty to fifty minutes to this time spent in religious activities—a maximum of 23 percent of the day's time.

The least religious day would be a non-chapel day at the Wesleyan-sponsored Dells Christian School (3 percent). The most religiously oriented content would be heard on a chapel day at Grace Christian Academy (sponsored by charismatic parents), or Baptist-run Springfield City Christian School (23 percent and 21 percent, respectively). The other two Baptist-run schools (ALCA, MCA) and the school sponsored by a Holiness church (CCCA) fell in between. Rose's (1988, 79) data show between 8 percent and 13 percent of the students' time is spent in "spiritual training" in a school sponsored by a charismatic community. In the ACE school she observed, chapel was held for thirty minutes three days a week, accounting for 5 percent of the students' work week.

Break time for play, naps, PE, and maintenance activities such as going to the bathroom, getting a drink, having snacks, sharpening pencils, and straightening desks of course take longer in the younger grades. Kindergarteners spend 57 to 71 percent of their day in these activities. The third and fourth graders at GCA whined that they didn't have as much break time as they used to. Their perceptions were correct. In first and second grades, about one-third of the day was spent in breaks, PE, and maintenance. In grades three and four, this was cut in half. The teacher's official schedule, posted on the wall, allotted 19 percent of the day for religious activities (8:30 to 9:45 A.M.), 35 percent for breaks and PE, and 46 percent for subjects. But actually the teacher usually started subjects a little after 9:00 A.M., and the days were arranged so that the students spent 5 to 9 percent of their time on religion, 17 to 22 percent on breaks and PE, and 71 to 74 percent on subjects.

By grade seven, breaks drop to around a quarter of the day's activities in most schools. But a self-paced (ACE) school curriculum can allow for as much as 40 percent of the day in breaks, depending on how fast the students do their PACES. Schools that use a self-paced system differ among themselves in the amount of break time they allow. So in some of these schools, students spend one-half of their time at their desks or cubicles, and at others, four-fifths of their time. When I visited ACE schools, I would see students who had caught up in their PACES doing errands and working on fund-raising acitivities.

This leaves one-fifth to four-fifths of the time for subjects. Kindergarteners only spend one-fifth to one-third of their time on subjects, between one and two hours. But first through fourth graders spend more than any of the other grades on subjects—58 percent to 80 percent of their time. In the upper grades, where students are changing classes in seven- to nine-period days, with one period for lunch, one for PE, one for Bible or a religiously oriented class, and two- to five-minute breaks in between, 50 to 70 percent of the time is left for subjects.

Subjects and Textbooks

Once settled into their classes, how much religious content do the students hear and read in their various subjects? Christian educators, especially those who lecture and write books on the subject, give as their ideal "integrating the Bible" into every subject, but the integration often has the appearance of the bricoleur-like add-on.[4] The various grades differed with regard to how much "sacred" material they heard on any given day. The first through fourth grades heard the least, because, as the teachers said, they were concerned with the students' "acquiring skills" in these grades. The third- and fourth-grade teacher at GCA (who had taught for some twenty-five years in public schools and two years in two different Christian schools) told me, "You'll find, in my class, much the same as public school, because these children need to learn those skills. But with the addition of the Bible" (Field Notes GCA 9/17/86). The kindergarten had more of a sacred flavor, because the first-year pupils were being socialized into the school routine. Beginning in grade five, more content is introduced, and this content can take on a biblical or conservative Christian slant. In the upper grades, certain subjects, such as science and history, contained more sacred material than, for example, language. Mathematics had the fewest references to things spiritual.

The ideological bedrock does have an impact on the content of the curriculum. For example, it explains the conservative Christians' insistence on special creation as the explanation for human origins, and on tracing God's ordaining hand in the continuing history of humankind. However, the subject matter of the subjects studied is not as religious as it could be.

A typical day for a seventh grader might include very little in the way of sacred material, or, on the other hand, he might hear this from his English teacher, instructing him about the dangers of checking inappropriate books out of the public library on library day:

What you read stays with you. It stays in your mind forever. It is never, never, never erased. What you see on TV and in movies is never erased in your mind. It's there in indelible ink, and it never ever goes away. And the more stuff like that that you put in your mind, the more it comes out in your attitude—your behavior. And the only thing we can do is avoid it. We never get rid of what we put in there. You gotta be careful about what you read. *I guard my mind.* I don't watch certain things on TV; I won't watch them because I don't want them in my mind; they'll never go away. Think about that. Satan is after *your* mind. (Field Notes GCA 10/28/89)

In science class seventh graders may (or may not) hear another recitation of the conservative Christian interpretation of God's creation and orderly plan for the world. The content of their history class may be (and is in the A Beka curriculum) largely biblical history. They will not hear much about God in math class, even though their book may begin with a statement of how mathematics reveals God's orderliness. Music can include no sacred songs, or a mixture of sacred and secular songs, as well as some instrumental instruction, from the cacophony of sticks and shakers for the kindergarteners to the lilting twang of lap dulcimers for the seventh graders. Rose (1988, 82) notes that "the majority of school time . . . is spent on straightforward presentation of academic material" at a school sponsored by a charismatic community that she observed.

Depending on the textbooks used, any particular lesson can have both sacred and secular material contained within it. A curriculum which relies solely on references to the Bible, church history, Christian schools, and character-building maxims can be imagined. The books could be 100 percent spiritual in idiom, containing examples taken only from the Bible. So can a curriculum be imagined that is totally devoid of spiritual references. (This is what the manufacturers of textbooks for public schools work hard to achieve [see Cohen 1986].) Again, as with every other measure, the Christian school textbooks were an amalgam of both. The content of the texts is laden with a religious, church, or conservative Christian idiom, and also contains much that is secular in nature.

Parson's (1987, 72) look at Christian school textbooks concludes that "these books make no pretense of religious or philosophical neutrality. They are written from a fundamentalist perspective, with every subject bathed in scriptural interpretation and political conservatism." This is supported by the titles of the books. For example, A Beka's textbook for Science 5 is *Investigating God's World;* Science 6 is *Observing God's World.* The high-school biology text is *Biology: God's Living Creation,* and the world history book is *The History of the World in Christian Perspective.* However, diversity among the conservative Christians affects what the textbook publishers can sell. A parent told me that she had objected to an A Beka book used at her daughter's Christian school, where she herself had taught, because it contained a ghost story. She surmised that perhaps the fundamentalist Christians at Pensacola Christian College (the home of A Beka Books) weren't familiar with the dangers that she, a charismatic Christian, knew this held. Her daughter's teacher said that the book no longer contained such material, and they mused that perhaps some parents and teachers had complained to A Beka (Field Notes Heritage USA 8/9/87).

Parsons (1987, 73) notes that some of the more moderate and liberal Christian schools "often use the same books found in the public schools." In our sample of schools, all used textbooks or self-paced instruction designed for Christian schools, except Dells Christian School and Springfield City Christian School, which used a mixture of secular and Christian school texts. As Parsons (1987) notes, A Beka Books, Bob Jones University Press, and Accelerated Christian Education (ACE) are the "big three" publishers of curriculum materials for Christian schools, although I identified twenty-six others—most of whom do not cover all subjects for all grades.

The teachers spent time weighing the pros and cons of various curriculum materials. Abundant Life Christian Academy and Grace Christian Academy used mostly A Beka books. The textbooks generally begin with introductions which stress both the skills the student is to learn, and the Christian applications of those skills. For example, *Language 6:*

Grammar Work-Text for Christian Schools by A Beka has this in the inside front cover:

How forcible are right words! —Job 6:25

Language is . . .
. . . seeing patterns and working analytically.
. . . learning how to use words effectively to express God's love to others.
. . . seeing the structure and orderliness of my language and learning to do things according to pattern.
. . . developing the ability to apply my knowledge of grammatical structure to my own thoughts and words.
. . . evaluating what I read, hear, and observe.
. . . communicating my beliefs clearly, forcefully, and persuasively.
. . . working up to the standards set by my instructor at the pace established by my instructor.
. . . learning rules and following them.
. . . learning that there is a correct way to do things.
(Chapman and Rand 1977, ellipses in original)

Likewise, the A Beka Arithmetic 6 book's introduction lists sixteen things that "Arithmetic is . . ." including:

. . . knowing that there *is* a right answer.
. . . learning to see the addition and multiplication tables as part of the truth and order that God has built into reality.
. . . learning to master a received body of knowledge and applying it. This is one way of obeying the command of Genesis 1:28 to subdue the earth and exercise dominion over it. (Howe 1981, ellipses in original)

The remaining thirteen attributes of arithmetic listed are secular in nature. BASIC Education's (affiliated with ACE)[5] "Self-Pac Math #1067" lists eight goals for the student, including: "To recognize repeating decimals and terminating decimals" and "To learn to give of myself to God."

Springfield City Christian School used some Christian Light textbooks. Christian Light Publications is anabaptist in orientation, and publishes textbooks and self-paced booklets. The cover of a "Lightunit" self-paced instruction booklet says "God's light in Mathematics" (or Social Studies or whatever the subject), and contains a logo with the message "God's truth equipping God's people to do God's work."

Once inside the textbooks or the self-paced instruction booklets, we find again a mixture of the plebeian and the sacred. A look at randomly selected pages (amounting to 10 percent of the total pages) of some A Beka language texts (*Language 6 Grammar Work-Text for Christian Schools*, 1977, 1982, and *Grammar and Composition Book One: A Work-Text for Christian Schools*, 1977, 1982) showed that 20 to 25 percent of the sentences used in exercises were sacred in nature.

In these exercises from *Language 6*, for example, the students were to "diagram the subjects, verbs, and predicate nominatives" in the sentences, or to "circle all possessive case pronouns", or "cross out any incorrect words and make corrections where necessary [in the use of adjectives]". The sacred idiom is used in this way:

Was Martin Luther the leader of the Reformation?
Abraham is the father of the nation of Israel.
India is a crowded land of heathen people.
Adoniram and Ann Judson became pioneer missionaries to Burma.
I __ you before prayer meeting on Wednesday night. (future of *call*).

In this analysis, character-building maxims like these were coded as sacred:

If you are idle, you are on the way to ruin, and there are few stopping places upon it. —H. W. Beecher
Idleness is only the refuge of weak minds, and the holiday of fools. —Chesterfield.
Our minds are given to us, but our characters we make.
Character is formed by a course of actions, and not actions by character.

Another 3 to 6 percent of the exercises were patriotic or concerned with American history:

Mr. Franklin folded his paper, took off his glasses, leaned back in his chair, and fell asleep.
Abraham Lincoln grew his beard because a little girl told him he would look more distinguished with whiskers.
James Madison was President during the War of 1812.

The majority (69 to 77 percent) were secular—quite ordinary, like:

Was it (she/her) who brought the watermelon and the ice cream?
The two pirates in the play were really Jesse and (I,me).

That is (he,him) there at the desk.
The winners of the sweepstakes were Sue and (I,me).

A Language Arts "Lightunit" from Christian Light Publication's self-paced curriculum (written in conjunction with Alpha Omega) when analyzed in the same way, showed that 6 percent of the sentences used in exercises were sacred, 4 percent were concerned with patriotism or American history, and 90 percent were secular.

All of the word problems from two self-paced booklets for mathematics were analyzed. One from Christian Light showed 9 percent of the story problems used a sacred idiom, the remainder were secular. One from BASIC education had just twelve story problems. Of these, five (42 percent) were sacred. On the sacred side were word problems like these:

> Pastor Alltruth asked the ushers to see how many visitors' cards they had in their supplies. One usher had 2/3 of a box, another had 1 1/3 and a third usher had 1 2/3 box. How many boxes of visitors' cards were found? (Self-Pac of Basic Education Math #1067, ACE 1979, 5)

> Lakewood Christian School has an enrollment of 96 freshmen, 104 sophomores, 100 juniors, and 95 seniors. What is the total enrollment? (Lightunit Mathematics #701 Christian Light 1980a, 43)

On the secular side of the ledger were problems put into words like these:

> One-sixth of the students in a certain school are under 10 years old. If there are 126 students in the school, how many are under ten years old? (Basic Education Self-Pac Math #1067, ACE 1979, 2)

> What is the total cost of a $389 washing machine and a $299 dryer to match it? (Lightunit Mathematics #701 Christian Light 1980a, 39)

In any given lesson, there will be both secular and sacred examples. Alpha Omega Publications (self-paced instruction) describes its "A Reason for Writing" handwriting curriculum with emphasis on "manuscript," "transition," and "cursive" for seven grade levels as "the only Christian handwriting program featuring scripture verse as total subject material." (At the same time, the books have characters drawn in cartoon style on "bright, colorful, durable covers.") (Alpha Omega Publications ad, 1988). After analyzing the sacred/secular content of several textbooks, it is easy to see how the publisher could make this claim.[6]

DISCIPLINE: "JESUS WANTS YOU TO BE GOOD" AND BEHAVIOR MODIFICATION

The types of discipline the teachers use also reflect the amalgam of Christian and education culture. Although the children at the various schools I frequented were nearly unfailingly polite to me (if not always to each other and to their teachers), occasions for discipline did arise fairly frequently. In fact, the very first thing I was told about Christian schools was this from a Christian school teacher: "Christian schools do have discipline problems" (Field Notes 6/23/86). The Christian schools are not "islands of Unbearable Virtue"—like the one comic strip character Prince Valiant sometimes visits—where nothing gets done because everyone is so busy being polite to everyone else and offering to let the other fellow go first. They are places where teachers make Sisyphean efforts to try to tame the "sin natures" (as they define human nature) of kids, most of whom are from conservative Christian families.

The use of spiritual language in disciplining is very dramatic. In her attempts to get students to show courtesy to one another, the junior-high language teacher said, during chapel, "Show each other Jesus today, people" (Field Notes GCA 4/6/87). On St. Patrick's Day, the administrator advised the teachers: "If they say anything about pinching [anyone who doesn't wear green] tell them that's not a Christian attribute" (Field Notes GCA 3/17/87). At an early faculty meeting, the administrator of GCA, discussing a recalcitrant student, noted that not following the rules of the school was a sin. A teacher told a student (who was also her son), "Brandon, if you don't follow rules, you're in rebellion" (Field Notes GCA 10/15/86). The first- and second-grade teacher admonished the children at chapel to do "what God wants you to do"; you should "obey—do it right now and with a cheerful heart" (Field Notes GCA 5/8/87). The third- and fourth-grade teacher followed Bible time in her class with this prayer one day: "We should do our work well as an expression of our love for You—to please You. If it's sloppy it just shows we don't really love You. We will do our work well because we want to please You" (Field Notes GCA 3/17/87).

Before a parent takes his turn at leading chapel, the administrator asks the students to be still, with this object lesson:

Administrator:	One day I was talking to the third and fourth graders, and I said, if Jesus asked you to do your math page, what would you say?
Student:	Yes.

Table 9.3 Frequency of Disciplinary Measures

TYPE OF DISCIPLINE, WITH EXAMPLES	MINIMUM USE[1]	WHERE	MAXIMUM USE	WHERE
Directive: don't or do "No talking please;" "Sit down, sit down, you all sit down."	17%	SCCS 8–12	37%	DCS K
Behavior modification "John, you and Marcus can sit with me during play time."	0%	SCCS 8–12	26%	GCA 1–4
Invoking school rules "Boys and girls, who can tell me when we talk?" "We raise our hands if we have a question."	0%	ALCA 8–12	17%	GCA K
Giving a signal Finger to lips; Turn off lights; "Excuse me, boys and girls."	7%	GCA 1–4	17%	SCCS 8–12
Sarcasm/humor "Earth to Lori, are you there?" "You're gonna die if you don't sit down."	2%	GCA K	17%	SCCS 8–12
Teacher wants you to "Mrs. Sherwood is not pleased with all the talking I hear."	0%	SCCS 8–12	9%	GCA K
Praise "Very good listening."	0%	ALCA 8–12	8%	DCS K, SCCS 8–12
Interrogation "Leonard, do you have your own paper to color? Why are you coloring on someone else's?"	0%	ALCA 8–12	6%	GCA 5–7

	SCCS 8–12		DCS 1–4
Explaining the consequences "Kevin, you're not going to have any crayons if you keep sharpening them. They're sharp enough."	0%		5% (DCS 1–4)
Corporal punishment (including threats) "Conrad, if you cut that, you are going to get a paddling so you go ahead and cut it and get a paddling. It's your choice."	0% DCS 1–4, ALCA 8–12, SCCS 8–12		3% (GCA 1–4)
God/Jesus wants you to "You're doing this for Jesus, you're not doing it for Mrs. Turner." "David, would Jesus be pleased if you spit on him?"	0% DCS K, DCS 1–4, ALCA 8–12, SCCS 8–12		3% (GCA K)
Making comparisons "Lloyd is our best rester"; "I'm choosing the quietest one."	0% DCS 1–4, ALCA 8–12, SCCS 8–12		2% (DCS K)
Other[2]			
Total cases in the sample[3]	649		

[1] Read these columns as: "The minimum use of directives as a means of discipline during a day (grades K–4) or class period (grades 5-12) was 17% of the time at SCCS in grades 8–12." In order to check for minimum/maximum ranges within an entire day's worth of disciplinary actions (for grades K–4), or a whole class period's worth (for grades 5–12), the 66 different classroom situations were collapsed into eleven combinations of schools and grade levels: DCS K, GCA K, DCS 1–4, GCA 1–4, GCA 5–7, ALCA 8–12, SCCS 8–12, SCCS K, CCCA 1–4, PCA 1–4, CCCA 8–12. The last four of these combinations were subsequently omitted from "range" considerations, because they had Ns less than 10.

[2] Five other forms each accounted for about 1% of the total cases: Apologize, Go to the Office, Repeat the Behavior Correctly, Get a Talking to at Teacher's Desk, Unspecified Threat. .5% (3 cases) did not fit any of the named tyes. They include "You're too picky, Ronald; there are boys and girls all over the world who would love to have one little raisin," and "You have to sleep because Mrs. Wagner is going to watch what you do when you sleep."

[3] Each instance of discipline was recorded as one "case," and all methods of discipline the teacher used in that instance were recorded. The table here shows the first discipline method the teacher (or student) used in each of the 649 cases.

Administrator: Yes, you would. . . . Well, let's remember, that Jesus is coming to us in the form of Mr. Raleigh to-
day, . . . and if Jesus were standing before you, and
talking to you, you would be so still. Your eyes
would be right on him. Wouldn't they? Remember
that today. (Field Notes GCA 11/25/86)

At another time, to calm the students down before chapel, she told
them: "Your behavior stinks—in my nostrils—and I know it stinks in
God's!" (Field Notes GCA 12/8/86). She often told parents that their
children were "growing in the admonition of the Lord" (Field Notes
GCA 5/11/87).

Sometimes the Christian idiom and that of professional education
were combined, as is shown in this example of a parent's effort to
improve her son's behavior in school. Mixing scriptural power with
behavior modification techniques, she gave the teacher a small booklet
made of cards that she had devised. On the first card was written: "In all
things, (bad attitude, discipline . . .) —— —— is more than a CON-
QUEROR. Romans 8:37." Behind this card were stapled others, one for
each day of the month. She asked the teacher—if it wasn't too much
trouble—to put a check mark beside each day when her son was good,
and to give him the card to take home. "I told him, you have to be
victorious over those things. You can let them rule you or you can rule
them. I told him he would get a quarter for each day he got a check
mark. I don't know if it's right to bribe your kid, but—" The teacher
replied, "Well, I think you have to give them incentives, especially at this
age" (Field Notes GCA 11/18/86).

If you visited a Christian school, these dramatic and out of the ordinary
examples would be the ones you would remember. But a quantitative
analysis shows that, when the various instances of discipline which take
place every day are taken into account, these dramatic sacred-based ones
are drowned in the commonplace.

The analysis asks: On a given day in a particular classroom, what
forms of discipline are used in what proportions? The analysis gleans all
of the instances of discipline used in particular classrooms during entire
days (for the lower grades, who stay with one teacher all day), or during
entire class periods (for the upper grades). The 649 sample cases are from
six different schools, sponsored by Wesleyan, Baptist, nondenominational, and Holiness churches, and by charismatic parents (ALCA, DCS,
CCCA, GCA, PCA, SCCS). The 649 cases are taken from thirty-one
different days (spanning September 9, 1986, to May 20, 1987), with
thirty-one different teachers in sixty-six different teacher-students-subject

combinations (that is Mrs. Mitchell teaching sixth-grade science is one combination, and Mrs. Mitchell teaching seventh-grade science, or sixth-grade history, is another.) Eighty-nine different students were disciplined, from one time to twenty-seven times apiece. The choice of headings for the types of discipline is etic, based on the *observer's* categorization of instances of discipline into like groupings.

Although it was very dramatic (to an outsider) when teachers invoked God or Jesus to keep students in line, on any given day the number of times they used this (at most 3 percent of the time) was far outweighed by more commonplace modes. Corporal punishment, too (including threats), accounted for not more than 3 percent of the discipline given.

Directives which just told the students to "Do" or "Don't do" something accounted for between 17 percent and 37 percent of the discipline in a particular classroom on a particular day. The tone of the directive ranged from concerned—"Ohh, don't put the scissors in your mouth, honey"— and polite—"No talking please," to simple commands—"Button your mouths; get your hands ready"—which were sometimes tinged with sarcastic humor—"John, we don't need any duck sounds, sir."

B. F. Skinner is certainly no hero to the conservative Christians and in fact is much maligned as a signer of the second "Humanist Manifesto." His views of human nature and the ultimate "conditionability" of humans puts us, according to the conservative Christians, on a par with animals, where God did not intend for humans to be. Yet, behavior modification discipline techniques, which have Skinner as their ideological father, are used with abandon in the schools.

Behavior modification techniques—losing recess time or break time, accumulating and losing points which allow for material gain or free time, and so on—are the second most popular type of discipline, accounting for more than a quarter of the discipline in some classrooms. "We use trips and breaks. Kids will die rather than give up their breaks," an administrator told me (Field Notes MCA 5/12/87).

The third- and fourth-grade teacher at GCA learned about a behavior modification technique (though it wasn't labeled that) at an ACSI seminar, which she used with success in her class. The students accumulated and lost points for good and bad behavior, with a scorecard in view on their desks. They competed with one another for a prize at the end of a certain time period. At a faculty meeting, she was discussing this technique with the administrator:

Mrs. Dobbins: [The seminar leader] said to tell them, "You're in control of the situation here." But then I had always thought that God was in control.

Mrs. Mitchell:	Well I think you want to tell them God wants them to be in control.

In the ACE school Rose (1988, 130) observed, material rewards awaited students who met their curriculum goals or memorized their scriptures. "In the lower grades (kindergarten to fifth), a classroom store displays colored pens, bubbles, balls, toy cars, dolls, etc. Students can earn points and can save up for the prize that they want—the goals are tangible and visible."

Invoking school rules ("Boys and girls, who can tell me when we talk?"), using signals (turning off lights or putting a finger to lips to signal "be quiet," calling a pupil's name to signal a warning) and sarcastic humor ("Earth to Lori, are you there?"; "That's good, Douglas, I can roll my eyes like that, too"; "Are you allergic to clauses?") were each used a maximum of 17 percent of the time. Teacher requests ("Mrs. Sherwood is not pleased with all the talking I hear"; "David, I'd like to see you in your seat now"; "I don't hear my boys' and girls' voices. I want to hear your voices") and praise ("Very good listening") each were used just under 10 percent of the time, at a maximum. Praise was also given for school work, but those instances were not counted here where the object of analysis was—what happens when a pupil breaches the behavioral code.

The types of discipline used by the most schools and in the widest variety of classrooms were commands to simply "do" or "don't do" a particular behavior, sarcastic humor, giving a signal, invoking school rules, and behavior modification techniques. Also used in most schools were explaining the consequences of the students' actions, and making them repeat a behavior over again, correctly.

Methods of discipline were somewhat different at different grade levels. Directions or commands to simply "do" or "don't do" something were used frequently at all grade levels. Behavior modification techniques were used more frequently in grades kindergarten through four than in fifth through twelfth. "The teacher wants you to" and invoking school rules also fell away in the upper grades. Sarcastic humor was used more often in junior high and high school than in the lower grades.

A look at the types of discipline used in Grace Christian Academy's kindergarten on a day early in the school year (only the sixth day of school for most of the thirteen four- and five-year-olds) and a day late in their first year of school (their 171st day) shows some differences. They were reprimanded sixty-five times by their teacher on the early day, and six times by each other. The last time I visited the kindergarten, they were disciplined seventy-four times by their teacher and four times by their peers. This was a day when the kindergarten teacher, who I often thought had the patience of

Job, confided in me, "I don't know which is going to give out first—my patience or me." (But she cried when the little students left on the last day of school, as did the first- and second-grade teacher.) So the number of times discipline was called for grew by about 10 percent. The variety of types of discipline used also grew. On the sixth day, eight of the types of discipline were invoked; on the later day, sixteen different types were used. The most often used forms at first were invoking school rules (which the pupils were just learning), directives, and behavior modification techniques; these three types accounted for about two-thirds of all the discipline on that day. On the day near the end of the school year, directives, behavior modification, and signals that they had been taught during the year were most often used, these three accounting for nearly three-fifths of the discipline on that day. On both days, while the disciplinary actions which called upon God or Jesus were dramatic, they accounted for only 3 percent of the total disciplinary actions given (two each day).

In summary, of all the instances of discipline, only a few rely on God's will or God's word to put children on the right track. Only a few rely on threats of corporal punishment to set them straight. The rest are based on adding and subtracting privileges, and on invoking school rules or the teacher's will.

WHY COMPROMISE?

The Christian schools have not one, but two primary goals. They want to train young Christians, but train them for what? Not all, they realize, are bound for careers in "Christian service." Increasingly, the schools wish to train youngsters who will be business, professional, and political leaders in the America of tomorrow.

Answers to questionnaires given to parents at Grace Christian Academy and Dells Christian School (with a 65 percent and 30 percent response rate, respectively), exhibited both goals. In answer to the question "What would you like for your child to do and be when he or she grows up?" 56 percent of the parents gave a Christian answer, such as the very common "Whatever God calls her to do." Another 9 percent of the parents joined this with their secular hopes, such as "we would like to see her . . . have a business of her own." Thirty-four percent of the parents answered in purely secular language: "Whatever he wants. We do desire to steer him into some type of professional occupation with higher education a priority." Some were more specific: "mechanical engineer"; "teacher"; "I would like my child to become (a) a scientist studying plants, insects, and animals; (b) a dress designer; (c) a cartoon illustrator."

Clubhouse Jr., a popular magazine for young children published by Christian psychologist James Dobson's Focus on the Family, contained a two-page feature with this theme: "'*Whatever* you do, do it for Jesus!' says the Bible (Colossians 3:23). Here are some things people do when they work for God." Pictures include violinists in an orchestra, a roofer, a Navy fighter-jet pilot, a doctor, a mom, and a lawyer (*Focus on the Family* 1988b).

One day the administrator asked GCA's fifth through seventh graders how many planned to go to college. Every hand went up, and faces had a quizzical look, as if to say that the answer was "of course" they were bound for college. The students at Grace Christian Academy, Abundant Life Christian Academy, Living Waters Christian Academy, and Springfield City Christian School, are likely bound for college, and not necessarily Christian colleges. At Marantha Christian Academy, Porter Christian Academy, Calvary Cross Christian Academy, and Hamlin Christian Academy, they are more likely to go to Christian colleges or into military service or to take jobs. (In this, they follow the sociological truism that the strongest variable in determining a person's career is his or her father's occupation.)

A survey done by Springfield City Christian School for their ACSI accreditation determined the "future educational plans" of its thirty 1985–86 seniors. The "present intention" of 44 percent of these seniors was "Bible school or college." Twenty percent intended to go to "four-year college," 13 percent to "community or junior college," and 23 percent were "undecided" (SCCS ACSI Self Study (3), 3).

The students' own aspirations reflect their desires to do things which require an education. In Grace Christian's reading and spelling class, fifth and sixth graders described what they want to be when they grow up (Field Notes GCA 10/15/86).

Teacher: Each of you is being prepared for something. God has a plan for you. [For your assignment], write what *you* want to do—how you feel you're being prepared for it. . . . See the point is, the people you read about had experiences as a child, which affected them as they grew up: Clara Barton, Amelia Earhart, and Helen Keller. The best listeners will get to read theirs.

Later, they read what they had written.

Patricia: I want to go to college, and be a teacher for sixth and seventh graders. At age twenty-four or twenty-five I

	want to get married and have two kids, and then start teaching again. With my family, I want to live happily ever after.
Emily:	I want to go to college. Then I want to go to law school at State University, or be a teacher of kindergarten and first grades. I want to get married, and have two, three, or four kids. I want to marry a good husband.
Rachel:	I want to be a hairdresser. The influence I've had is that my mother taught me how to cut hair so the bangs will feather.
Tina:	I want to pass out tracts door to door, or be a doctor.
Denise:	When I'm thirteen I'm going to work in a shop after school until I graduate.
Patricia and Emily:	You can't do that; you have to be fifteen or sixteen.
Denise:	I want to go to college and be a vet. I want to marry, and have three kids and live in Springfield, Missouri.
Brandon:	I like the outdoors, ships, fresh air, and guns. I would like to be an author, and grab about $20,000 from it. But $20,000 when I grow up because of inflation would only be worth about $10,000. I do not like to stay in one place; I'd like to go to Egypt, Israel, or South America. I'd like an organized life and job.
Polly:	I want to go to college and be a veterinarian.
Warren:	I want to make good grades, so I can go to college and play football. Then after college I want to be a Navy commander, and play football, live in California, and play on the Chicago Bears team. I'd like to be a star, make lots of money, and live in a mansion.

The students are concerned with their academic progress. When achievement test results were given out, students were proud of high marks, concerned about failure, and wanted to know "how they did" compared with others who took the test (Field Notes DCS, GCA, PCA). The first and second graders were anxious about their achievement tests, and even though the teacher explained that, unlike the tests she made up for them, these tests were *supposed* to include things they would *not* know, some of them cried when they didn't know an answer, and others refused to continue with the test (Field Notes GCA 3/31/87; 12/4/87). Students from various schools who knew I was a college professor discussed their concerns about being prepared for college. However, the analysis of the students' prayer requests and praise reports showed that those related to school work only 3 percent of the time.

The parents' and administrators' stress on making an impact on American society puts an emphasis on education, American style. This is played out, as we have seen, in a sizable imputation of traits, language, techniques, and materials from the culture of the education profession. As the pastor and administrator of Porter Christian Academy put it, "[I tell the students], if you want a piece of the action, prepare now" (Field Notes PCA 4/8/87). The administrator at Grace Christian Academy discussed the goal of the school at a faculty meeting.

> God has really been working on me lately about the purpose of this school. The primary goal of the school, is to send these children out academically prepared with Christian attributes. (Field Notes GCA 11/18/86)

An article in the journal of the American Association of Christian Schools agreed with her:

> The stated primary goal of Christian education is developing Christlikeness in the students. Be that as it may, the Christian school cannot depart from traditionally accepted standards for professional preparation and competency and hope to sustain community respect. Somewhere a proper line of demarcation must be drawn by the Christian school administrators which can render both to God and Caesar their due. (Nicholson 1987, 9)

How do Christian school personnel find that line marking what to include and what to eschew within their schools? As befits their Christocentric philosophy—that Christ working within you is the locus of power, and that God's will lies behind all happenings—they ask for direction from God.

Making Decisions: The Revitalization Process at Work

It is not surprising that conservative Christian educators would turn to God when going about the revitalizing process, for to the conservative Christian all things are sacred. In making decisions, conservative Christians manifest the philosophical differences that they have with mainstream American culture. For them, God is the basis for power; the explanation for events is God's will; "Nothing happens by accident." Accordingly, the basis for making decisions is God's direction. "God leads, guides, and directs" the conservative Christians' footsteps, and it behooves people to "discern God's will."

And yet, if we look at decisions made within the schools, we will see that they are not made on purely ideological bases. Almost any decision has both practical, secular parameters as well as sacred, ideological ones.

THE ANATOMY OF CURRICULUM DECISIONS

Several decisions relating to curriculum show the mix of secular and sacred considerations that inform them. Some of these decisions are made in a school using secular material which wishes to change to a Christian curriculum; others are from a school that is using a Christian curriculum and wants to supplement with secular material; still others are made in a school that is changing from one type of Christian curriculum to another. The impetus for seeking change can be concerns about "humanistic" content, or about how well the books teach the subject matter. Sources of information affecting the decision can be Christian, such as an Institute for Creation Research seminar, or secular, such as receiving sample books from a friend who teaches in public school.

Dells Christian School teachers had used a variety of secular textbooks, including Economy Readers, and were neither dissatisfied with them nor concerned that using these books made their school any less a Christian school: "Our *teachers* are different [from public school]" (Field Notes DCS 4/30/87). But that changed when the sponsoring church's new pastor, who had children in the school, became interested in the school's curriculum. He read Paul Vitz's (1986) report on the content of public school textbooks, and he had heard people say, "If you're going to use the same stuff as public schools, than what's the difference?" Then he found in one of the first-grade readers a reference to the idea that listening to music can make you feel good; although it wasn't about rock music per se, it reminded the pastor of kids becoming engrossed in rock music (Field Notes DCS 4/30/87).

The administrator had considered Economy "one of the safer readers," and was also considering Lippincott, "but the A Beka salesman said that they had changed" toward stories which reflected "violence and changes in the American family." And so the DCS staff began to look at materials for teaching reading designed especially for Christian schools by Rod and Staff, Bob Jones University Press, and A Beka. After a long discussion with an A Beka salesman, the administrator and her secretary, a graduate student in political science education, talked about how they would make their decision.

They discussed "story content." The administrator wanted to see traditional portrayals of families, and not one-parent families. "I know that a lot of families are one-parent families [including children in Christian schools]. But maybe we can change the frame of thinking. If kids are taught [about the traditional family form], maybe things will change. Because I know a lot of people go into marriage thinking—well, if it doesn't work out I can always get out of it" (Field Notes DCS 4/30/87). She wanted the stories to portray different races, and she wanted women and men to have dissimilar roles in the stories.

The new materials would have to be "eye-catching to children . . . We already threw one out [Rod and Staff]. The material was good, but there were either no pictures, or they were black and white. You have to grab their attention or they're not going to read it."

They discussed the thought that Bob Jones University materials were more "analytical" than A Beka's. "I want my children to be able *to think*. I don't want just, what I call regurgitation." "A Beka is a lot of memorization and drill. . . . A Beka is drill, drill, drill, drill."[1]

The administrator was interested in the kinds of "teacher helps" available, and was impressed with this aspect of A Beka, but also didn't want the teachers to feel that their creativity was stifled by the A Beka curriculum.

She was not enthusiastic about an A Beka pre-kindergarten reading program. Pre-kindergarten "kids are not ready; they do not have the motor skills. . . . I'm not a pusher for reading [in kindergarten]. If they learn, fine; if they don't, fine. We're pushing them so young. When are kids going to be kids?" (Field Notes DCS 4/30/87).

She also was not enthusiastic about using A Beka's video program. "Something deep down inside me doesn't like it." The secretary suggested that perhaps it was the "lack of social skills." The administrator, agreeing, said it would be lacking in the "relationship with a teacher. They can't hug her. She can't relate to them." The secretary added, "and they expect to be entertained by TV." The administrator allowed that it might be useful in Spanish, and "it may be the only way we can go past the sixth grade," in a number of subjects (Field Notes DCS 4/30/87).

Her ruminations, then, reflected concern for "Christian"—or at least "safe-for-Christians"—content, as well as for a variety of educational variables. There were material considerations as well; cost was a factor. If A Beka were chosen, the administrator wanted to buy "the whole program," in order to get the curriculums and teacher's helps. "You get the whole curriculum in the lower grades, but in the upper grades, you have to buy it for $100.00." The cost of the books themselves was also a factor, because the *school,* not the parents, purchased the books, keeping them for reuse in future years. The school even purchased "consumable books" for the students' use. So there was concern with the "cost of changing (texts)"; it would be a "big cost outlay. . . . We were just getting to where I didn't have to worry all the time [about money]." Bob Jones material was already used in math and science, and the administrator thought that using the same publisher in the subject of reading "might be easier. . . . We're familiar with it" (Field Notes DCS 4/30/88).

While Dells Christian School was seeking Christian readers to replace their secular ones, Grace Christian Academy, which had been using A Beka, was looking for secular supplements. The administrator had decided that there was a need to have supplementary textbooks available at the school. Behind her decision were two thoughts: "I've found that teachers teach differently—and need something on hand—horizontal materials—that that teacher who is maybe not so creative can have at hand. She can pick it up and say, 'Oh, I can have the students do that' (Field Notes GCA 2/18/87). I've noticed that some teachers don't seek out things; they have a tendency to follow A Beka down the line." (Field Notes GCA 2/19/87).

Also, she thought that students who had been exposed to secular textbooks would be better able to recognize their non-Christian aspects in later years. She had been looking at textbooks now used at her secular college alma mater, and found them to be "too humanistic." Thinking that this is what the school's students would meet when they go to college, she decided: "If the students look at other textbooks [while in the lower grades], they will be better able to withstand the pressure and pick and choose when they go to college" (Field Notes GCA 2/19/87).

The potential choices for "horizontal supplements" derived from (1) a list of teaching materials from another Christian school in a larger city that the administrator had visited; (2) "freebies" given by publishers to public school teachers and passed on to the administrator; and (3) books she had left over from her own days of teaching in public school.

The first- and second-grade teacher thought that her students could benefit from more reading material. Information about potential material to use was gleaned from (1) vendors at the ACSI meetings (including secular publishers like Open Court); (2) a list of curriculum materials obtained from the school the administrator visited; (3) advertising received after writing to the publishers on this list; and (4) information provided by an Open Court sales representative who visited the school. At the suggestion of this salesperson, the administrator and two teachers attended a statewide (secular) readers' conference, returning with armloads of catalogs. As they pored over the information they had received, the administrator said, reflecting a concern for "story content:" "It's easy to see just by going down the table of contents that some of these are not for us. . . . There's a lot on the Middle Ages [magic, witchcraft]. And there are things that are not classics there—that don't add anything" (Field Notes GCA 2/19/87, 3/23/87, 3/24/87).

At first the decision was made not to buy supplemental books for first and second graders, even though the teacher liked Open Court. The administrator felt that there was just "too much to work around" (i.e., secular content of the unsafe variety) in them. "That RISE (Open Court) book—all the stories I'm drawn to they get somewhere along the line [in the A Beka curriculum]." But, while attending a summer workshop at her alma mater, the administrator learned more about Open Court from a fellow student, who said "how good it was and how it followed phonics well." The decision was then made to order the supplementary books for the first and second graders because "it follows the phonics method of A Beka well" (Field Notes GCA 6/2/87, 6/30/87).

In preparation for choosing books to be used in this supplementary way as well as possibly changing some texts, the administrator played a tape in which James Dobson (Focus on the Family 1986) interviewed Paul Vitz, whose study of public school textbooks received much media attention. She said, "Listen to this so we'll know what we're looking for when we preview these books." At a faculty meeting one month later, the administrator clarified the criteria for choosing textbooks:

When reviewing these textbooks, think about: Is it *worth the cost?* Is it worth changing or supplementing? Remember the cost to the parents.

If it's a reader, does it *blend with your phonics?*

Does it *complement what we're trying to do here* and not take away from it. Will you not have to spend a lot of time explaining, "well, we don't believe in that"?

We've got things sitting on the shelf down there—that teachers have ordered. I just want to be sure that we *use* what we buy, so that we are good stewards of God's money. (Field Notes GCA 3/24/87, 4/28/87)

In reviewing some of these secular history texts, the administrator commented on the "continuity" (which she judged to be poor). The "comparative approach" of covering "the social aspects of France, Germany, etc., and then the economy of France, Germany, etc., rather than taking a country as a whole . . . is too hard for this age group. That's not the way we think" (Field Notes GCA 4/20/87). She also looked at their "handling of religion." Was Christianity mentioned, and if so, how? She was impressed with one book because it discussed Jesus, said he died on a cross, and that when onlookers came, his body was not there (Field Notes GCA 4/20/87).

The young junior-high history teacher (especially trained in math but filling in in history, as well) previewed Bob Jones University's history textbook. "I like this one better [than the currently used A Beka textbook]."

The same chapter as they're in [in their A Beka text]—the Islam world—starts with a *story* about a boy and his family. They were living in Medina and were driven out when Muslims came. It's not true, but it could be; it's the kind of thing that happened. *There aren't so many facts and figures.* A Beka's chapter on the same thing is just information. The questions are the same as A Beka—the same information—but presented in a different way. It has *cartoons and pictures.* It has *things for teachers* for each chapter: puzzles and crosswords, etc. It can *cover more of the world,* because the chapters are shorter. For example, Byzantium isn't covered in A Beka, and is in here. I've been reading to them from it; they like it. It would be *too expensive* for them to have both of them. One bad thing: *it doesn't start with Creation,* like A Beka does. It starts with Abraham rather than Adam. (Field Notes GCA 4/28/87)

The name of the publisher didn't enter into her decision, since she didn't know who published the book. At a faculty meeting, she said: "I like that history book—I think it's *easier* but I don't know if easier is [a valid criterion]." The administrator replied, "No—that's what we're looking for." "Then I think we should change that," the history teacher concluded.

Regarding the teaching of science, the administrator and a parent who was a science professor at State University spent time during the summer comparing A Beka science texts with secular ones. Their analysis led them to the conclusion that A Beka science was not wanting in content (although of course it was different in perspective) when compared to the secular texts. Still, the administrator, who was also the science teacher, was not satisfied with the "continuity" in the A Beka science textbooks, especially for seventh grade, and for that reason switched to Bob Jones University textbooks after the school year had begun. She had the students keep their A Beka books for reference, and she used both of them alternately.

Seeking better ways to teach science (in a fundamentalist Christian mode) had prompted the teacher to attend a week-long seminar sponsored by the Institute for Creation Research. While there, she met a teacher from another school in her home state, and subsequently visited that school. During this visit, the administrator was impressed with a science curriculum that used experimentation kits which included all the needed materials for each student. She requested information about the kits from the (secular) companies which marketed them. Another teacher noticed her poring over the information she received from several sources, and noted that a science professor (at the secular college where both she and the administrator had received their degrees) "knows about those." That provided yet another source of information, which the administrator utilized.

In the end, the decision to change the science curriculum was put off to another year. The kits were more expensive than textbooks. The advertising literature and the science professor made it clear that a teacher must be committed to using the kits and to keeping their materials stocked. The school was moving to a new building and the administrator decided that the cost of this move was "enough for next year . . . I think it's too expensive. I think this year we'll get a new building." The volunteer computer and PE teacher, a student at State University, had told his professor in a course on science curriculum that the school was interested in this "hands-on" approach. The administrator was pleased that "he's trying to get us some of the [experiential] boxes. But I don't know. I think if you get the basics, that experience will come—even if it's in college—if you get the basics" (Field Notes GCA 5/15/87).

So one school sought to move from secular to Christian texts, another sought to supplement Christian texts with secular ones; still another moved between types of Christian curricula. Maranatha Christian Academy, a kindergarten through twelfth grade school sponsored by a fundamentalist independent Baptist church, was moving away from ACE to A Beka in the lower grades. The administrator explained his reasoning:

> We're not upset with ACE, but concerned about *burnout,* with starting the kids on it so young and going all the way through. We will go to seventh grade with A Beka next year, if we have a teacher. We'll go to eighth grade with A Beka the next year, if we can find teachers who are qualified and believe like we do. . . .
>
> We have K4 A Beka kindergarten [for four-year-olds]. I don't really recommend it, if the mother is at home, not at all. But if not, it's better than baby sitting. If the parents want to come and pick them up at noon, that's fine, or they can stay until 3:00 P.M. K5 is 9:00 A.M. to 3:00 P.M., and they have to have that. K5 A Beka is necessary for them to go into A Beka's first grade. . . .
>
> We use A Beka Video for algebra, and next year Spanish, and maybe plane geometry. The algebra gives homework and a lecture, but I teach it, too. But it *helps because it's broken down into 170 days of lessons;* I don't have to figure out what to do each day. . . . There are books which come with it. A Beka charges twenty-five dollars a month. I figure it's worth it for the money, to have the lessons planned. A Beka says you don't need a qualified teacher with the video, but having seen the algebra work like it has, I doubt that. But it worked better than ACE for algebra, because then I had eighteen kids taking algebra in my Learning Center, and you answer the same questions over and over [as they work the problems in their ACE PACES]. (Field Notes MCA 5/12/87)

Thus, the Dells Christian, Grace, and Maranatha curriculum decisions all reflect concern for cost of the materials, their palatability to students, their consistency with teachers' educational principles (for example, teaching reading by phonics), as well as the availability of teacher aids and a story content that does not detract from the conservative Christian message.

Decisions concerning hiring teachers also reflected spiritual *and* educational concerns. At DCS, the administrator considered an applicant who was Catholic. If she were "just a catechism Catholic," she wouldn't do; but she might be a "Christian Catholic" (Field Notes DCS 5/29/87). The administrator was more concerned about the applicant's reluctance to punish children by spanking them than about her religious doctrine. Later though (probably after discussion with the pastor, who interviewed candidates about the "spiritual aspects," while the administrator "took the educational aspects"), she said that she was no longer considering this applicant for an interview because "Catholics have a different way of looking at some of the Biblical things than we do" (Field Notes DCS 7/27/87).

IMPETUS FOR CHANGE AND
INFLUENCES ON DECISIONS

As with so many other areas of life in Christian schools, making decisions is a combination of influences from education culture and Christian culture, joined with practical considerations. The impetus for changing readers can be concern about content that too realistically reflects certain aspects of modern American culture. The impetus for having secular supplemental textbooks can be teachers who do not otherwise seek out supplemental materials and students who need to know what they will be "up against" when they get to college. The impetus for desiring supplemental readers in the lower grades can be to improve students' skills. The impetus for changing history textbooks can be a set of secular educational concerns, once the content is approved. The impetus for looking for a new way to teach science can be a perceived lack of continuity in the current textbooks. The impetus for changing from self-paced instruction to the traditional classroom can be worry about student burnout.

Once these factors have pushed toward a desire for change, the path toward the decision is strewn with a variety of influences, both Christian and educational in nature. Factors such as the degree to which the content is safe for conservative Christians, features which make it an effective teaching tool, consistency with the educational principles of the staff, cost, and logistics combine in teachers' ruminations about curriculum.[2]

As we saw in these examples of decisions concerning curriculum, Christian concerns are most likely to be manifested in story content and not in the epistemology of how the teaching is to be done.[3] Christian concerns are reflected, actually, in the negative sense. It is not that content must be Christian; as we have seen, schools use secular materials, and even textbooks made for Christian schools contain much that is secular. Rather, there are certain things they must *not* contain.

Magic, profanity, and nudity must be avoided. Of course, materials on science must not be based on evolution. DCS's administrator was concerned about modern family structure and nontraditional sex roles, and GCA mentioned magic and witchcraft. Both GCA and DCS eschewed elements they saw as part of "humanism," such as "values clarification" (GCA) and "situation ethics" (DCS).

GCA's staff sought out field trip opportunities, and with several universities and community colleges nearby, there were many possibilities. Story content was a concern here, too. They were sorry they had attended one children's play at a local university, because it contained "spells and incantations." They had called ahead to check the content, and had been assured that there was "no magic" in it. (Evidently there was a breakdown in communication over what was meant by "magic.") But they were glad they had gone to the Nutcracker (and no mention was made of its magical content). (Often classics are forgiven some magical or otherwise objectionable content.) They were sorry they had gone to see "Where the Red Fern Grows" because it had contained some profanity. They were disconcerted when they took students to a square dance, because beer was sold. They decided not to take the students to see the movie "The Mission," because, although it concerned a missionary, it contained nudity. (They did, however, show a video of "Through the Gates of Splendor" about missionaries, which included scenes of unclothed South American Indian people.)

Once the story content is cleared as *not* being objectionable, concerns for educational techniques take over, expressed in the words and principles of America's professional educators; added to these are practical concerns such as cost.

Although it is possible to separate the influences on decision-making and to categorize them as either sacred or secular, as we have done here, the conservative Christians would not describe the decision-making process in these terms. Instead, they would say that the way these decisions are made is that "God directs our footsteps." The school is God's school; the choices are God's choices—ordained by God.

Discerning God's Will

The conservative Christian prays about a number of concerns—where to send his child to school, whether the school should have a new building, what curriculum to use, whether and where a graduating senior should go to college—as well as about many other much less momentous decisions. In this chapter we will explore the mechanics of *how* these decisions are made—how do the conservative Christians discern God's will for their lives?

The Christocentric conservative Christian world view does allow for practical, secular causes for events. But to these are added a godly or diabolical hand, so that ultimately, "nothing happens by accident." If God's will is the explanation for events, and if power, success, and peace are obtained by the Holy Spirit working within a person, then the grounds for making decisions will be God's leading. It is necessary, then, to ask for, and to listen to, God's leading in all things; people should not just "follow their own individual selves." This is, again, at odds with the ways of American individualism.

Lana Townsend, a parent who had attended a wide variety of churches, spelled out the differences between individualistic and Christocentric decison making. She felt that individualistic (she would say "unregenerated" or "unsaved") people "just sort of muddled their way through life." For her, the conservative Christian way is a " 'daily being led' kind of life-style" (Interview LT multi-church 3/14/88).

The value of decision-making from a Christocentric perspective was strong for conservative Christians of many denominational stripes. Marie Riley, a teacher at a school sponsored by an independent Baptist church (Abundant Life Christian Academy) reiterated the differences between Christocentrism and "man's" way.

> We. say we're Independent Baptists. We're Independent Baptists in that our church is not officially tied to anything else. But we call ourselves Dependent Baptists because we depend on God. Too many people worry about what's right for them in man's sight. Part of the concept of Christianity is that we care for men, we like other men,

we should be compassionate, but we don't live for other men. In the sense that our lives are led, guided, and directed, the core of our life should be what God has for us. And if He's pleased, then it doesn't really matter how we measure up in other people's eyes. (Interview MR Baptist 8/21/87)

She also agreed that "daily being led" is the conservative Christian way.

It's the way you live—every minute that you live, knowing that the way you're living is what is right for you, in God's sight. . . . I take this from my pastor, because he constantly gets those questions from young people—they're saying, "How do I know God's will for my own life?" He says, "Don't sit here today and say 'Fifteen years from now, where will I be?' " He says "take it minute by minute, hour by hour, day by day. If you know that what you're doing right now is not contrary to God's will, then you're in God's will. And as this hour leads into the next, and this day leads into the next, and this week leads into the next, you, then, are living in God's will." . . . If you don't have it now, and you're not concentrating on it now, it's one of those things you won't have tomorrow or the next day, because it's something you should have started on yesterday. (Interview MR Baptist 8/21/87)

At Grace Christian Academy (operated by charismatic Christian parents), the administrator described a similar day-by-day walk with God during a faculty meeting prayer:

And Father we just know that You are right there. We are with you, Father. We are yoked with You, Father. The next move, as You move, we'll move easily with You. (Field Notes GCA 2/24/87)

In order to make decisions concerning any aspect of their lives—momentous or quotidian—the conservative Christians say that they "discern God's will." In so doing, they are practicing a form of what anthropologists would call divination—"the endeavor to obtain information about things future or otherwise removed from ordinary perception, by consulting informants other than human" (Rose 1911). Divination, in this sense, is a neutral term which is not necessarily linked with "enchanters, witches, charmers, consulters with familiar spirits, wizards, or necromancers" as it is in Deuteronomy 18:10–11; and divination is not new to

Christianity. For example, the Moravians who settled Old Salem (now Winston-Salem, North Carolina) in the 1600s made decisions by lot, following Proverbs 16:33: "The lot is cast into the lap; but the whole disposing thereof is of the Lord." As we will see, the mechanics of discerning God's will contains aspects of "fortuitous" divination (passively finding meaning in omens), and "deliberate" divination (actively seeking God's help) (Lessa and Vogt 1965, 299).

GOD LEADS, GUIDES, AND DIRECTS

The conservative Christians use scripture to support their conviction that God does "lead, guide, and direct" their lives so that they are "not left to drift aimlessly."

> The Scriptures are very specific in their promises that God will direct our paths. In Isaiah, for example, we learn that we will be guided by divine illumination (9:2), and that this guidance will be continous (58:11). [See also Isaiah 9:2 NIV; Psalms 48:14 NIV; Psalms 73:24 NIV.]. . . .

> We also learn from the Scriptures that we are to trust entirely in the Lord for guidance. "Trust in the Lord with all your heart, and do not lean on your own understanding. In all your ways acknowledge Him, and He will make your paths straight" (Proverbs 3:5–6). [See also John 16:13 NIV; Psalms 23:2 NIV, Luke 1:78–79.] (LWCC nda)

GOD IS INTERESTED IN ALL OF LIFE

The conservative Christians believed that "there is no area in your life that God's not interested in" (Interview MR Baptist 8/21/87), although they differed somewhat on how *specific* God makes his directions. Lana Townsend said that

> the Scriptures give general directives for all areas of life and some very specific ones. Which house to buy, which neighborhood, what route to take to work, where to shop for groceries are all things which we like to feel sure God is both included in and directing us

about.... But there is a difference between a decision to buy the wrong house, ("wrong" because of unknowns such as termites, bad wiring, etc.), and a decision to deliberately commit an act the Scripture designates as sin. (Interview LT multi-church 3/14/88)

On the other hand, Sarah Ramsey, a teacher who had been attending a charismatic church, said, "Sometimes I think God doesn't care so specifically. When I was praying about [whether to change churches]—I can't say I really *heard* this—but it was as if He was saying, 'Well, Sarah, it really doesn't matter. Do whatever makes you feel better. As long as you're serving me, and have a relationship with me, it really doesn't matter' " (Interview SR charismatic 1/30/87). Mrs. Riley, the Baptist teacher, agreed that asking God's mind in every situation could go too far.

I don't think there is one area in your life that God's not interested in. But I think some people carry it to the extreme, in the sense that they make God their excuse for making bad choices because they have said I prayed about it. I have heard people do that. I think you can be ridiculous about certain things. "Do I buy a blue blouse or a white blouse?" That's maybe important in some ways, but I think God gave me sense enough to know. . . .

Some people pray, "Which do I wear, the shoe with the three-inch heel or the two-inch heel?" I have a little trouble with that, because I think God gives us good sense. . . .

Now I have known people—I haven't seen them, but I can picture them—having a major prayer meeting right in the middle of Downtown Department Store. I wouldn't criticize anybody who prays, but I sometimes wonder if we don't make ourselves look ridiculous in the eyes of these we want to influence—we want to convert—by making God appear to be a simpleton because we act like one. Because I think God made us superior creatures; we have marvelous minds. . . . When I go to the grocery store, I don't ask God to tell me before I walk in if I should spend $47.32 or $37.93.

But I think in the areas of life in which we're unsure, and sometimes in those small areas, sometimes I ask the Lord: "How do I speak to this question? Was I right in the way I treated my children? . . . Give me the strength to go and tell my own children that I was wrong." (Interview MR Baptist 8/21/87)

Certainly, it is thought that God is interested in what goes on in Christian schools. He "raised them up," and he is involved in the day-to-day life within them. The administrator at GCA prayed:

Father, You know the needs that this school has, and Father we lift them up to You jointly together right now . . . We ask that You *would* lead, guide, and direct every footstep and every word that is conceived out of all of our mouths and everything that our hands set to do. . . .

And because of that, we will not look back, and we will not look side to side, but we'll just keep our eyes on You, because we know, that You are the author and the perfecter of this. (Field Notes GCA 3/3/87)

A teacher at GCA said: "I come in in the morning and I say—'What should I do now?' and I'm nervous and I don't know what to do. And He says—'the fifth graders have a test today'—so I get out that test, and He says 'the sixth graders have a test tomorrow,' so I get that out, and so forth" (Field Notes GCA 11/21/86). When a new teacher at GCA was changing the bulletin boards in her room, she wondered aloud how to get ideas for new ones. The administrator counseled her to ask God about them (Field Notes GCA 2/3/87).

It was thought that God would "work things out" to best advantage (in the long run). For example, at GCA, the responsibility for chapel was rotated among the various techers. One, a good storyteller with a flair for the dramatic, was deemed particularly good at chapel presentations. When the schedule was calculated, chapel fell to this teacher more often than her turn, because of school vacations, and so on. A relieved colleague, less confident of her own speaking abilities, said laughingly, "The Lord works it out so that Nancy does chapel."[1]

God prepared the adminstrator for a set-to with parents over homework. God had given her a way to teach math techniques. When I asked her how she knew about this or how she found out about that, she would say, "God." "God gave me a good way to teach three-digit multiplication. Use colored chalk, and it shows what to carry." When I asked, "How did God show you that?" she said, "I say God; I thought of it—like everybody thinks of things—but I thank God for giving me the talent to think of that. Instead of [saying] 'I did it.' It's like you have a partner—and you give them a pat on the back" (Field Notes K. Mitchell 8/13/86).

STEPS IN DISCERNING GOD'S WILL

Conservative Christians from fundamentalist independent Baptist churches, charismatic churches, and those who have been affiliated with many kinds of churches had the same conviction that God "directs their footsteps" along a path he has planned. Over and over again, they described the same methods for discerning God's will.[2] Hunter (1983, 82) describes an evangelical formula "for testing a plan of action. . . . If the biblical teaching, the subjective witness of the Holy Spirit, and one's life plan line up like harbor lights or are consonant with one another, it must be God's will and therefore one should proceed with the plan." A charismatic community's lesson on "Discerning God's Will" agrees with and adds to these three "harbor lights."

> God has given us certain points of reference in order that we may clearly chart our paths in such a manner that our walk as individuals is consistent with His will. Specifically, there are [five] such guideposts available to us as we seek to determine the details of His plan for our lives. These are (1) an inward conviction developed through prayer. . . , (2) confirmation in scripture, (3) Godly counsel, (4) circumstantial evidence [and God's provision], (5) the peace of God. (LWCC nda)[3]

Inward Conviction or Leading

How do believers discern God's will for their lives? An inner conviction or leading that sometimes arises in prayer is one of the "guideposts." The leading is a feeling of "being compelled." It's a "niggling that keeps after you and compels you. It comes from the inside out. The Scripture says springs of living water come out of your belly." "The strong urgent leading is . . . conviction" (Interview LT multi-church 3/14/88). Some informants described the leading as more subtle than compelling or niggling; they said that "God doesn't push; He just tells you" (Interview GH 11/21/86). "He never pushes; the Holy Spirit is a gentleman" (Interview DR charismatic 10/24/86). Some call it a "still, small voice" (Interview DF charismatic 11/24/86; Field Notes K. Mitchell).

In any case, the leading arises if the believer "seeks His face daily" in prayer (LWCC nda). The leading can take the form of a "voice," "images," or a "sense of satisfaction." Sheila Compton, a parent who had attended Baptist and now charismatic churches, explained how she received God's message.

> [When it's God's leading], you know. God will open doors. I don't want to say I've heard an audible voice, but at the same time I have, at least once or twice. I haven't a vision in the sense that I'm sitting here and all of a sudden the kitchen's gone and I'm in this cloud and I see all this stuff. But God has shown me things, and it's not necessarily—I won't say through dreams—but it's as I'm praying; it is images. I guess in a way it's a vision. You go back to the Old Testament especially, and see how God talked to Moses and how he talked to Abraham, and the prophets in the Old Testament. He talks to us the same way; it's just that most people aren't willing to receive it. (Interview SC charismatic 8/27/87)

Baptist teacher Marie Riley said:

> [I haven't heard God talk]. Not out loud. I haven't. I know some people have said they do. I hear God speak to me through the Bible. As I pray, I've never heard an audible voice inside. Some people hear an audible voice inside; I don't hear that, either. As I pray there is a presence or there is that peace. . . . There is something inside of me, and I know I am communing with Him and I am in communication with Him. I have seen answers to prayers. Again they're not audible; they have been answers in the sense of the satisfaction of having completed something about which I've prayed: the accomplishment of something—sometimes even a material gain or something; the birth of my children. (Interview MR Baptist 8/21/87)

Some do not deny hearing God speaking to them. Gail Halsey, a teacher at GCA, explained how to know the difference between "your own voice" and "His voice": "You hear your own voice in your head. His voice comes from the heart down here [pointing to her heart]. It's like it's inside you. . . . Your voice is busy, anxious. That's not God. God's voice is calm and deliberate" (Interview GH charismatic 11/21/86)

It is the Holy Spirit element of the Christian Trinity that is most often invoked as the source of the leading or conviction. "As we pray . . . God will give us conviction by the Holy Spirit" (LWCC nd). "The Holy Spirit lives within every believer . . . and He can show you" (Interview SC charismatic 8/27/87).

"The Holy Spirit is one called alongside to help us with every aspect of living out the life of Christ" (Interview LT multi-church 3/14/88). The teacher of GCA's Bible class for fifth and sixth graders reiterated this, saying: "The Holy Spirit sheds light on our path. He will lead us in all areas of our lives. How to do right. He leads us in who to marry, where to move—all areas of life—depending on how closely we walk with him, fellowship with him, and listen to him. We have a different light than the world's" (Field Notes GCA 1/19/87).

The conservative Christians distinguish among the "body (the five senses), the soul (mind, emotions, will) and the spirit (intuition, conscience)." The body and the soul are repositories of the "world's knowledge." For the believer, the spirit contains "God's knowledge" (Interview LT multi-church 3/14/88). The conscience and intuition, which every human being has, in the believer become the seat of the indwelling Holy Spirit. The conscience is a "mechanism that God has given to people that's an instrument to be let to the Lord" (Interview DR charismatic 10/24/86). When making decisions,

> unbelievers have the process of elimination based on circumstances, natural intuition, perceptions, and knowledge on which to base decisions. But intuition and conscience are avenues God intended for His use to guide and pattern us for His purpose. But in the natural man (unregenerated [unsaved] man) they are corrupted. When a person is saved, God (by the Holy Spirit) enlightens our conscience and sharpens our spiritual intuition so that these avenues are useful for guidance from God. (Interview LT multi-church 3/14/88)

Parent Delores Raleigh explained that "there is a God-shaped vacuum inside of us. . . . It's like a test tube inside of us. It's filled with something. There are only two spirits; . . . like a test tube, it can be filled with one or the other. There's the world—the devil—[placing her hand across her heart horizontally], and God [moving her hand to the vertical position]" (Interview DR charismatic 10/24/86).

The conservative Christians see the right relationship of the three components of the human being—body, soul, and spirit—this way: "We are meant to be a spirit being first, a soulish being second, and then a physical being after that, as well. . . . Now the way we live, especially in this country, I was always raised to be a soulish person first. . . . You reason everything. If there's not a reason why not, then you can do it; . . you can do it, if you want to."

So for the believer, there needs to be "a fine tuning to the Spirit of God, because we're not used to walking as our spiritual being. We are used to walking as a soulish man, led around only by our mind and our own reasoning, and what we can figure out" (Interview DR charismatic 10/24/86).

In an illustration from Dells Christian School's handbook (see figure 5.1) the Holy Spirit, with a much smaller "my spirit" inside it, is leading the "will, mind, emotion" (the "soul"), and bringing up the rear is the "body". At chapel at Maranatha Christian Academy, sponsored by an independent Baptist church, the principal and assistant pastor described this right relationship with the Holy Spirit by saying: "You get in the backseat and the Holy Spirit drives the car" (Field Notes MCA 3/6/87).

As the Baptist principal's homily shows, fundamentalists, as well as charismatics and evangelicals, make a place for the Holy Spirit and its leading.[4] The assistant principal at Maranatha would begin his chapel discussion of scripture by saying: "I don't know how the Lord showed this to me, but he did" (Field Notes MCA 1/16/87).

> We fundamentalists were so scared of what those charismatics and liberals were doing that we ran from the Holy Spirit. And you have to have the Holy Spirit. . . . If you're reading the scripture, and you don't know what something means, don't ask me; ask the Holy Spirit first. . . . The author of the Bible is not dead. . . . He's alive in the Holy Spirit. So ask the Holy Spirit. He can interpret it for you; He knows what it means, because He wrote it. (Field Notes MCA 3/6/87)

When it comes to making decisions within Christian schools, examples of praying for God's direction abound. Every level of the Christian school ministry and business counsels that one should pray to seek God's leading. Replies to inquiries requesting information from curriculum manufacturers are form letters asking that the recipient pray about whether to use this particular curriculum. ACE suggests that schools should "ask your students to pray about whether God wants them to come to [ACE's college] International Institute."

Lockerbie (1972, 116), describing how decisions are made at the evangelical Stony Brook School, says that it is necessary to "pray for God's best solution." And indeed, this is done, daily. The Dells Christian School administrator prayed about whether she should take this position, after a series of circumstances seemed to leave it in her lap (Field Notes DCS 12/10/86). At a Grace Christian Academy PTF meeting, it was necessary for the chairman of the board of directors to appoint a nominating committee to choose candidates for new board members. As he stood at the front of the crowded room, he was slow to make his choices, explaining that he was "waiting for God's direction" (Field Notes 1/12/87). During a lengthy PTF meeting discussing the school's need for new facilities, the chairman said: "In terms of where to proceed from here. . . . We [the board] need a little direction. I don't want to rush you, but I need some direction. Let's take a few minutes and be quiet; be still and have a moment where we can rest. In your own terms, ask God what He thinks. . . . Let's just be quiet and ask God for direction."

Thus, decisions affecting a school's physical plant, the administration, and the curriculum are submitted to God in prayer. So are discipline problems. At a GCA faculty meeting the administrator's closing prayer included:

Father, we seek great peace and calmness over the seventh-grade boys, Father. You know their nature. You know why they do the things that they do, Father, and Father we are trusting in You to give us *Your* strength and understanding, Father, as we work with them. . . .

Let our patience not be short . . . Father, and reveal to us their needs, Father, and help us to meet the needs of those boys, Father. Whatever it is that we need to do, You *show* us, Father. And Father, we just are trusting in You. . . . You sent them here for a reason, and this is a life-changing year for them and we'll hold on to that hope Father, that You have given to us. (Field Notes GCA 12/02/87)

At a faculty meeting two months later, the administrator said: "I know if we continue to pray, God is going to show us—soon—what to do with the seventh graders" (Field Notes GCA 2/3/87).

At times, prayers seemed to direct God as much as they sought his direction. Or at least, they exhorted God to lead in certain directions. For example:

Father I lift up the PTF meeting especially, and that the parents would come in receptive and willing and open, Father, to efforts the board is making concerning their children. And Father, I lift up the families who are still in prayer—who are indecisive concerning the placing of their children here for next year—and I ask that You would . . . give them a comfortable peaceful decision, Father, concerning their children. And that, they would know, Father, in their hearts, what this school is. . . . We just ask, Father, that unity—a spirit of unity—be present. (Field Notes GCA 3/3/87)

Confirmation in Scripture

After the leading or conviction of the Holy Spirit has been felt, the believer "must sometime evaluate it according to the Word" (Interview LT

189

multi-church 3/14/88). The importance of checking one's leading with the scriptures was emphasized time and time again. "It's got to square with the Word. . . . the *written* Word, the visible Word" (Field Notes GCA 1/30/87). Whenever the administrator at GCA questioned something she had read, or something she had heard in a "teaching" in church, on the radio, or on television, she turned to reading the Bible (Field Notes GCA 11/13/86).

> The inward conviction should . . . be tested by the subjective confirmation of the Scriptures. It must be measured in the light of scriptural principals. The importance of this step is emphasized in Isaiah 8:20, with this warning: "To the law and to the testimony! If they do not speak according to this Work, it is because they have no dawn." A conviction can lead one astray if it is not in agreement with the Scriptures. (LWCC nda)

If a person "has ever taken the time to integrate large portions of Scripture into their spirit mind or 'heart,' " then "another kind of leading of the Holy Spirit is the kind of 'knowing' that springs up out of the resources of the Word that has been hidden in a person's heart. This is the 'rivers of living water' " (Interview LT multi-church 3/14/88). "Read the Word; get it into your heart; you meditate on it; you get it in there. Memorize it, but not just memorize it, it gets down into your heart" (Interview DF 11/24/86 charismatic). Students were often reminded to get "those scriptures down into your heart." In Bible 5/6, the teacher exhorted the students to:

> Feast on the bread. Feast on God's word. That's how we fellowship with God—get his Word inside of us. . . . Our prayers, God says, are like a sweet-smelling savor, in His nostrils. "The smoke of the incense, together with the prayers of the saints, went up before God from the angel's hand" (Revelation 8:4 NIV). God enjoys our prayers. (Field Notes GCA 1/19/87)

The Math 7 students at GCA were told that:

> Reading God's Word, praying, and listening are three ways of getting Godly wisdom. He said to get it, it's not just going to come knocking on your door is it? You can't just expect God's Word to come to you. You have to pick the book up, and you have to read it. . . . And if you're doing those things, then you can ask God to help

provide the everyday knowledge that you need in your math and in whatever else. (Field Notes GCA 11/03/86)

Seeking Godly Counsel

Seeking the counsel of "mature individuals who know the ways of God, and have been walking with Him with spiritual understanding for many years" (LWCC nda) is also recommended. "Seek counsel from several Godly friends" (Interview LT multi-church 3/14/88). And yet, the admonitions that you cannot depend on any human being; that humans take scripture out of context; that humans twist scripture; that God, Jesus, the Holy Spirit is the only one you can trust, would seem to mitigate the worth of seeking godly counsel.

Administrators did ask other teachers what they thought of teacher candidates—"What did you think of her, spiritually?"—and it could be said that the considerable reading and listening to Christian tapes, radio, and TV that some of the administrators and teachers do is a way of seeking godly counsel (Field Notes GCA 5/5/87). A charismatic parent, Shelia Compton, said she saw this kind of "godly counsel" as functionally specialized, so that "what we do here in this house is if we're being attacked physically—or we need to stand for physical healing—we turn on Richard Roberts; plug in an Oral Roberts tape; read an Oral Roberts book. If we're being attacked financially, then I'm going to Kenneth Copeland. Because that's what he's anointed to preach on" (Interview SC charismatic 8/27/87).

Finding Circumstantial Evidence and God's Provision

The next step in discerning God's will is to be awake to circumstances and provisions (or lack thereof) which show whether God approves or disapproves of the plan.

While we may decide to launch out in a given direction in full faith that it is the will of God, we should be aware that the final confirmation is His provision for our needs. Provision is a primary means God has of restraining His over zealous servants who are extending themselves beyond His will for their lives. By not following with provision, He communicates to us that either (a) the time He has established has not come, or (b) the direction in which we are going is wrong. (LWCC nda)

Confirming circumstantial evidence can come in many forms. It can come from the words of another person, from a particularly enlightening scripture, or it can be inferred from other signs.

A PERSON BEARING WITNESS. A source of confirming evidence can be "one or more 'unknowing' sources who say something that bears witness with the inner witness the person already has."

The confirmer is unknowing in the sense that he/she is unaware that what they said has any application specific to the other person's life at that time. (Interview LT multi-church 3/14/88)

For the charismatics, who believe that certain persons are called to be prophets, confirming evidence can come from such a person.

Occasionally God sends a person to confirm things for another of his servants. This would fall under the "grace gifts" or charismata, that is, word of knowledge, wisdom, or discernmment. This kind of confirmation is invalid if it is not *confirmation;* the person's comments must line up with what *you* are getting from God already, and His Word. (Interview LT multi-church 3/14/88; see also Interview SC charismatic 8/27/87)

SCRIPTURES COME TO LIFE. Sometimes it is taken as a "sign" of circumstantial evidence when specific "scriptures may come to life on a particular day" (Interview LT multi-church 3/14/88).

A student in the fundamentalist Baptist school that Alan Peshkin (1986, 117) observed told him: "In English, Mrs. Reynolds . . . [will] say, "OK, turn to such and such verse in the Bible. I want you to find adjectives, pronouns, and verbs." I look at the verse, you know, and I think about the verse, and sometimes something comes to me that really, you know, the Lord sent and used that class to send to me."

A parent at GCA, Delores Raleigh, concurred:

You can read passages in the Scriptures and you know they're right and you know they're good. . . . There might be a word of of encouragement, or it can be a word of direction. . . . It can quicken to you that which you need. . . .

It's by the Spirit of God that that happens. Otherwise why would you be reading that one verse—that's really pertinent to you—that ministers to you and shows you maybe what to do, or just gives you encouragement in a situation? (Interview DR charismatic 10/24/86; see also Interview SC charismatic 8/21/87).

You know how Grandma Jeannette will say "God led me to this verse"—well that's what happens. (Field Notes MCA 3/6/87)

GOD GIVES SIGNS OR OPENS DOORS. Sometimes people ask the Lord to "give them a sign" and if "doors are opened" then it is taken as evidence that the direction they are taking is the Lord's will. "Where an opportunity might arise or something, I might say that might be a sign to you [of God's will]. . . . I would say to someone "well maybe this is a sign to you that your life should take a different course, or you should do something else" (Interview MR Baptist 8/21/87).

Signs from God are mentioned with some frequency in the Bible. A metaphor used frequently today is from Judges 6:36–40:

And Gideon said unto God, If thou wilt save Israel by mine hand, as thou hast said, Behold, I will put a fleece of wool in the floor; and if the dew be on the fleece only, and it be dry upon all the earth beside, then shall I know that thou wilt save Israel by mine hand, as thou hast said. And it was so: for he rose up early on the morrow, and thrust the fleece together, and wringed the dew out of the fleece, a bowl full of water. And Gideon said unto God, Let not thine anger be hot against me, and I will speak but this once: let me prove, I pray thee, but this once with the fleece; let it now be dry only upon the fleece, and upon all the ground let there be dew. And God did so that night: for it was dry upon the fleece only, and there was dew on all the ground.

Today, "throwing out the fleece" is a way of "seeking God's will." Ammerman (1987, 87) notes that in the Independent Baptist church she studied "putting out a fleece" meant "to test an alternative." A person would venture into something new, and wait to see whether God supported it, with "provision." "Some people jump into career choices or whatever just arbitrarily making a decision . . . and if it works out, fine, and if it doesn't, fine. And they would term that throwing out the fleece, as a test or a sign" (Interview MR Baptist 8/21/87).

The same principle, though not the specific metaphor, is used when a person watches to see whether a particular thing "works out," as a sign of God's will. Teacher Gail Halsey described "the first time I ever asked God anything":

> It was about changing my major. I was in math, and I was getting to hate it. I had taken a few statistics courses over the summer, and I loved it. It made it practical, because those math courses can get pretty abstract. So I said, "OK God, if You want me to do this, You make the paper work go smoothly. So that I won't have to walk across the campus twenty times and get all frustrated." And I went to my course advisor and found him in for the first time, and he said, "Oh sure, all you do is fill out this form and take it over there and take your transcripts." And I filled out the form right there and when I went over [to where he had directed me], I met my new course advisor: *he* was *in*. And I made *one* trip across the campus. (Interview GH charismatic 11/21/86)

Signs of God's provision figured in plans made by Julia Dobbins, the Baptist teacher from Grace Christian Academy. She and her husband were embarking on a missionizing crusade overseas.

> We have known about this crusade for six years, and have been asked to go for the past three years. But we just always said "No way." Then—neighbors were talking about a trip—going overseas— and it just hit me—yes—why not? So I talked to George, and I said "Honey, we're not gettin' any younger, and we're in good health now, and we could do this for the Lord. We don't have any payments—not for car or house—just the rent and usual things." He has five weeks vacation he can use, though we won't need that much. So I said, "Let me see if the school board would let me go; that would be another sign." Then we met a man who has been on that crusade before. So it's just all coming together. (Field Notes GCA)

Later, when an accident caused the couple to have to purchase a new car, the cause was thought to be the devil trying to "come against" their work for the Lord. The couple prevailed however, continued planning for the crusade despite the setback, and did eventually go. If things work out smoothly (in the long run), it is seen as a confirmation that it is the Lord's will.

Asking God to "open a door" is a common way of requesting a sign. A parent at Dells Christian School told me how she came to enroll her child in the school. To find schools, "I looked in the phone book. I said 'Lord, if it's meant to be, open a door.' And when I called, they wanted my son. And I was able to get the money to pay for it" (Field Notes DCS 5/29/87).

So God's provision, or lack of it, is a sign that a person is (or isn't) doing what God wants him to do. God will "open doors" or "nail them shut." Charismatic parent Shelia Compton explained that she asked the Lord to guide her about being involved in a church music ministry. "I submitted it to him. I said, 'You may not even want me in this stuff; tell me and I'll get out. Let me know; slam some doors; nail 'em shut' " (Interview SC charismatic 8/27/87). Describing how she knew that God wanted her to be involved in political activity, she told how she was able, with God's help, to arrange transportation and child care in order to go to her first major meeting. These things didn't occur "accidentally." It "was God" at work, supporting her involvement (Interview SC charismatic 8/21/87).

Evangelical Lockerbie (1972, 72), as well as fundamentalist Baptist administrators at Maranatha Christian, and charismatics at Grace, explained God's willingness to make provision this way: "God supports His work." "We are working for Jesus Christ." "We're serving Jesus Christ; we're serving God." "Jesus is the head of this school" (Field Notes MCA; GCA). It was said that God provided the supporting pastors, the board members, the administrators, and the teachers. This was taken as a sign that they were his schools, and that he wanted them to continue.

FINDING SIGNS: EXPLAINING EVENTS CHRISTOCENTRICALLY. The curriculum decisions made by administrators and teachers were thought to embody elements of circumstantial evidence which showed that God was leading their footsteps in the right direction, and eventually to the right decision.

The very ways the stories about these decisions are told shows the difference between individualistic and Christocentric expositions. When I describe decision-making about curriculums, I discuss attending workshops, gathering information, and talking to others who use the materials. When the conservative Christians describe it, their words stress their conviction that none of this just happened. For example, an individualist would say that the Open Court textbook sales representative just happened to be in the area, and coincidentally told GCA's staff about the upcoming reader's conference. Not so the conservative Christians, who see it as God leading their footsteps. The individualist would say that the administrator happened to hear a fellow student at a seminar discussing Open Court materials. But when the administrator described these situations, she emphasized the fact that various information fell across her path *without her actively seeking it out.* She noted that the student was not in the same seminar she was; she was sitting near this person at lunch, and the student spontaneously began talking about Open Court (that is, the administrator didn't ask her about it). An individualist would say that it was coincidence that one of the teachers happened to see the administrator looking at advertisements for experiential science teaching aids, and mentioned to her that a former professor had more information about them. An individualist would see it as a likely chance occurrence that the administrator would meet a teacher from another Christian school at an ICR Seminar located at a Bible college. The conservative Christian would see these things as coincidences, too, but not as coincidences of chance; rather, they are a coincidental sign of God's leading. They are translated as the marks of God's leading at work.

An administrator at a school run by charismatic Living Waters Christian Community makes it clear that he learned of a new curriculum through the Lord's leading. He had gone to a seminar about the curriculum, and visited a school which used it.

> The Lord allows it to happen through contacts and circumstances. I visited that school where I saw the curriculum—not because I wanted to visit that school—but there was something else I wanted to visit in that place—and the school was there, too. I didn't know it would show me anything, but it did.

> It isn't coincidence, but that's what people would say it was—that it was just coincidence. I didn't know about the seminar; I called to check on a book this person had written and he told me about the seminar. . . . The Lord confirms that. At the beginning of the year, I didn't know . . . [that I would find these things]. In fact, they had sent me flyers and brochures for years, and I had just put them in the file. I wasn't interested in it, and I was prejudiced against it. And you can say, "well I wish I had learned about this or paid attention to this four years ago," but you can't say that, because God's timing is perfect.

> You're always praying He's going to bring what you need at the right time. You're building up a bank account. You're asking God not to let you do anything that would hurt the children. Because God knows our hearts. And He knows that we want to please Him. (Field Notes LWCA 2/26/87)

Experiencing the Peace of God

The conservative Christians repeatedly said that a feeling of peace showed the believer that he was in God's will. "The end result of following the leading is peace of mind . . . confident peacefulness" (Interview

LT multi-church 3/14/88). There is a "peace of mind—not a feeling of turmoil" (Interview SR charismatic 1/30/87).

> As we seek to determine His will, if the peace of God leaves us (i.e., if we have moved from the watered garden of Isaiah 58:11, to the dust bowl of Psalms 68:6), that is the time to stop and examine the situation. (LWCC nda)

> There's a peace. There's a peace inside when you know you're doing the right thing. You know. It might not fall into place immediately, but it will start to fall into place, and it will run smoothly. That doesn't mean that it's not going to get out of kilter one day; you're not going to be like an army regimented. But it's gonna flow. When it doesn't flow. . . you know you're busy in too many of the wrong directions. (Interview SC charismatic 8/27/87)

> The peace of God is a fruit of the spirit. The peace of God is like the umpire of your heart. It's telling you right from wrong. (Interview DF charismatic 11/24/86)

> You know. Just as you know it's time to eat, you know. I don't know how to describe it anymore than that. (Interview SC charismatic 8/21/87)

MAKING DECISIONS

Examples of making decisions with God's help abound, and range from the sublime—like whether to send a child to Christian school, whether to change a major, where to find a job—to the commonplace—like whether to come to school with a cold. God's help was given to mothers agonizing over their children's futures, and to a graduate student when he was not quite prepared for a test. Let two examples of how believers make decisions suffice to show the application of the discernment process we have described.

Mrs. Raleigh tells how she decided to sent her daughter to Christian school. She discusses the leading, the scriptural affirmation, the positive circumstances and provision, and the peace of God which accompanied her decision.

> I knew since Beth was in kindergarten that she shouldn't be there— that she should be in Christian school. The Lord showed me that. But I

said, "what am I going to do about that—there is no place." And it got stronger and stronger. It's in the Word. . . . Deuteronomy 6. . .

The government is ordained by God—the federal government and state government and so forth—is ordained by God, but to govern, not to teach. I found that I didn't have to give up my children to the state. When they were in public school, whenever they were out of school, I felt guilty; I always had to explain to the state. There was always a question—"where *are* they?" I kept relinquishing them, every day, day in and day out. They were not being taught God's principles; they were taught worldly values.

We went to [another school to visit]. We didn't like ACE and there were some other things there. . . . We were ready to send them to City. Then we met with Kathleen. [At that time] there was no building, no school. We were the second or third parents to sign up. It was the biggest leap of faith I've ever made. But it was God's idea. It was His desire to have this school. He brought the people together to do it. . . .

I knew enough to pray and to ask God what to do, and for Him to make a way. And to me—at that time—for God to make a way for a school was—I might as well have said bring Mars to earth; it seemed almost impossible. But yet I knew that's what she needed. And that's why when the school came about it was a miracle. . . .

It was just—God did it. People were obedient to . . . what He was doing. There's a difference, you know, in that and people doing it on their own. (Interview DR Charismatic 10/24/86)

The volunteer physical education and computer programming teacher at GCA describes his God-led job search.

When I was looking for a job, I wanted to stay in Dells. At that time, I was absolutely head over heels in love with my church; . . . I didn't want to leave it.

I prayed about it. I said "Lord, I may be just being selfish right now." . . . And I said "Lord, I'll go anywhere You want me to go. But I just wanted to let You know that I really want to stay—I just have this incredible desire. But if that's not what You want . . . then just tell me where to go." . . .

Four companies were after me. I even decided to make the phone calls [to the companies]. And when I picked up the phone I started shaking and I was so uptight that I couldn't. I wasn't frightened but I just couldn't make that phone call. And when I put the phone down I felt overwhelming relief and peace. . . .

I thought God has withdrawn his . . . peace. Peace is God's nature; when you take God's nature out, what's left over is what's out in the environment—the devil. . . .

He was pulling back, and saying, "I'm not in this decision you're making." . . . I couldn't do it. . . . I didn't make the call, and we're back in unity again. We're walking side by side. . . .

My professor started talking to me about this job he had. I thought he was talking about a part-time thing. He said, "you can start in November; you can start working full time for me." And it was a $19,000 a year job. I thought it was going to be about about $10,000 a year. . . .

My spirit started doing handsprings. I didn't have to ask anyone. . . . I said, "This must be You, God. Man, this is great!" Hindsight, of course, is a good test as to whether you got it right or not. . . . I said, "God You really did, superabundantly provide what I could ask for . . . and what I wanted."

It gave me an opportunity to grow. It gave me an opportunity to witness. Several people—well at least one that I know of—came to the Lord from my being on that job, and others certainly were witnessed to. . . . It's a broad picture put into focus. He knows the beginning and the end. I needed to learn to be led by God. (Interview DF charismatic 11/04/86)

THE FUNCTIONS OF DISCERNMENT

The conservative Christians would say that when people are saved, they gain peace *with* God. This is the peace accompanying the promise of salvation and everlasting life. The only other alternative, as they see it, is eternal damnation in hell. When they are saved, eternal life is secured. This is "*becoming* a Christian." Then, if they commit themselves to daily discerning what God's will is for them, and to living within God's will, they gain his help in matters of everyday living in this life. They gain the peace *of* God. This is "*being* a Christian." The peace comes from using various means of "asking God what He thinks," using him as a "partner" to help make the "right" choices in decisions of everyday life—both great

and small (LWCC nda; Interview MR Baptist 8/21/87). Put more collo-
quially (and in a way with which some conservative Christians would not
agree): "I know what it's like to be outside [of God's perfect will]. I know
[how that feels]. If you're outside of it, things happen to you—like something happens to your car. It will need a $600 repair bill. If you're in
God's will, it might be it needs a spark plug for fifty cents—or nothing at
all happens to your car" (Interview GH charismatic 11/21/86).

Discerning God's will, like divination in general, has psychological,
sociological, and ritual functions. The psychological functions are easy to
fathom, for we all have felt a peace (lack of turmoil) after a decision has
been made.[5] Just as being "anointed" engenders a feeling of rightness, so
does asking God what to do as you make decisions add a feeling of
security in doing the right thing. The feeling that decisions are right or
correct must be enhanced if they are thought to be in accordance with
God's will; this assurance must surely bring the "psychological release
that comes from the conviction that subsequent action is in tune with the
wishes of supernatural forces" (Herskovits 1938, vol. 2, 217).

From the analytical perspective of social science, the conservative Christians participate in this form of help with decision-making for the same
reasons people everywhere do: "Divination permits the man who is immo-
bilized by a difficult decision to make a choice, and to make it with
confidence" (Lessa and Vogt 1965, 298–300). All of the decision-making
examples we have used partake of the function of "inspiring the persons
who must execute the decision with sufficient confidence to permit them
to mobilize their full skills and energies, unimpeded by anxiety, fear, or
doubts about having made the best choice among the alternatives available" (Wallace 1966, 173; Bascom 1941).

In discerning God's will, the conservative Christian gains both an answer to a temporal question and spiritual peace. It might be said that
another latent psychological function lies in the fact that "through the
ritual performance which divination entails, he is also giving overt expression to his doubts, suspicions and fears. And this, at least in some measure, is an end in itself" (Beattie 1967, 230). The prayers that "went up"
from GCA as it experienced the disjunctures encumbent upon a change in
social structure (from church-sponsored to a parent-led board of directors) were a sometimes anguished description of current difficulties, and
an expression of fear that others might be on the horizon. At the same
time, they were statements of assurance that God's help would prevail in
his school that he had "raised up."

The sociological function of producing and expressing group unity
came into play, too, during these prayers (Radcliffe-Brown 1964, especially chapter 5, the description of the dance.) The prayers were not

prayed in private; it was not just God who was listening. As the prayers were said by the administrator, holding hands with all the teachers in a circle, they all "came into agreement" with what she was saying. Agreement was symbolized by the intermittent responses—"Thank You Jesus. . . Yes Lord. . . Praise God. . . Praise Jesus"—interspersed by the teachers as the administrator spoke. Teachers who were deciding to leave their jobs at the school stopped coming to these morning prayers.

Discerning God's will also performed the sociological function of "accomplishing a more rapid consensus within a group, with minimal offense to the members . . . for the choice was made [or at least supported] by an outside power" who is "beyond cavil and beyond reproach" (Wallace 1966, 172–173; Park 1967, 236). An example is asking for God's intervention into GCA's decision to seek a new building. In this case, the board of directors and a majority of the parent shareholders had to agree to expend money to relocate the school, and had to agree on which of several alternatives to choose. As they pondered a plan proffered at a PTF meeting, one parent spoke what was on several (but up to that point not all) minds: "Personally, I don't see how God could lay it out any plainer" (Field Notes GCA 3/9/87).

The act of discernment is also ritual, and thus shares ritual's function of expressing (and reaffirming) the ideology that lies behind it. "Divination is a rite: it is not just a way of doing something; it is also, and essentially, a way of saying something." Certainly, the conservative Christian who consults God's wisdom "wants to know the answers to the questions which he has in mind" (Beattie 1967, 230). But in doing the asking, he is also expressing his Christocentric ideology; he is reaffirming his *dependence* on God. He is expressing that he's not just "doing this on his own"; he's asking for God's leading; and he is giving thanks to a "partner." "*Mores* do not live on of themselves but must be recreated by ritual, ceremony, and the acts of constituted authority in the experience of each individual" (Park 1967, 254). Asking God to show his will for your life, and exhorting the children to do the same, recreates the Christocentric ideology of man's dependence on God afresh, everyday.

The Christocentric worldview of the conservative Christians fulfills all of the needs religion, magic, and divination have been found to meet. "In a world rendered fearful and worrisome by uncertainty, chance, and inadequate understanding of a wide variety of natural phenomena," they provide answers (Lessa and Vogt 1965, 359). Their ideology with its attendant rituals provides answers in areas of uncertainty, removes the possibility of chance ("nothing happens by accident") and proffers creationism to explain natural phenomena. Thus, all of the questions of life—the deep and enduring ones concerning the meaning of life, death, and life after death—are answered by their philosophy. And so are the questions—some serious, some quotidian but niggling—of everyday life in a school, like whether and where to seek out a new building or a new curriculum, and what to put on the bulletin boards. For "there is no area of life in which God is not interested."

The main reason for following God's will is that by doing so, He is glorified. When He is glorified, two things happen: (a) those in the world about us develop a greater awareness of His reality and are thus more strongly motivated to seek His peace by calling on His Name for salvation, and (b) our own awareness of the fact of His being and His care for us is increased—which then, in turn, brings us into a greater measure of His lasting peace. (LWCC nda)

You guide me with your counsel, and afterward you will take me into glory (Psalms 73:24 NIV). (LWCC nda)

12

Conclusion: Choice and Compromise

The anthropologist's function is to understand a culture on its own terms, to interpret it given the tools and theories at hand, and to describe it to outsiders. This already challenging task is made all the more so when that culture is a controversial one surrounded by ready-made stereotypes, as is true for Christian schools. While I was learning about Christian schools, a colleague declared that he knew about such schools: "All they teach is how to memorize Bible verses; they're not interested in teaching the kids to read or write or count." Another asked, "Do they spend all day on Bible?"

The rhetoric of the conservative Christians paints them as a different people, "separate from the world," striving to be "not unequally yoked together with unbelievers." Some studies of Christian schools have said that the conservative Christian church, home, and school comprise a total institution where the goal of maintaining separateness and difference is met (see Peshkin 1986, 1987). On the other hand, Hunter (1986; 1987, 157) has found a good deal of "accommodating to modernity" among conservative Christians, and notes that "the caricature of Evangelicalism as an inert fortification of antique cultural traditions is certainly wrong." This research supports Hunter's conclusion.

Indeed, the conservative Christians themselves know that they are making compromises with the culture that surrounds them. This brand of fundamentalism was born in the USA and is in some ways overwhelmed by American popular culture. Inside the schools, competition and materialism coexist or compete with the gentle fruits of the spirit that the conservative Christians identify as "love, joy, peace, longsuffering, gentleness, goodness, faith, meekness, temperance." Prayer requests and praise reports of the pupils were much more likely to be concerned with trips to Disney World for themselves, or with teenage relationships, than they were with, for example, healing of others' bodies or souls.

Other components of the Christian school cultural matrix derive from education culture. In this microcosm of the professional education cultural scene, parents are asked to participate in Parent/Teacher Fellowship, and held at bay during parent/teacher conferences. Teachers attend workshops on critical thinking and obtain continuing education credits. Forms of discipline based on behavior modification techniques ("You'll lose the points you have accumulated if you do that") are used much more often than those based on religious principle ("You're doing this for Jesus").

INTERPRETING THE COMPROMISES

The question then becomes why do we find compromises, rather than the establishment of a total institution. Further, why do we find the particular compromises that we do? Why does this culture have these traits, and why does it *not* have other alternative ones? To find answers, we have looked at the relationship between conservative Christian culture and the encompassing American society. We have plumbed the process by which culture-bearers become actors engaged in making and unmaking their cultural surroundings. In that vein, this research has been a case study in the practice of culture-building, in the ways that conservative Christian administrators, teachers, parents and students create Christian school culture.

BUILDING CHRISTIAN SCHOOLS AS A
REVITALIZATION PROCESS

The light we have shone on conservative Christendom's building of Christian schools illuminated it as a revitalization process—characterized by a "conscious, organized effort by members of a society to construct a more satisfying culture." (Wallace 1960, 30; see also Ahlstrom 1975; Carper 1984; Jordan 1982; McLoughlin 1978; Marsden 1980; Marty 1981; Nordin and Turner 1980.)

Borrowing Wallace's (1966, 160) terms, the conservative Christians' model of an ideal society is their *goal culture*, which they readily described as harboring "no competition, forbearing and forgiving, and the fruits of the spirit." This is the essence of the Christian walk. "Contrasted with the goal culture is the *existing culture*, which is presented as inadequate or evil in certain respects" (Wallace 1966, 160, emphasis his). The American way of life, and particularly "secular humanism," is the denigrated existing culture for the conservative Christians. The Christian schools themselves are the *transfer culture* which connects the existing culture and the goal culture. It is here, within the Christian schools, that the revitalization process—"the process by which cultural materials . . . are analyzed and combined into a new structure"—is carried out (Wallace 1966, 39, 16, 211, emphasis his).

In the Christian schools, therefore, we can see a case study of how decisions are made, consciously and unconsciously, when people go about the business of creating a culture, of how they decide what to keep and what to eschew. Let's first discuss this question analytically, or etically, and then summarize the native, or emic, answers provided by the conservative Christian worldview itself.

Creating a Culture: Why Compromise?

A school is a more consciously built culture than the ones which we are born into, and all along the way, decisions as to how to run it must be made. The conservative Christian revitalization process employs a "revivalistic" rhetoric which describes its aim as restoring "a golden age believed to have existed in the society's past" (Wallace 1966, 165). They speak of a rosy *Little House on the Prairie* past, and parents admiringly say that their first look at a Christian school was like "stepping back in time" (Field Notes 9/17/86).

Yet, what actually occurs within the schools is "assimilative, which imports many of the customs of the . . . dominant group, and combines them sycretistically with native customs" (Wallace 1966, 165).[1] On the one hand, the conservative Christians teach their children that they are a separate people, a people apart from the world. The little ones are taught to sing "Be careful little ears what you hear; be careful little eyes what you see." The older pupils are taught that "the devil is after your mind." Yet for all these exercises in polarization and boundary maintenance, the conservative Christians are well aware that they have made accommodations to modernity, though they may not label them as such.

Compromises and accommodations ensure the continued existence of both conservative Christian culture and the schools themselves within American society. If the Christian walk is to survive in American society, it must be walked the American way. In the early part of this century, theologian Ernst Troeltsch wrote that "the fact remains that all intransigence breaks down in practice and can only end in disaster. The history of Christians itself is most instructive in this connection. It is, in the long run, a tremendous, continuous compromise between the utopian demands of the Kingdom of God and the permanent conditions of the actual human life" (Pauck 1968, 78; see also Troeltsch 1960, 511).

It should not be a surprise that conservative Christian educators create a school culture that borrows from the surrounding culture. How successful would a more "alternative" alternative be? Like any new cultural form, if it is to endure, the Christian school must create palatable and meaningful compromises which "objectively synthesize a relation between [for them, competing] cultural categories." Sahlins (1976, 217) reiterates this necessity, using the example of the fashion designer, who we *think* "plucks his ideas out of thin air. . . . But the fashion expert does not make his collection out of whole cloth; . . . he uses bits and pieces with an embedded significance from a previous existence to create an object that works, which is to say that sells—which is also to say that objectively synthesizes a relation between cultural categories, for in that lies its salability."

Characteristics of Conservative Christianity

Certain features of conservative Christianity—for all its emphasis on separation and difference—render it amicable to a compromising process.

A TRADITIONAL RELIGION. It has the earmarks of a traditional religion, in Weber's (1948, 1963) terms, where all things are sacred and ideology is played out on an ad hoc basis (unlike "rational" religion where abstract ideology is separate from everyday life and manifested in an abstract, logically coherent way.)

This aspect of conservative Christianity means that as they make the day-to-day decisions which constitute the creation of a new culture, Christian educators work in the bricoleur mode applied to culture-building by Lévi-Strauss (1966).

USING THE BRICOLEUR APPROACH. The bricoleur is the jack-of-all-trades who works with what is at hand. The bricoleur's opposite, the cultural engineer (who would be more comfortable in Weber's rational religion), would employ a process of clarifying the values the conservative Christians desire for their goal culture, and then would examine alternative ways to instill these in their children. For example, if the ideal target or goal culture is one where material goods and competition have little value, then, how do you train children in the desired mode? Perhaps this would require an Amish-like isolation that these Christians are not willing to pursue. They do, after all, want their children to succeed *inside* American society.

Instead, like Lévi-Strauss's bricoleur, they pick and choose from what's available, and make alterations to themes and artifacts of popular culture, rather than using an entirely new pattern. They create ways for Christian children to compete in locating and quoting Bible verses and in collecting toys with Christian themes. Rather than creating new ways for children to play, the Christian toys are My Little Ponies and Care Bears and Their Friends with Bible verses appliquéd on them.

But how is it possible to reconcile bricoleur-like compromises with the overarching ideology that prides itself on being separate and different? Contained within the conservative Christian culture is an arrangement of values which allows for the necessary synthesis.

ALLOWING FOR ACCOMMODATION: UNCHANGING SACRED POSTULATES AND CHANGING SOCIAL ARRANGEMENTS. The conservative Christian culture, as is true of societies in general, has a "hierarchial arrangement of values. . . . What may be called 'ultimate' or 'basic' values," reside "at the highest levels." "Instrumental values," concerned with the specifics of how people in a society should act, are at the "lower levels of the hierarchy." Values at the highest level are "vague"; they are not specific or concrete. These nonspecific "ultimate sacred postulates" are possessed of sanctity— "the quality of unquestionableness imputed by a congregation to postulates [that are] in their nature neither verifiable or falsifiable" (Rappaport 1979, 155, 209). The fact that ultimate sacred postulates are vague and devoid of material referents (which makes them immune to falsification) renders them adaptive in the long view of a society's changing history.

> Vagueness is not a flaw but an adaptive characteristic of the ultimate. Propositions about God typically are devoid of material terms and therefore in themselves specify no particular social arrangements or institutions. Being devoid of, or at least low in, social specificity, they are well suited to be associated with the general goals of societies, namely their own perpetuation, for they can sanctify *changing* social arrangements while they themselves, remaining *unchanged,* provide continuity and meaning through those changes. Their typically cryptic nature is also important, for if they are vague the association of the ultimate and eternal with the immediate realities of history requires continual interpretation. Interpretation and reinterpretation do not challenge ultimate sacred postulates, but only previous interpretations of them. (Rappaport 1979, 155–56, emphasis mine)

In the assimilative transfer culture found in the Christian schools, the retained native Christian traits are at the highest levels of belief. The basic or ultimate fundamentalist Christian message—how to be saved to live eternally, and what happens if you are not—is steadfast. In the generic statement of faith smelted from many such statements from a variety of Christian schools, this basic message was given voice this way: "Salvation is attained by the grace of God through the blood of Jesus. Whoever believes in Christ and will accept Him as Lord shall receive eternal life."

The compromises appeared in the realm of values about behavior: what students could wear, collect, play, listen to; with whom they could interact; how they would be taught and disciplined; but not in the very deepest (or highest) realms of belief.

The conservative Christians say that the Bible contains specific rules for living, and they hold national conferences to ferret out Biblical solutions to modern-day problems (Coalition on Revival; Congress on the Bible; Appalachian Conference to Rebuild America). However, the fact that a variety of specific concrete behaviors are supported by different schools, all of which subscribe to the same ultimate sacred postulates, shows that there is flexibility of interpretation at the instrumental or social arrangements level of building a Christian school culture.

The relationship between unchanging ultimate sacred postulates and changing social arrangements was conveyed by an administrator and teacher when a jeans-clad student who attended one of the new charismatic churches asked why her classmate from a Holiness church (who happened to be absent that day) always wore skirts. Her teacher admonished, "It's not a salvation issue."

Characteristics of the Culture-Builders

Some characteristics of the Christian school culture's constituency also encourage compromising in the bricoleur mode.

BACKGROUND OF TEACHERS. The personnel who are creating the culture—the actors in the Christian school transfer culture—have been culture-bearers in the surrounding culture. Teachers who have been trained in secular universities and who have taught in public schools bring with them a set of cultural traits which they alter within the Christian school setting.

DESIRES OF PARENTS. Marketing to sophisticated Christian parents also helps to explain the embracing of parts of modern education culture. If your goal is to produce well-educated Christian young adults, who can be further eudcated in "the college of their choice"—not necessarily a

Christian college—and who will become leaders in the America of to-morrow, certain concessions to the educational establishment will be made.

DIVERSITY OF STUDENT BODY. The diversity of church and doctrinal background among their student bodies pushes the schools to stay in the realm of the ultimate sacred propositions about which all agree. It is easy to see that a church that opened a school only for its own children could dictate specific instrumental social arrangements, based on church doctrine. But diversity in doctrine leads to generic in praxis.[2] Administrators told me this from the first day of my fieldwork. At first I heard them but did not heed them. They were telling me that since there are students from several churches in each school, the doctrinal edges are honed down.

> We don't teach church doctrine here. (Field Notes HCA 10/28/86; see also Field Notes CCCA 5/11/87)

> At DCS, the kids have different religions; we teach about God and Jesus. (Field Notes DCS 1/7/87)

> We have kids from all backgrounds . . . and we're not there to specifically make Baptists out of them. We're there to provide a Christian atmosphere. (Interview MR ALCA 8/21/87)

> We're trying to bring several churches together here . . . Fundamentalists, nondenominational, charismatics, all come to the same point. As long as it's from a Biblical standpoint . . . because schools are servicing children from more than one church, they cannot afford to mingle into church philosophy. It's like walking down a hallway. There are many doors—like classrooms in a school corridor [that represent the different churches]. . . . As a school, you have to stay in the hallway and teach children in a way that's beneficial to the society as a whole—not to any particular church—and not be negative toward any particular church . . . no matter what the door post says.

> We're all doing our best to know what the Christian life-style is; to harm as few as possible; to draw as many as possible unto Christ. It shouldn't be so that your doctrine makes someone else stumble or fall away. . . . As Christians we'll all be in heaven together. (Field Notes GCA 12/21/87; see also Field Notes CCCA 5/11/87)

> We're all trying to do what God wants us to do; trying to keep Christ at the center. (Interview LT multi-church 2/15/88)

None of the churches are called Faith Baptist Academy or Faith Full Gospel School, or Faith Wesleyan School. All are called simply Faith *Christian* School or Academy.

The schools are at least partially motivated by the self-interest of keeping their doors open when they decide to allow for diversity in the student body (see Ortner 1984 on interest theory). Marketing research undertaken by curriculum purveyors suggests that schools across the nation are in increasing numbers making this decision (Mooers 1989). These decisions serve to soften the school's own serving up of particular church doctrine.[3] Just as the public schools endeavor to strip away all references to religion that would offend a wide variety of believers and nonbelievers, so the Christian schools (all but those who are solely for the purpose of educating children from one church) have a less difficult, but similar task. They must produce a generic, "blandified" form of Christian education that is not offensive to a variety of conservative Christians.[4]

Thus, using only conservative Christianity's ultimate sacred propositions allows for a variety of interpretations of social arrangements, including arrangements that embody a good deal of compromise with the surrounding culture. The criteria used in these culture-building decisions can be explored within anthropology's framework for explaining cultural form.

EXPLAINING THE FORM OF THE COMPROMISES

To compress 100 years of anthropology into the simplest of terms, the explanations for the reasons that a culture is formed as it is have been of three types. In the eyes of the materialists, a culture embodies certain traits because they are practical, utilitarian, and adaptive for survival of the population, given their particular external environment. The mentalists, or idealists, on the other hand, see a culture's traits as resulting from the playing out of an internal cultural pattern or structure. They say that the culture has these traits (some of which might be so awkward as to appear almost maladaptive), because the pieces of the culture fit together into the cultural pattern. (Of course there have been many subtheories developed from these two.)

The third is a synthesis of the other two. This perspective recognizes the limitations of environmental adaptation, but recognizes them as just that—limitations. Thus, environmental constraints determine what a culture *cannot* do, or it will not survive; but they do not determine or predict precisely what a culture *will* do. For example, a maladaptive trait would be a taboo on reproduction for 100 per cent of a population; the religious communes created by the Shakers adhered to this rule, and there are few Shakers left today. But a broad range of alternatives *is* survivable; it is survivable for proportions less than 100 per cent of a population to be celibate. Survivability cannot predict what a culture will do within this broad range of sufficiently functional alternatives. Most anthropologists agree that all societies contain processes of situational adjustment (coping with external circumstances, adaptation) as well as processes of regularization (the imposition and confirmation of internal cultural form) (Moore 1976). Most anthropologists agree that culture cannot be viewed simply as epiphenomenon.

The factors that are important in determining the outcome of the compromises made within the Christian schools may reflect either an expression of ideological concerns or an adaptation to environmental exigencies.

Expressing Ideology

Deeply held ideals color the way the conservative Christians evaluate the cultural material available to them, and influence the compromises they make. One such value is their particular view of the self. Their reading of the scriptures yields specific ideas about human nature and the relationship with the divine, which produce a view of the self as a "bondslave for God," to use a metaphor with roots in the Bible which has blossomed in fundamentalist literature. It is necessary to "die to self" and give your own will over to the will of God.

This ideological bedrock lays the foundation for the content of the curriculum. It affects the desired relationship between teacher and student. It is a factor in determining what behavior is acceptable within the school walls (and—in the case of some schools—outside the school walls); it influences the methods of discipline used when those behavioral norms are overstepped. At the same time, it leads to conflicts which signal, perhaps, compromises yet to be made. Apparent within the schools are conflicts between the conservative Christian God-centered self versus the American individualistic self; between the fruits of the spirit versus competition; between "we can do nothing ourselves (without Christ)" versus "you can do anything (possibility thinking)."

Adapting to the Environment: Practical Exigencies

Although the basic conservative Christian ideology (the "salvation issues") and the Christocentric view of the self hold an umbrella over (or build a tent around) the possible interpretations of social arrangements available to the Christian schools, certainly these interpretations are subject to practical constraints, as well. The limitations of the environment itself are a factor; the material status of the Christian schools helps to determine the decisions made within them. This includes the availability of funds (which affects the availability of space) and the availability of time.

For example, the logistic assignment of students to classrooms looked at first to have ideological undertones, but turned out to have been made on a practical basis. A school with many "combined classrooms," or rooms housing more than one grade, might seem to be playing out the desire to go back to the one-room schoolhouse—to manifest the halcyon *Little House on the Prairie* days of the desired revivalistic goal culture. Instead, the combined classroom was the result of the limited number of teachers (who will work for low pay, who are conservative Christians, and who are qualified) and of the small number of students in any one grade. The combined classrooms are not a desirable part of the transfer culture that is embodied in the schools. Teachers don't like them, and professional organizations offer workshops to help them "handle this problem."

To carry logistics one step further, even the way students are seated in the classrooms also is mostly a practical concern. At one school, the five-year-old kindergarteners sat in down-sized students' desks all day, except for naptime, playtimes, and lunch. This was due to the high enrollment in kindergarten and to the small size of the classroom. When the school moved into a new building with larger classrooms, a play kitchen and "activity tables" were added. The desk-sitting had not been, as I at first surmised, an ideological decision, perhaps, to help, "bend the will without breaking the spirit" of the children. It had been a practical decision. As the school saw it, what else was there to do? (The reader might be able to develop alternatives, but that does not detract from the fact that the school perceived this as a decision based on practical, not ideological, concerns.)

The logistics of the ACE (Accelerated Christian Education) schools, where the students sit in individual cubicles, could be said to be more ideologically based. This seating arrangement is consistent with the individualized plan of the instruction, and with keeping the school orderly: "Let all things be done decently and in order" (I Corinthians 14:40). As one administrator told me, "The ACE school is the quietest school you'll ever be in" (Field Notes 10/28/86; see also Rose 1988).

However, the information ACE sends to persons who are considering starting schools stresses the low cost of the ACE system. It can also be put into place in a short time, as an administrator who had a vision for a school in April, took instruction in using ACE at the Texas headquarters during the summer, and opened an ACE school in September, told me (Field Notes ACE 11/11/86).

Thus, even choosing curriculum materials has practical boundaries. Besides cost, ease of use for the teachers is considered. An administrator, who was not personally entirely approving of the ready-made curriculums sold by the major Christian textbook publishers, told me that many Christian teachers are "not well trained" and so the curriculums provide them with lesson plans and background information which they may not already have, or have the time to find, on their own (Field Notes ICR 8/11/86). Even teachers who are well trained may not have the time to create their own lesson plans. At some schools, teachers, besides teaching a variety of subjects and grade levels, have various church duties, and go to church several times a week. Thus, they may rely on the ready-made curriculums.

The funds available to the schools are limited, and so some of the decisions they make on ideological bases are eventually circumvented by practical concerns. For example, at one school, new books were chosen both because they fit ideological needs and because it was thought that they would do a better job of teaching the material. But the school moved into a new building, and the change to new books was considered an additional expense that could not be made at the time.

Adaptation to the environment need not be thought of as only adaptation to the *physical* environment of climate and availability of sustenance, or even money and time. Adaptation to environment includes the neighbors, as well as the terrain.

Adapting to the Environment: The Surrounding Culture

Some of the compromises made with Christian schools could be seen as reactions to increased need for marketing in a culturally pluralistic society (see also Hunter 1983). Parents want their children to be able to go to the college of their choice (with God's direction)—not necessarily a Christian college—and to pursue the career of their choice (with God's direction)—not necessarily in Christian service. They are to be Christians in business, politics, the professions, and so forth.

Administrators considered some compromises with the world as necessary because "you can't take it all away." The students don't live in conservative Christian enclaves. They (mostly) do have televisions. Many have siblings in public schools (in grades higher than those provided in Christian school, or taking advantage of athletics or other extracurricular activities). They may know what they "have in Jesus," but they know what they're missing, too.

Generally anthropologists see practical material concerns as the limiting factor, and ideology as determining what choices will be made from among a variety of sufficiently functional options. In this case study, standing this on its head would be more applicable. In making choices where it is necessary to check for "story content" (such as in curriculum decisions), content that smacks of "humanism" is rejected. But once that has been cleared, choosing from a variety of options is a matter of applying several educational principles within a framework of practical financial and logistical strictures. When it comes to other items, such as the material culture the children are allowed, the content limitation is even more nebulous, allowing for Care Bears posters and Darth Vader lunch boxes, at the same time as *some* of the children eschew Smurfs, Garbage Pail Kids, and Jem rocker dolls.

Thus it is clear that each Christian school has not taken its founding church's ideology and fashioned it into a school. While they have done some of this, they have also borrowed from education culture and have been drowned in the surrounding popular culture. Have the actors in this revitalization process—this attempt to create a new culture—succeeded or failed?

To ask a more specific and less value-laden question, have they been able to create a new structure based on their ideology? The answer must be—only partially. Bruce Lockerbie (1972, 151), a longtime Christian educator, asserts that there is no philosophy of Christian education. Other Christian educators, who teach courses and write books on the philosophy of Christian education, would disagree with him, but if his point is that Christian educators have not created an alternative schooling that is as tightly wound around their ideology as it might be, then it is well taken. Wherever their own ideology conflicted with that of the surrounding culture, compromises were made.[5]

How do the conservative Christians, who engage in a good deal of polarization, square their view that they are separate from the world with the accommodations that they have made? The anthropologist, seeking analytic answers, looks to ways the compromises are adaptive for survival in the environment, or to ways they fit together into a cultural pattern which reflects the most important ideas of the culture. But the conservative Christian ideology yields a different explanation.

THE CONSERVATIVE CHRISTIANS' EXPLANATION FOR THE COMPROMISES

For conservative Christians, walking the Christian walk and maintaining a Christocentric worldview means that they are daily being led by God. If they will listen, God will direct their footsteps into the pattern he has ordained. This is no less true for the schools that he is thought to have raised up.

This desire to stay under God's authority and in "his perfect will" yields a means of making decisions which is used daily within the Christian schools—a process which anthropologists have called, in other contexts, divination. It is necessary to discern God's will about decisions large and small—momentous and quotidian. The school staff, in effect, divines God's will in decisions about opening a school, and once opened, what curriculum to use and what to display on the bulletin boards. "We don't want to just do this on our own. We do what God would have us do" (Interview LT multi-church 2/15/88). Thus, for the conservative Christians, the choices and compromises made within the Christian schools are ultimately ordained by God.

IMPLICATIONS

It might be said, to paraphrase Thoreau (1861), that "in diversity is the preservation of the world." This is certainly true in terms of genetic variation, which affords a measure of assurance that a new virus or other threat to our biological selves will not wipe us all out. It is true, as well, in the cultural realm. Future changes in physical or social environment (what the climate is and who the neighbors are), may render adaptive a cultural trait which is now neutral.

Whether the diversity provided by conservative Christianity is good or bad, adaptive or maladaptive for American society will, in the long run, be a question for philosophers and social critics, and not for the anthropologist, whose job it is to describe and interpret a culture, to make the concepts important in one culture understandable to readers in another.

For the critics *and* the proponents of the New Christian Right, there is much to ponder. But for those who *fear* the conservative Christian culture, it may be well to remember that it is embedded in the American culture that surrounds and penetrates it. At the same time, perhaps that very embeddedness will prevent it from offering the mitigating influences to mainstream American culture's materialism and individualism that have been sought by social critics since Tocqueville.

Methods

This appendix describes what an anthropologist does, what the principles for good anthropological practice are, and how those principles are manifested in day-to-day practice. I refer to my fieldwork diary, two three-inch notebooks where I kept track of the "non data" portion of the research—my interrelationships with the people who were teaching me about Christian education. The first entry is September 27, 1984; the last (as of this writing), August 31, 1989.

The goal of anthropology's ethnographic enterprise is to promote understanding among people by creating a description of one culture that will let members of another culture understand it better. Cardboard cutout stereotypes of a culture and its people give way to more well-rounded portraits, complete with contradictions and inconsistencies. George Spindler said that when anthropologists write descriptions of faraway cultures, they "make the strange familiar," and that when they write about culture in their home countries, they "make the familar strange." In this case, I found that the conservative Christians were not as "strange" (different) as had been supposed; perhaps this study, then, serves to make the seemingly strange a bit less strange.

In order to write a description, it is necessary for ethnographers themselves to come to an understanding of an unfamiliar culture. The method used to collect data for this study was predominantly the *participant observation* method which is the essence of anthropology. In this method ethnographers do fieldwork, by participating in the culture under study, at the same time as they are observing it.

It has been said of ethnographers that they don't read the background material on the groups they wish to learn about, preferring instead the one-on-one interviewing and observing techniques which are the hallmark of participant observation. Most ethnographers do not deserve this criticism, and indeed, the background research for this study began in 1983, in the library; besides a review of secondary literature which resulted in a 150-page bibliography, this research included collecting and analyzing primary literature from numerous organizations that support Christian schools. The fieldwork began in June 1986, and is still ongoing;

but it was full-time, thanks to a generous grant from the National Science Foundation (BNS8520070), and a Radford University Faculty Development Leave, from August 1986 throught August 1987. The places where data were collected, and the amount of data collected, have already been described in chapters 1, 2, and 3. Here, I will concentrate on how the data were collected.

Participant observation proceeds through certain stages, whether it occurs in a faraway land with a culture very different from the ethnographers' own or whether it occurs in their native lands. The labels we use to identify these stages vary, but I think it is valid to say that we tend to experience the stages of *making entrée, culture shock, establishing rapport,* and *understanding the culture.*

MAKING ENTREE

My initial contact (or *informant,* as anthropologists call the people who give them information) was a Christian school teacher who had been a student of mine several years ago. We attended a secular seminar for teachers together, and after class I asked her questions about her church and school. She brought me books and materials her administrator had given her to pass along to me, knowing of my interest. (These materials included the "Humanist Manifesto.") She told me of an Institute for Creation Research seminar for teachers that her administrator was attending. I asked if I could go along. Much later, she confided that she didn't know whether to encourage my involvement in this way, and that she prayed about it.

I did go to the Institute for Creation Research (ICR) Seminar with Kathleen Mitchell, the administrator at Grace Christian Academy (GCA), and as she tells it, I got in her car (never having met her before our prearranged rendezvous at her home), started asking her questions, and didn't stop for a year and a half. We were roommates at the seminar for a week; we attended classes together, ate together, went on shopping trips together. And so our acquaintance rapidly grew into friendship. On our last day at the seminar, our suitemate, Frieda Jumps, a Baptist pastor's wife who taught at a school sponsored by an independent Baptist church, noted, "I'm going to feel so unimportant next week; no one is going to be following me around writing down everything I say" (Diary 8/15/86).

Kathleen was as interested as I was in various kinds of Christian schools and their similarities and differences. She would ask any administrator or teacher she saw dozens of questions about their schools, and take me along to hear. This was so much more valuable than devising my own questions; I heard what concerns Christian educators themselves have. In this way, and later by spending day after day at the schools, I was able to learn what conservative Christians say *to each other* in informal everyday conversations, at faculty meetings, and in classroom repartée, as well as in more formal presentations such as lectures at conferences and in published books on Christian education. I also observed how they present themselves to outsiders, in writing and in interviews.

When I talked to people or interviewed them, I had few preset questions. I asked administrators what they thought I should know about Christian schools, and asked questions that allowed me to compare the schools. I asked a number of informants: "How do you discern God's will?" They were quite willing to tell me, and my only other questions were follow-up to help me understand more clearly. These discussions took place in a variety of settings: during arranged appointments in administrators' offices, during whole days spent in parents' and teachers' homes, with the tape recorder running while we talked and their husbands and children came in and out, between classes (and sometimes during classes) at schools, in vans traveling to field trips, and wherever parents were waiting for children. They talked; they were willing to teach me, and knew I was willing to learn; I listened.

My entrées into the other eight schools were made by making phone calls, arranging to visit the school to talk with the administrator and teachers and, at most schools, observe classes. At first, I feared that school personnel would not be receptive to my coming; all I had to give in return was my promise to listen to what they had to say about Christian education and to write objectively about it, so that others might understand it better. I explained the goal of my research by explaining that I wanted to learn about the Christian school movement from the people involved in it—to gain their perspective. I wanted to become immersed in their culture. I clarified that I was not going to discover anything they didn't already know; in fact, that was precisely what I wanted to discover—what they knew and took for granted. I explained that I was *not* evaluating, and that the schools and their personnel and students would remain anonymous. I pursued each school rather doggedly.

Some schools made no particular notice of my coming, forgetting which day we had said I would come. Others posted notes on the faculty mailboxes reminding them of my visit. If I visited often enough, eventually little notice was taken of my presence; I ceased to be a visitor. As is usually the case in research of this sort, people were "just glad someone is interested," as Kathleen Mitchell said (Diary 8/10/86), and liked to talk to a willing listener: "I can't believe I've talked this much"; "I've jawed you like I'd known you all my life" said some informants when I first met them (Diary 1/16/87; 5/24/87).

CULTURE SHOCK

Generally, culture shock refers to things in the culture that are surprising to the ethnographer, are misunderstood by the ethnographer, or are uncomfortable because they don't fit with the ethnographer's own cultural background.

Little that I met in the Christian schools or literature shocked me. Years of previous reading had considerably lessened the shock value of even the most extreme statements of intolerance toward other churches or different life-styles. I was more suprised by the unanticipated moderate statements in which teachers sometimes advocated tolerance. What surprised me, then, were times when their culture did not meet my expectations; when they were not as different as I had expected; when church ideology was not the determining factor that I had hypothesized.

An example of this surprise was that the plain clothes I had chosen to wear to the ICR seminar were out of place. Other instances that pointed to the students' similarity to American kids in general came during early days at Grace Christian and Maranatha Christian Academy. A van in sudden need of repair caused me to volunteer to take students from Grace Christian to their parents' meeting spot in a nearby town in my camper-topped pickup truck. As I talked to the van driver in the seat beside me, I struggled to keep the truck on the road while the elementary and junior-high students tumbled and rolled and roared in the back. I wondered aloud whether we should open the window through to the back, and she said we were just as well not hearing them any louder. At Maranatha, known as the strictest school in Southeastern Valley, while I talked with the administrator in his office, students literally bounced off the walls in the corridor.

One aspect of the conservative Christian culture that is bound to be unfamiliar and somewhat discomfiting to the outsider is being "witnessed to" as a means of encouraging conversion, which conservative Christians are bidden to do. The first such instance occurred early on, at the ICR seminar. A school missionary questioned whether I was "a Christian" and then questioned whether I *could* ever understand Christian education. He thereby doubted the whole anthropological enterprise. Later, Kathleen asked me if I felt threatened by his words. As we spoke, our suitemate, Frieda, expressed concern for my soul, as well. I explained that

I could not become involved with any ideology on a *personal* basis while I was doing my fieldwork, or I would not be objective. What readers would find my work useful then? But, Frieda asked, what if I died before my fieldwork was through? I determined to be flattered by these concerns for my soul's future, rather than rankled. They were, after all, expressing the desire, as they saw it, to spend eternity with me. (However, it's difficult to become *too* flattered, since *everyone* is approached with the chance to convert.) I admit, however, that I took to the women's witnessing better than the men's. Kathleen and Frieda explained that there are different ways of witnessing, and that a person has to determine what will appeal to the potential convert—you have to determine "where he's at." It seemed that the women were good at making these judgments. The men, on the other hand, tended to use a pat approach, for example, asking the question, "Are you sure you would go to heaven if you died tonight?"

Geertz (1973, 230) noted that "scientific studies of religion ought [not] to begin with unnecessary questions about the legitimacy of the substantive claims of their subject matter." It is possible to "dissociate" from concern for the truth or falsehood of religious doctrine; it is possible to "suspend belief, or disbelief." Of course, ethnographers do not become unfeeling automatons upon entering the field. They react inside when hearing statements that don't match their own values. But "the promise of anthropology requires that the individual should agree to distinguish between his absolute convictions and his specialized activity as an anthropologist" (Dumont 1986, 205). In my case, my own convictions, and mismatches with them, went into my diary; the field notes themselves remained anthropological activity. Kathleen well understood my need to stay removed from ideological entanglements, and explained this to others along the way.

I have labeled culture shock a stage of fieldwork, as if it is to be gotten through and passed, never to be felt again. This is not exactly the case; it waxes and wanes, taking its turn with rapport.

ESTABLISHING RAPPORT

Establishing rapport generally occurs side-by-side with being given, or taking on, a role within the society, a role that is negotiated between ethnographer and informants. In my case, I asked Mrs. Mitchell if I could come to the pre-school workdays at her school and meet the teachers. Not without some hesitation, she permitted me to come. I helped with the incredible flurry of activity that accompanies the annual opening of a school serving seven grades. As I tore tests out of test banks, I talked with the teachers about my intention to learn from them about Christian schools. They laughed at the thought of teaching me. One of the teachers seriously pondered my task. She asked, "How are you going to remain objective? Even captives eventually get to like their captors."

Her statement would recur to me when I realized that I, too, had seen the vans with "Faith Christian School" emblazoned on the side and had applied the usual sterotypes to them. At first, I was embarrassed to ride in these vans myself, thankful that no one I knew would see me. Later, I began to note a loyalty in my feelings toward the schools, giving no thought to being associated with them, rooting for "our team" at ballgames (telling my husband about the bad foul calls against "our team"), and looking out for the children on field trips.

During the time of my fieldwork, the teachers, administrators, parents, and students at these schools were my peer group. I was away from my usual colleagues, and my loyalties shifted to the new peers. One day at lunch at Grace Christian, I found myself gazing peacefully across the sea of little faces at the long tables (while the teachers bustled all around me microwaving the children's lunches and trying to keep them from being *too* loud). My gaze was sufficiently ethereal that Mrs. Sherwood asked, "What are you looking at?" My lack of concern about being associated with "the Christians" paralled my growing lack of concern and self-consciousness about their possible response to my note-taking.

The degree of participation in participant observation can vary along a continuum from none at all ("nonparticipation" or "passive participation, in Spradley's [1980] terms), to quite a lot ("active" or "complete" participation). The degree of participation I undertook—that is to say, my role at the schools—varied from school to school, from classroom to classroom, depending on how the teachers and I negotiated it. At some schools I was observer. At others I was observer and teacher's aide. Acting as a teacher's aide could include solitary activites such as helping with photocopying and cleaning up, or more interactively helping some little students with their lessons while their teacher worked with others on a special project or a different subject. Often I was confidante. But I was always a passive observer in the sense that I wasn't in charge of or responsible for anything. This lack of responsibility was refreshing, following as it did ten years of college teaching.

Some symbols of establishing rapport came when, at one of the pre-school teacher workdays at GCA, I was in the library taking note of the book collection, and one of the teachers called out, "Do you want to join us for prayer?" Thereafter, I was present at every morning faculty prayer on the days I came to Grace Christian. In November, like a lover slowly moving into a paramour's apartment, I brought in a hanger to hang my coat in the closet, and left my big water glass on a shelf above the hanger (Diary 11/6/86).

Having established rapport there, I began to visit the other schools. Once having learned the routine and structure of one school, it was easy for me to make comparisons and contrasts with the others. But I found that if I went to Grace fewer than two or three days a week, my rapport there would wane a bit; there were things I should have seen, the teachers would say. So throughout the fieldwork, I came to GCA at least two days a week.

The comfort the administrator and the teachers felt with me grew, so that fairly quickly I was able to participate in Parent-Teacher Fellowship and faculty meetings and the like. At the first PTF meeting, Kathleen Mitchell told the parents that they had probably heard from their children that someone was sitting in on their classes; she introduced me to them as "sort of on staff." After that meeting, and throughout the year, parents would approach me to tell me how they had made their decisions to enroll their children in Christian school.

At each school it was necessary to explain that I was *not* evaluating the teachers, and that I could not be seen as an educational consultant; most teachers at first assumed that I was a professor of education. I explained that I had no expertise that would allow me to take on those roles. Then, it was necessary to follow through on this by *not* offering opinions, criticism, or even praise. It was not difficult, due to pre-fieldwork preparation, for me to avoid expressing opinions on religious or social issues. However, I did not realize I had opinions on educational issues, and had to guard against voicing those as they occurred to me.

My cultural background is one in which praise and compliments come easily, and my diary shows a constant battle against making these kinds of comments, which came naturally for me. My fear was that if I sometimes complimented, then when I didn't, it would be taken as disapproval; and perhaps teachers might do more of what I seemed to approve of than they otherwise would. Whenever teachers *asked* for my opinion (which some continued to do), I would say that I was not evaluating, and try very hard not to offer an opinion. Neutrality was the word of the day.

It was necessary, of course, to thank the teachers for what they were teaching me, but at the same time to avoid any kind of commentary. I tried to change their perceived statuses of evaluator and evaluatee to our more appropriate roles as collaborators in teaching me about Christian schools. Still, that teachers looked at me as an evaluator was given away by jokes like Frances Nichols's "Don't come into my class until April" or their protests that "I'm not doing anything special or profound today," after which I would assure them that this was not necessary for my goal of learning about everyday life in the schools (Diary 9/86).

The first day I observed Nancy Sherwood's class, Kathleen Mitchell asked her, "Did you feel intimidated?" Mrs. Sherwood replied, "Nope. I just went right on." Mrs. Mitchell agreed, "Nothing intimidates us" (Diary 9/2/86). The first day I visited Mrs. Turner's kindergarten class, I had placed a little chair in the crowded classroom's back corner, and asked her, "Will this bother you, where I'm sitting?" She said "I'm not as organized as I wanted to be." I reminded her that I was "not evaluating, just learning." When the day was over, I thanked her for letting me sit in; "I hope it didn't bother you." She replied, "It didn't. I thought it would, but it didn't" (Diary 9/9/86). When Kathleen introduced me to Sarah Ramsey, the music teacher, she said, "Melinda will tell you whether you're doing it right or wrong." I said, "All I can tell you is whether you're following the pattern." Kathleen, laughing, agreed, "Right; she will tell you whether you're following the pattern."

When I returned to Grace Christian for the Christmas program in 1987, six months after I had left the field, Kathleen Mitchell asked me, "Well, was that [program] better than last year?" I replied, "You folks seem to feel better about it than last year." "But, you're out of it now, so I thought—," Kathleen protested my noncommittal answer. "That's not a fair question to ask her," Mrs. Turner said. I agreed, "That's right, no evaluation" (Diary 12/14/87).

At other schools, teachers were pleased with the thought that "we're teaching a college teacher" (Diary 5/7/87). Even so, administrators and board members would eventually say, "We know you said you weren't evaluating, but we didn't say we wouldn't ask you: is there anything you see that you think we should be doing differently?" And again, I would explain that I had not been observing with that thought in mind.

Another role which I had to avoid was that of a spy of sorts. The administrators would ask me questions about the teachers, about what the parents said, about other schools, and about what the students did when the teachers were out of the classroom—questions that I side-stepped as best I could.

Yet another role the teachers sometimes wanted me to play for the students was "college professor who knows how hard it is in college, so you'd better study now." I did play this role for the teachers, on their cue ("What's it like in college, Dr. Wagner?"). These were the only occasions when they called me "Dr. Wagner."

The teachers made various explanations of my presence to the students. Mrs. Nichols said to her sixth-grade class, "We have a visitor. Does anyone know why she is here?" The administrator's daughter, Emily, and her good friend Rachel raised their hands: "She's taking notes." "What is she taking notes on?" "Us," the girls said, playfully preening their hair. Mrs. Nichols continued, "She is here observing, helping out, just here." The students had heard enough; they wanted to continue with their prayer requests (Diary 9/22/86). One student asked a teacher, "Where's that woman who sits in the corner and writes?" (Diary 9/22/86), and another would ask the administrator, "Does she write down everything we say?" (Diary 11/3/86). Fifth grader Carl asked me, "How many of those note pads do you have?" (Diary 9/29/86). At Christmastime, a student told me, "I know what we should get you for a present—paper and pens!"

Among the students, I sometimes felt like Peggy Sue, who, in the movie "Peggy Sue Got Married," goes back in time to her high school, but with her adult mind. I did not want to be an authority figure over the students for two reasons: I didn't want to usurp their teachers' authority, and I didn't want them to change their behavior around me. They showed some concern about my writing, especially the students who were accustomed to being disciplined by behavior modification techniques which rely on lists of miscreants. Kindergartener Ronald asked, "You're not writing for Mrs. Turner, are you? How many names do you have on there?" But they must have quickly seen that I did not tattle on them, and they had no problem at all in not seeing me as an authority figure. Unless a teacher specifically put me in charge when she left the room, the students would carry on with their usual shenanigans behind the teacher's back, posting a sentry at the door to announce, "Mrs. __ is coming," as a signal for all to quiet down.

The children also made very good informants, having no difficulty assuming my naïveté. For example, at Dells Christian School, kindergartener Toby made a place for me to sit at the down-sized table and chairs where we ate lunch, leaving room for Lawrence's two pretend friends. Then he taught me how to say grace (Diary 2/12/87). The kindergarteners would tell me to get in line with them, to come outside to recess with them, and invited me to their parties. The students included me in the stories they made up, and sometimes in their praise reports. I was made an honorary member of some classes, and an honorary graduate of Grace Christian.

Several students were curious about what an anthropologist does, but two fourth-grade girls at Calvary Cross Christian Academy seemed to capture it best, by, with no prompting from their teacher or me, becoming anthropologists themselves. Cecilia wrote on a three-by-five inch piece of note paper:

A lady came to our school who was very nice she was waring a black scert and a striped blose. She had brown hair she has banges and her hair is down to her shoulders. She is doing an S.A. on the 3 and 4. She stares at us and the room. She has a funy perse and a note pade that she writes on the information her name is Miss Melinda Wagner. Writen By Cecilia Downs. (Diary 5/11/87)

Doreen's field notes were more note-like, and written in red ink on three-by-five cards:

Visitor M.W. 5/11/87
Melinda Wagner
She took some notes on the classroom
She was pretty
She stayed to 2 o'clock!
She looked at the *scorekeys* for *3rd* & *4th*
She was nice!!!
She called out some words for Word Building 48
She was waring a black skirt and striped blouse and a *ring*
and a watch she has short brown hair and green eyes!!!
She went out on first break with us and on two three
church to practice.
She had a white string pocketbook
She works at a college as a teacher
She is 39. (Diary 5/11/87)

Alan Peshkin (1986) writes that during his fieldwork in a Christian school, he sometimes knew things about the school before the teachers did. This occurred with me, too. (Although ethnographers should never let themselves believe that they know and hear *everything*.) At a PTF meeting, a new teacher was glad I came and sat down beside her, because I was the only one she knew! At the graduation ceremonies, I imagined that I felt more a part of the schools, more familiar with the teachers and the students, than did the parents, most of whom had never visited other than to deliver and pick up children, and to attend PTF meetings and special programs. When I came back to school programs after leaving the field at June graduations, students squealed and hugged me and parents welcomed me. By then, my relationship with the teachers had changed from research collaborator who was also a friend to a friend who was sometimes a research collaborator.

The feelings and thoughts one has during fieldwork—of friendship and loyalty, disjunctures with one's own value system, observation, understanding, and analysis—become a kind of dance of pulling in closer and pushing away. I wondered, later, why I had not gone to GCA on my birthday. Birthdays being a major concern there, the students were very disappointed when I didn't come that day. The administrator gave me my present when I came the next week. It was a plaque which read "A Faithful Friend is a source of strength/And he who has found such a friend has found a treasure." It was surrounded by birds and a wood frame, with an inlay that read "GCA '87." It was my style and I knew that Kathleen had picked it to fit me. Had I not come to school on my birthday as a subconscious way of pushing away a bit? At the Grace Christian graduation ceremony, the administrator presented me with a gift, and the students loudly applauded their approval. (It was easy for the students to like an anthropologist, who had no responsibility for them or control over them.) As I went up to the podium to accept the gift, I did something I had not done before—I turned off my tape recorder as I left my seat. Was this a symbol that Melinda Wagner the fieldworker had tuned out, and that Melinda Wagner the person was accepting the gift?

It would be naïve to think that I was the only one pondering our relationship. I can't know all that was in their mental diaries that detail their decision to let me into their world, and our long time together. We both were entrenched in an introspective *pas-de-deux* of presentation of self. One thing that did surprise me was that they didn't seem to talk about me and my characteristics among themselves; they asked me the same questions about my home life and background, one by one.

Sometimes we discussed our relationships, and reminisced about the early days of fieldwork. Nancy Sherwood said she prayed about my request to visit the school, and thought, "You'll be lucky if Kathleen lets you do that." But, she said, "it worked out all right." Kathleen said "the first thing I had to do was forget that she had a Ph.D. Because that could be intimidating, you know" (Diary 1/28/87).

Kathleen confided that "sometimes I go home at night and think, I wonder if I should have said that [to me]," just as I had wondered, myself, about comments I had made that might, for example, be construed as evaluation. A parent divulged, "When you came in, some of us wondered, what is she going to say?" (Diary 8/27/87). During the time the media was focused on Jim and Tammy Bakker's problems, they worried that my study would be akin to the newspaper articles. We discussed the difference between journalism and data gathering of the anthropological sort, which tries to understand the "natives' " point of view. Mrs. Turner captured the essence of anthropology's goal when she said, "But it's funny how you understand people better when you get to know them and understand why they do things" (Diary 1/28/87).

At first Mrs. Mitchell wanted, as much as possible, to be in control of the information that I heard (and tried, unsuccessfully, to shield me from the most extreme books and tapes). But in the long run, they could not filter what they did at school due to my presence, which was ubiquitous. They still had to run a school, and "whether you're there taking notes or not, it doesn't matter." They believed that they were doing the right thing at the schools, day by day manifesting God's will, and so most of the time they did not worry about how I might perceive it. "We don't have anything to hide" (Diary 4/7/87; 1/28/87).

That I was accepted is symbolized by a change in the tenor of the entries into the diary. The notes of reluctance from the teachers were sounded in September. Later, they would say, "I missed you in class today," or "What will we do without your help (sweeping, and so on), when you go to the other classes?" They said they missed my "smiling face." After January, the teachers would often comment that I was "blending into the woodwork" as far as they and the students were concerned. "You're just an invisible observer, like you want to be" (Diary 2/10/87; 3/2/87). But the relationship is a push-pull for the informants as well. There were plenty of comments demonstrating that they didn't mind—even liked—having me around. But there was also "There's Melinda; she's studying us and getting paid."

UNDERSTANDING THE CULTURE

The fieldwork proceeded in the general way outlined by English anthropologist E. E. Evans-Pritchard (1962, 148) years ago. He said that the anthropologist "lives among [a people] as intimately as he can, and he learns to speak in their language, to think in their concepts and to feel in their values. He then lives the experiences over again critically and interpretively in the conceptual categories and values of his own culture and in terms of the general body of knowledge in his discipline. In other words, he translates from one culture into another." He compares what he has observed in this culture to ethnographers' descriptions of other cultures.

Anthropologists take the specifics they have observed and generalize from them; they pin them to a theoretical backdrop. This is analogous to taking a photo and blowing it up to a larger size. If the original photo was taken with a sharp lens and fine-grained film, the blown-up image is still acute. If, however, the lens is out of focus or the film is coarse-grained, the blown-up picture is blurry. Just so, a record of human behavior must be clear and detailed if the analysis of it is to be valid.

Field-note taking used the principles I think most ethnographers use, perhaps not specifically labeling them as Spradley (1980) does; for example, "the language identification principle" requires that the ethnographer carefully record who said what, so that various vocabularies used by different people, having various statuses, in different circumstances, can be learned. His "verbatim principle" requires that the record of what people say be exact and detailed. The "concrete principle" means that observations of what people do must be made, again, in exact, detailed language. Following these principles works to keep the ethnographic film fine-grained. If patterns and generalizations are to be sought, the analysis cannot begin with field notes which are themselves already generalizations; it must start with what was seen, heard, tasted, smelled, and felt.

These principles, Spradley (1980) notes, are meant to overcome the ethnographer's tendency—student or professional——to translate and simplify, to assume an understanding of what's going on. My own naïveté about education and school culture, as well as about conservative Christian culture (except for what I had read) were an advantage in describing and analyzing the Christian school cultures. At the secular education seminar I had attended in order to gain some familiarity with this culture, I was befuddled by the seminar leader's pronouncements to the assembled teachers, like "Now people, if you will come through concept construction and formation you'll bring them to mastery, right on grade level, on that competency" (Field Notes 6/27/86). Thus, not being blinded by prior familiarity, I took nothing for granted; it was all new to me. I could easily create cultural alternatives in my mind, which allow for seeing what *is* there by noticing what *isn't* there.

As I sought patterns, I wrote down each time an activity occurred. Near the end of the school year, Kathleen Mitchell saw me writing notes while prayer requests and praise reports were being said during chapel time. She leaned over and said, "Are you still writing down that we do prayer requests and praise reports?" As I opened my mouth to reply, she said, "Patterns, right?" We had had several discussions about the anthropological method, and she had learned her lessons well.

It is exhilarating to learn about an unknown culture one-on-one from other people. Field work demands, as Dorothy Lee (1986, 83, emphasis hers) says of motherhood; "full commitment to the situation, with all one's senses and other capacities *there*, alive and straining and alert." It is tremendously satisfying to be able to become a part of a different community, to get into other peoples' lives, and to feel accepted by so many different people (Diary 9/3/86; 5/24/87). It felt good when a teacher didn't notice me at the door of a church before commencement, and said, "You just blend in over here. You're beginning to look like us"

(Diary 5/25/87). But anthropological fieldwork brings with it a triple bind, putting the fieldworker between a rock and two hard places. It is necessary to obtain good field data, using these principles, so that the report will be as objective as possible; anthropological ethics clearly demand that informants know what the ethnographer is doing; and it is necessary not to intervene or to interrupt the ongoing flow and history of the society. It is necessary to attend to these three goals simultaneously.

In ethnography, like archaeology, the dig is the most fun, but then there is the lab work—the analysis—to see what has been learned. Eric Wolf, in an often quoted statement, said that anthropology is the "most scientific of the humanities, and the most humanistic of the sciences." There has long been a tension within anthropology between those who see anthropology's goal as an emulator of the natural sciences and those who prefer humanistic understanding. The tension is ongoing and healthy, it seems to me, for a slide into either one camp or the other will make anthropology less than it is.

In the days of anthropologists Franz Boas and one of his many students, Paul Radin, the ethnographer was to act merely as pencil or recorder. Ethnographies were verbatim records of transactions with informants, including however many versions of the origin story were collected, including however many blueberry pie recipes were collected. Today, the ethnographer is storyteller, rendering the concepts that make up one culture understandable to people in another (Spradley and McCurdy 1972). But the story must be based on empirical data. I have tried to avoid the "trust me" tone of some studies. I have tried to avoid statements that begin "It is my impression . . ." One way to do this is by means of quantitative analysis. For example, my impression of the use of discipline would have been that Christian symbols were often invoked, because that's what made an impression on me, being different from my own experience. A quantitative analysis of field data showed otherwise. Of course, a quantitative analysis is only as good as the field data on which it is based. Alas, the reader will have to trust me on my claim that the data were meticulously recorded.

I am partial to Spradley's (1980) image of the ethnographer as "mapmaker" charting unknown territory, saying "let's see what's out there," unfettered by a rigid preconceived research agenda. The original focus of the research, as stated in the research proposal and design, was to trace the links between an independent variable of conservative Christian ideology and the dependent variables of values, norms, curriculum, social structure, and artifacts found in Christian schools. With this in mind, together with the "let's see what's out there" mode of thinking, I borrowed another page from Spradley's (1980) book, watching and noting everything at first. Fairly quickly, the focus shifted from tracing conservative Christian ideology to tracing the sources of a syncretistic culture. From October through March, while I continued to watch everything, I took special note of certain things and kept an index of field notes which described any appearances of those things. Some of these indexed items resemble Spradley's (1980, 88) cultural "domain," which is a "category of cultural meaning that includes other smaller categories." For example: What are all the kinds of discipline used? What are all the reasons to say "praise God?" What are all the things to do when you are supposed to be taking a nap? A variety of ideological and structural keywords were recorded in this index. This keeps track of what one *is* seeing, so that it is clear what is *not* being seen. After March, I broadened out to the big picture again, while still maintaining the index.

When studying subgroups within their own culture, obviously academics have to avoid being less than objective due to their own ideological convictions (they have to suspend both belief and disbelief). In the case of some subgroups, they have to guard against an intolerance of intolerance. But it seems to me that there is a more subtle threat to our neutrality. We tend to presume that everyone is as concerned with ideology, language, and thought as we are. We expect that the discourse of religion, especially, takes place on a sophisticated and high plane—different from the everyday and common. When the Episcopalian Book of Common Prayer is updated so that "Save me, O God; for the waters are come in unto my soul" (Psalms 69:1 KJ) becomes "Save me, O God! For the waters have come up to my neck" (Psalms 69:1 RSV), we wince, along with David Martin (1982). When Christmas becomes "Jesus is the reason for the season" and a sprig of holly printed onto a message button; when children wear "God is awesome" T-shirts; when teachers can buy pop bottle–shaped stickers that say "God loves you and Soda I"—we wince again. It offends our sensibilites; it upsets our epicurean natures.

These relatively naïvely pursued trends of popular culture are important and worthy of study and understanding; popular culture is culture. I nearly fell into this anti–pop culture bias myself, as I found myself admiring some of the schools better than others. As I analyzed, I realized that those who had done the least compromising with popular culture, who maintained the most difference, were favored; they were closer to my ideal of religious—in other words, simpler. Within this study, I have tried to put the syncretistic popular trend of many conservative Christian school cultures in perspective by comparing it to traditional religion, in which the sacred and the vernacular are intertwined, and contrasting it to rationalized religion, which separates sacred and secular.

As in most fieldwork, it was at first difficult to convince people that I was indeed interested in learning the minutiae of their daily lives. But after a while the Christian educators seemed impressed with my perseverance in coming to the schools and their various activities to learn about them. On one of my many visits to chapel at Maranatha, the assistant principal would say, "You're Mrs. Diligent, aren't you?" (Diary 5/24/87). Kathleen Mitchell laughed at my desire to collect artifacts and said, "Wherever you're putting all this will never be the same." As I attended every activity in which the parents were involved, including fund-raisers, she said, "You take this anthropology seriously" (Diary 11/21/86). A parent would say: "At least she got to know us."

Notes

Chapter One. Introduction

1. I can think of two possible reasons why Peshkin (1986) saw more attributes of a total institution than I did, even in schools sponsored by independent Baptist churches like the one he described. First, the school he described was closely tied to the American Association of Christian Schools, which was then in its infancy. The schools I observed, although affiliated with AACS and other organizations, are farther removed from that founders' ideology. The grass-roots schools don't always follow national organizations' principles and strictures; they adapt them to meet their own needs. Second, in the intervening years between Peshkin's fieldwork and mine, my guess is that Christian schools in general have become more diverse in their student bodies. Schools that may have begun with students from one church later opened their doors and cast out a wider net for potential students. This has supposedly been a national trend (Mooers 1989) and would serve as a stimulus to compromises within the schools. (See chapter 8 for further discussion of this point.)

2. The "Humanist Manifesto" I and II were exhibits at this trial. These were the first documents given to me by a Christian School administrator to show me "what we're up against."

3. See also Gallup (1979), and these reports: "A Nation at Risk" (National Commission on Excellence in Education 1983); "What Works: Research About Teaching and Learning" (U.S. Department of Education 1986); "A Nation Prepared: Teachers for the 21st Century" (Carnegie Forum on Education and the Economy 1986).

4. Like ethnic minority groups who grow tired of answering to someone else's call, the conservative Christians create new labels for themselves. My *charismatic* informants called their churches "Full Gospel," "Faith," or "Word" churches. "Full Gospel" churches say that they believe *all* of the gospel, including that the "gifts of the spirit" are "for today" (which fundamentalists deny).

The teachers who advertise in the AACS Placement Letter give their preferred church affiliation in words such as simply "Baptist," or more specifically "Independent Baptist," "Independent Fundamentalist Baptist," "North American Baptist," "Independent Fundamentalist," "Bible," "Reformed Baptist or Doctrine of Grace," or "Evangelical." But the schools seeking personnel do not list their church affiliations in the placement letters, although the name of the sponsoring church (but not a denominational affiliation) appears in the AACS National Directory.

The term *evangelical* was rarely used. *Fundamentalist* was used by independent Baptists to describe themselves when they were making distinctions between themselves and charismatics and *liberals*, and one informant asked if she could be labeled fundamentalist charismatic, because she thought she was conservative theologically, but believed in the gifts of the spirit, too.

5. Several polls have used positive responses to three questions to identify conservative Christians, called either "evangelical" (Gallup 1981) or "fundamentalist" (*Los Angeles Times* 1986). Respondents were asked whether they believed the Bible is the actual word of God, if they had ever had a born-again experience, and if they had ever encouraged others to accept Jesus as their savior. For Hunter (1983, 140–141), an Evangelical "is a Protestant who attests to the inerrancy of Scripture and the divinity of Christ and either (1) believes that Jesus Christ is the only hope for salvation or (2) has had a religious experience—that is, a particularly powerful religious insight or awakening that is still important in his everyday life, that involved a conversion to Jesus Christ as his personal savior or (3) both (1) and (2)."

6. This interpretation depends on "dispensationalism." Since the length of some of the dispensations (periods of time) in the earth's history are thought to be unknown, the dispensationalists can't estimate exactly how old the earth is.

7. See Barr (1978); Cole (1931); Cully (1963); Dollar (1973); Gasper (1963); Jorstad (1981); Melton (1978); Piepkorn (1979); Sandeen (1970) for history. See Ahlstrom (1975); Fowler (1982); Hill (1981); Hunter (1983); McLoughlin (1978); Marsden (1980); Marty (1975, 1976, 1981); Moberg (1975); Quebedeaux (1974, 1978) for typology.

8. See Hunter (1987) regarding what the family structure actually was, how it changed, and the conservative Christians' reactions to the changes.

9. Marsden (1980, 160) is quoting from the *King's Business*, Editorial XII (March 1921, 217), and Editorial XI (December 1920, 1111).

10. Authors who have been concerned with how conservative Christians did (and do) deal with modernity have included Hunter (1983, 1987), Marty (1975, 1976), and Quebedeaux (1978). Heinz (1983) and Hunter (1983, 11) have been interested in the process of "bargaining" in the realm of the symbolic world view. Heinz (1983, 147) has said: "The choice of specific symbols and the ignoring of others need critical examination." This research examines these choices.

Chapter Two. Christian Schools in Southeastern Valley

1. ACE is preparing for the "School of Tomorrow" with programmed learning on computers. To critics who ask about the human element, they reply that the students will have more contact with the teacher (supervisor) when they need

it, because the computer will handle routine tasks so that the teacher will be freed of much paperwork.

2. A non-denominational school within the Holiness (Wesleyan-Arminian) tradition in Cincinnati, Ohio, is named God's Bible School and College. It is noted in the catalog (p. 27) that the name "has become well-known in the circles of the Holiness Movement. This name is significant in the stress it places on the priority of a Bible education and on the fact of the interdenominational, nonsectarian character of the organization. It also emphasizes the fact that its purpose is to train students to give God priority in life."

3. The King James version of Matthew 18:15–17 is:

15. Moreover if thy brother shall trespass against thee, go and tell him his fault between thee and him alone: if he shall hear thee, thou hast gained thy brother. 16. But if he will not hear *thee, then* take with thee one or two more, that in the mouth of two or three witnesses every word may be established. 17. And if he shall neglect to hear them, tell *it* unto the church: but if he neglect to hear the church, let him be unto thee as an heathen man and a publican.

4. Other scriptures used to explain and justify dress codes are these which pertain to "identification with the Lord and not with the world":

Let no man despise thy youth; but be thou an example of the believers, in word, in conversation, in charity, in spirit, in faith, in purity. (I Timothy 4:12)

Prove all things; hold fast that which is good. Abstain from all appearance of evil. (Thessalonians 5:21–22)

5. In faculty meetings, it was sometimes lamented that some parents were not undergirding sufficiently.

Chapter Three: Through Classroom Windows

1. Both of these teachers and one other left in mid-year because the school's organizational arrangement changed from church-sponsored to parent-controlled.
2. The "Ms." is an approximation of the Southern dialect that says Mz rather than Missus. It does not imply that the students are using Ms. to address a woman regardless of marital status. For Ms. Palmer, who was divorced, it did serve this purpose as well.

Chapter Five. Ideological Boundaries: The Christian Sense of Self

1. Many scholars have discussed the differences between traditional and modern societies, noting the distinctive senses of self, or kinds of "will," associated

with each one (Toennies 1957), and have created different labels for the two orientations. For example, what I have termed "collective" is called "collateral" or "diffuse" or an "unindividuated" self (Marsella 1985, 290). Dumont (1985, 94) uses "holism" where I use "collective" to stand for societies "where the paramount value lies in society as a whole," and uses "individualism" as I do, "where the individual is a paramount value." Others use "sociocentric" and "egocentric" (see Rosenberger 1989; Shweder and Bourne 1984). See Dumont (1986) and Troeltsch (1960) on the history of the individualistic mode and Christianity's place in it.

2. Both individualism and the conservative Christian view of self (Christocentrism) are individualistic in that they both adhere to the "modern idea of man as an individual," as opposed to "the traditional notion of man as a social being" found in "collective" cultures (Dumont 1986, 152).

3. In modern American society, the self has been reified, but to emptiness, say some social critics. On the back cover of *Habits of the Heart* (Bellah et al. 1985) an interviewee is quoted as saying, 'In the end you're really alone, and you really have to answer to yourself." On the inside front cover is this quotation from Christopher Lasch: "The interviews underlying this book support the contention that our culture produces not an imperial self but a beleaguered, empty and minimal self, one that retains only a tenuous grasp on its surroundings and on its own identity." In a similarly critical tone, Dumont (1986), in defining Toennies's *Naturwille,* the spontaneous carrying out of the "social will" which occurs in traditional Gemeinschaft communities, and *Kurwille,* the "rational will" common to modern Gesellschaft societies, says that *Kurwille* is characterized by freedom of choice exercised in a world without wholes.

4. That modern-day Americans see themselves as the sole locus of their volition is evident within every freshman college class. Teachers of sociology and anthropology who struggle to show students that their choices have been partially determined by their social status and culture fight an uphill battle against the ironic maxims of that very culture.

5. The modern person's independence, autonomy, and choice of values are all overrated. As Dumont (1986, 61) rightly noted: "The ideological affirmation of the individual is accompanied empirically by an unprecedented degree of interdependence." Luckmann (1967, 97) agrees: "The sense of autonomy which characterizes the typical person in modern society" is "somewhat illusory." "The individual's capacity is obviously limited. Analytically, *either* he exerts his choice between existing virtual values, or existing ideas, *or* he constructs a new idea-value (which must be rare)" (Dumont 1986, 260, emphasis his). Modern people are freer than primitives, who have fewer choices. But they are not infinitely free because they are still a part of larger systems. Everything they are "free" to do may not be adaptive for their own survival. "Although men are metabolically separate from one another, and although consciousness is individual, men are not self-sufficient and their autonomy is relative and slight. Men are parts of larger systems upon which their continued existence is contingent" (Rappaport 1976, 33).

6. There is something unfortunate about the words "embed," "immerse," "deny," and "submerge," often used to describe a collective identity. They imply a full-blown individualistic self which was subsequently drowned in a collectivity. That is not the case. "It is the peculiarity of the West that it assumes individuality as potentially present in the human infant, and even in the embryo" (Hocking 1968, 95). The semantic problem is reminiscent of English philosopher Bentham's words concerning Locke, "the modern champion of individualism," who "forgot that he was not of age when he came into the world. Men according to his scheme come into the world full grown, and armed at all points like the fruit of the serpent's teeth sown by Cadmus at the corners of his cucumber bed" (Halévy 1928, vol. 1, app. iii, 418, quoted in Dumont 1986, 74). A baby in a collective culture grows up with a completely different sense of self, and it is not one where individuality is totally lacking (see Moore 1968).

On the other side of the ledger, a collective orientation is not totally lacking from modern-day American society, either. As Dumont (1986, 75) says, the "holistic conception" was never completely done in. Tocqueville suggested that the American penchant for voluntary organizations, and religion, would keep American culture from being totally individualistic. Bellah et al. (1985) found that in the United States there *was* a "second language" of concern for a collectivity, but that it was drowned in the "first language" of individualism, so much so that interconnections among human beings were not recognized, for lack of means of expressing them.

7. Collectively oriented cultures do, of course, recognize the distinctiveness of one human from another. About this, Dumont (1986, 62) makes a clarifying distinction. The expression "the individual" is characterized by the combination of two elements:

1. the *empirical* subject of speech, thought and will, indivisible sample of the human species (which I call for analytical clarity the particular man, and which is found in all societies or cultures); [the individual as indivisible is taken as a given, as stated by Christian philosophers Duns Scotus and William of Ockham in the thirteenth and fourteenth centuries. (Smith 1968; see also Kirkpatrick 1977)]
2. the independent, autonomous and thus essentially nonsocial *moral* being, as found primarily in our modern (commonsense) ideology of man and society.

8. Marsden (1982, 161) notes that fundamentalists have been viewed as highly individualistic. He agrees that they are, in certain ways, "in the sense of advocating classical liberal economics and in emphasizing the necessity of an individual's personal relation to Jesus." Also, "their view of the church is nominalistic; they see it as a collection of individuals." The stereotype was furthered by early twentieth-century "theological liberals who were building the social gospel movement" because they were "quick to point out such individualistic traits and to contrast them with their own more communal

emphases." However, Marsden (1982, 161) points out two strains to the contrary, saying that "in fact fundamental churches and national organizations are some of the most cohesive non-ethnic communities in America." More cogent to our point here, Marsden (1982, 162) points out that "despite the profession of individuality, fundamentalist churches and organizations tend to be highly authoritarian, typically under the control of one strong leader. Although fundamentalist preaching sometimes stresses making up one's own mind, in fact the movement displays some remarkable uniformities in details of doctrine and practice that suggest anything but real individualism in thought." (See also note 12 below, regarding the differences between modern-day individualism and Christocentrism.)

9. Even though it is not a collective sense of the self that the conservative Christians desire, it is true that Christianity would seem to contain the ultimate in family symbolism. Jesus is the Son of God. Mother Mary is respected or revered. Kin terms are found in the etymologies of words used in the early church. Bellah (1970, 91) notes that "Abbot, the word for the head of a monastic community, is from the Aramaic for father. Pope, which in the early church was synonymous with bishop, is from the Greek for father. These terms, together with the common term father for priest, were used to indicate the appropriately family relationship that should obtain within the Christian community."

Bellah (1970, 91) also knows that the Reformers rejected paternal terminology, emphasizing that Christians are directly related to the triune God, and do not need the clergy for mediation. Still, the familial terminology lingers on in the Holiness tradition of calling adult peers in the church "Brother" and "Sister." (The pastor is not "Father"; he is "Brother" just as are all the other adult males in good standing in the church.)

10. The current doctrinal controversy concerning this point hinges on to what degree humans are involved in their own saving. All of the conservative Christians believe in "God's grace" as opposed to "man's works." But Reformed Baptists and the Presbyterian Church in America are clearer descendants of Calvin; they believe in "unconditional election" and "irresistible grace." They say that Baptists, on the other hand, believe that "a man must participate with God in his saving" (Field Notes 7/27/89).

11. To some degree, this battle is still being fought. In June 1988, the Southern Baptist Convention passed a resolution that states: "The doctrine of the Priesthood of the Believer in no way contradicts the biblical understanding of the role, responsibility, and authority of the pastor" (Poole 1988).

12. What is the relationship between Calvin's individualism and earlier and later forms? Troeltsch (1960) finds Calvin's individualism to be of a different breed from that of Catholic, Lutheran, and Enlightenment thinkers. Troeltsch (1960, 589–590) says:

This individualism differs not only from Catholic and Lutheran individualism, but also from the optimistic, rationalistic individualism of the Enlightenment [which we would label "individualism"]. Founded upon a crushing sense of sin, and a pessimistic condemnation of the world, without color or emotional satisfaction, it is an individualism based upon the certainty of election, the sense of responsibility and of the obligation to render personal service under the Lordship of Christ. It finds its expression in the thoughtful and self-conscious type of Calvinistic piety, in the systematic spirit of self-control, and in its independence of all that is "creaturely." The value of the individual depends wholly upon the merciful grace of election and it may give honor to none save God alone.

The Christocentrism of modern-day conservative Christians fits this description with the following exceptions: Predestination has been mostly dropped, the denigration of all that is creaturely has been softened, and the charismatic branch of the family tree has added color or emotional satisfaction.

Dumont (1986), on the other hand, sees Calvinism as an "intensification" of individualism, but he is mainly concerned with the relationship of the individual to "the world." He finds that early Christianity rejected the world, but, following a path of continuing flexibility with regard to "Caesar," the world was accepted by Calvin's day. He thus finds in Calvin a "prototype of modern man" (Dumont 1986, 261).

However, when concerned more particularly with the locus of the self and power, as we are here, the difference between Calvin's individualism and modern individualism seems as great as the conservative Christians say it is. The ideal sense of self I found within the conservative Christian groups did not match the characteristics discussed in this chapter for modern middle-American individualism. They themselves see it as one of their main points of difference with mainstream American culture and go to lengths to instill this view of the self in their schoolchildren, and to criticize other views of the self, such as the popular American "do your own thing," and New Age beliefs which borrow from the Eastern idea of a spark of the divinity within our own selves. If the modern-day conservative Christian (Calvinistic) view of the self were merely an intensification of the American self, such protests would not be necessary.

13. The authors of this part of the Bible (Romans) realized that they were using metaphor to describe how individuals should be—should feel and act—in their relationship with the deity:

I put this in human terms because you are weak in your natural selves. Just as you used to offer the parts of your body in slavery to impurity and to ever-increasing wickedness, so now offer them in slavery to righteousness leading to holiness. (Romans 6:19 NIV)

I speak after the manner of men because of the infirmity of your flesh: for as ye have yielded your members servants to uncleanness and to iniquity unto iniquity; even so now yield your members servants to righteousness unto holiness. (Romans 6:19 KJ)

14. During my fieldwork, Dobson's popular films were shown at a Church of God, a Methodist Church, and at the Grace Christian Academy Parent-Teacher Fellowship, and his name was mentioned approvingly by Dr. Donald Howard, president of Accelerated Christian Education. The Dells Christian School administrator used Dobson's books as sources when she was writing a handbook for the teachers about discipline, and Grace Christian teachers listened to his tapes at faculty meetings.

15. The Confucians see a paradox in their valued father-son tie which parallels the Christian paradox: "The father-son tie is a constraint, a limitation, and a bondage; yet through its constraining, limiting, and binding power, it provides a necessary means for self-cultivation for the father as well as the son" (Wei-Ming 1985, 240).

Chapter Six: Being Christocentric

1. Although scholars of Christianity like Gibbon (1960) and much later Dumont (1985) dismiss millennialism as something that was of importance only to the earliest Christians, it is real to today's conservative Christians (Harding 1984, 1987). Evangelical educator Lockerbie (1972, 159) says that eschatological time must be taken into account in the Christian school's plans. "The Christian school regards the consummation of the Ages as its ultimate Commencement" (Lockerbie 1972, 160).

2. The promise of divine favor, instead of being partially

confined to the posterity of Abraham, was universally proposed to the freeman and the slave, to the Greek and to the barbarian, to the Jew and to the Gentile. Every privilege that could raise the proselyte from earth to heaven, that could exalt his devotion, secure his happiness, or even gratify that secret pride which, under the semblance of devotion, insinuates itself into the human heart, was still reserved for the members of the Christian church; but at the same time all mankind was permitted, and even solicited, to accept the glorious distinction, which was not only proffered as a favor, but imposed as an obligation. It became the most sacred duty of a new convert to diffuse amongst his friends and relations the inestimable blessing which he had received, and to warn them against a refusal that would be severely punished as a criminal disobedience to the will of a benevolent but all-powerful Deity. (Gibbon 1960, 147)

3. The administrator frequently agonized over her position as a woman in a role her ideology reserved for men. She justified it this way: She had prayed for a man to come and take over the position, and none had come forward; it was

better that a woman fill the position than that the job go undone. Also, she had no men working under her (other than in a voluntary status); this, she thought, prevented a bigger problem (although she did think it would be good for the students to have a male teacher).

In the nine schools I observed, there were two female administrators. In three more, male pastors were the named administrators, but women actually did the administrative work; the pastor-administrators were, in fact, often absent from school grounds. In one of the schools, a man had the nontraditional role of kindergarten teacher.

4. If the child is switching to public school in the upcoming school year, however, the ridicule turns to things like "Daddy said I could be in Boy Scouts next year, when I'm in public school, because it meets at my school, right after school's out" (Field Notes GCA). This reversal is not as likely with older students who will be going to public school because they have run out of grades in Christian school, although they too, begin to talk about athletic and extracurricular opportunities.

5. Even seemingly negative occurrences, which threatened to weaken the school's social structure, such as teachers resigning, were eventually squared with God's leadership. Since "God wouldn't do anything to hurt the children," ultimately the resignations were seen as God's pruning.

6. At least this is the *language* used by middle Americans: "Insofar as they are limited to a language of radical individual atuonomy . . . they cannot think about themselves or others except as arbitrary centers of volition. They cannot express the fullness of being that is actually theirs" (Bellah et al. 1985, 81).

7. Geertz (1973, 174) warns that these polar contrasts (ideal types) of Weber's cannot contain all the variety to be found in the religions of the world. Many nonliterate primitive religions have, for example, been informed by self-conscious criticism, and "in societies with rationalized religion," a "popular religiosity of a traditional sort persists." Yet he still finds the dichotomy useful, and basically his ethnographic observations fit the model. The "traditional" religions of clan, tribe, and village, he notes, are "concrete, action-centered, and thoroughly interwoven with the details of everyday life." Their approach to the problems of meaning are "implicit, circumscribed, and segmental." The "rationalized" world religions are indeed possessed of a "greater conceptual generalization, a tighter formal integration, and a more explicit sense of doctrine" (Geertz 1973, 175).

8. Gibbons's (1960, 153–154) discussion of the early evolution of Christianity shows something of this sort occurring with the move from the polytheism of Greece and Rome to the monotheism of Christianity. The Christians were hard-pressed to avoid any semblance of ritual activity supporting polytheism because it was everywhere; it pervaded people's actions without them thinking much about it. Any important transaction of peace and war was accompanied by sacrifices to the gods. The games and festivals were dedicated to the gods. Of course, weddings and funerals were influenced by the pagan spirits,

but so was "every art and every trade, including "the arts of music and painting, of eloquence and poetry."

It was the first but arduous duty of a Christian to preserve himself pure and undefiled by the practice of idolatry. The religion of the nations was not merely a speculative doctrine professed in the schools or preached in the temples. The innumerable deities and rites of polytheism were closely interwoven with every circumstance of business or pleasure, of public or of private life; and it seemed impossible to escape the observance of them, without, at the same time, renouncing the commerce of mankind, and all the offices and amusements of society. . . .

Even the common language of Greece and Rome abounded with familiar but impious expressions, which the imprudent Christian might too carelessly utter, or too patiently hear. . . . If a Pagan friend (on the occasion perhaps of sneezing) used the familiar expression of "Jupiter bless you," the Christian was obliged to protest against the divinity of Jupiter. (Gibbon 1960, 153–154)

Chapter Seven: Walking the Christian Walk the American Way: the Fruits of the Spirit Versus Competition

1. Conservative Christians want to be Christocentric rather than egocentric, but they also want to be individualistic rather than collectively oriented. For them, the latter smacks of socialism and communism, which they abhor.
2. Youth ministers try to use teenage peer pressure as an evangelizing tool. Several of GCA's young people performed a skit at one of their churches. In it four teenagers are in a car. The car goes out of control, and they are killed. In the next scene, three of the teenagers are going to heaven and the fourth is trying to follow, but he is being pulled from behind, not allowed to follow.

Fourth:	Why can't I come with you?
Three:	You aren't saved.
Fourth:	But I went to church with you. I went to Christian school with you. I did everything you did.
Three:	But you aren't saved.
Fourth:	I wish you had told me.

A song sung on field trips at ALCA had this chorus:

How I wish we'd all been sa—aved.
It's too late to change your mind,
the sun has set and
you've been left behind. (Field Notes ALCA 4/10/87)

Chapter Eight: Walking the Christian Walk the American Way: Separation Versus Worldliness

1. There is at least one Christian marketing research firm, Barna Research Group in California.

2. It is not just the conservative Christians who are creating Christian "kitsch" (*Time* 1987a, 52–53). When the Pope visited the United States in September 1987, the market exploded with such things as Pope-on-a-rope soap, buttons with the Pope's pictures saying "GO AHEAD, BLESS MY DAY," and a yard sprinkler with the water coming from the likeness of the Pope's hands, called "Let Us Spray."

3. The Holiness church makes more major adjustments to worldly things. For example, one year the teacher who took the yearbook to be printed and bound was asked what they wanted on the cover. She said she didn't really know, and the printer said he would fix them up, so she left in it his hands. When the books returned, they sported a peaceful scene of a girl standing on a sandy beach looking out at the ocean, and the school's theme, "Reflections," in big letters. The only trouble was that the girl was wearing shorts and a short-sleeved shirt. So the teachers tried to modify them by covering them over with black marker, making sleeves to the elbow, and a skirt. But the black marker modifications tended to rub off of the slick cover surface (Field Notes CCCA 5/06/87).

4. Performers who sang in the Christian nightclubs, called Christian coffeehouses, said the establishments had a hard time financially because Christians were reluctant to pay a sufficient cover charge to keep them open, and of course there were no liquor sales to keep them afloat (Field Notes GCA 4/14/87). A Christian teen club was considered for the Southeastern Valley, but the promoter decided to give the market further study.

5. One of the Holiness-sponsored schools was well aware of the need for clear and obvious lines, both in the figurative and the literal sense. A teacher explained that they required sleeves to be to the elbow, or longer. As she pointed out, the elbow is an obvious place, or line, and "there has to be a limit somewhere; if not, you could end up with no sleeve at all" (Field Notes CCCA 5/6/87). If you look at the human arm, you can see that it is true that the only places which could be said to create a definite line are the elbow and perhaps the wrist. Even the shoulder is an equivocal "place."

6. See also Hunter (1983) concerning an increased capitulation to modernity, specifically "rationalization" among evangelicals—in the form of the packaging of spirituality, the civility of evangelizing, and the subjectivization of faith so that it is "more relevant."

7. An unfortunately unidentified participant in the discussion following the presentation of my paper, "Alternative Christian Schooling: How Alternative Is It?" at the Society for the Scientific Study of Religion meetings in Chicago, Illinois, October 28–30, 1988, made this good semantic point.

8. One administrator with whom I talked had an experience rare in the creation of Christian schools. He took the job of opening and administering a new school only after the parents who hired him agreed to pay him for a year of study and planning. When it came time to open the school, however, funds were lacking, and it was necessary for him to turn his attention to fund-raising (Field Notes 10/6/86).

Chapter Nine: Education Culture in the Christian Classroom: Snoopy and Scripture, Phonics and Prayer

1. Some states have certain requirements for private schools, such as a minimum number of days or hours of instruction, or that certain subject areas be taught. However, the state in which the schools studied are located has no regulations for private schools.
2. The national Christian school organizations are concerned that the Christian schools be seedbeds for "evangelization," but none of the administrators I talked to saw this as a main mission of their schools. (All, of course, welcomed it when it did happen.) They were interested, instead, in "discipleship," ministering to children who are already in Christian homes. They thought—some from experience—that evangelization opened the door to a "reform-school" mode, and caused many problems which could be avoided by the greater homogeneity secured by an emphasis on discipleship.
3. The separate strands of the cultural plait became almost palpable when I took my mother along to a regional convention of the American Association of Christian Schools. Being interested in the teaching and guiding of children, she listened intently. Since she had not been trained in being neutral about what she heard, when the speaker used pop psychology terminology and said something like "The different ways we communicate and respond are going to make the parent respond in different ways. . . . When you talk to parents, at conferences, don't cross your arms, lean forward a little—but not right in their faces. Nod once in a while. Smile. . . . Have an 'I'm proud of this work' folder," my mother nodded vigorously in agreement. When, on the other hand, the speaker called up fundamentalist Christian ideology or social analysis such as the view that the "cause of the revolution" in sexual mores and violence in our society was Elvis Presley and his rebellious rock music, my mother unconsciously breathed a sigh that only I could hear (Field Notes AACS 10/9/87). I could have developed a sigh/nod index to measure the extent to which the conservative Christian and American popular cultural strands were part of the presentations.
4. Others think that the goal of Christian schools should be teachers' modeling of Christian behavior to the students.
5. BASIC education is older editions of Accelerated Christian Education materials, marketed separately to schools who want to use self-paced instructional

materials, but who do not want to adopt the entire ACE system (Field Notes CCCA 5/11/87; Mooers 1989).

6. A teacher at ALCA told me about articles in resource literature for Christian school teachers that raised the question of whether students were being "overdosed" on Bible, since they hear it in Bible class and in many other classes, too. Most Christian educators see the goal of Christian education as the "integration of the Bible into every subject." But the authors of these articles feared that students may eventually "tune out" the Bible (Field Notes ALCA 3/18/87).

Chapter Ten. Making Decisions: The Revitalization Process at Work

1. This is the conventional wisdom on A Beka. Christian educators feel that A Beka materials are ahead of public school grade levels by about a grade, and that a student who has missed A Beka's kindergarten program will have some difficulty with its first grade, and so on. (Most teachers judge it a positive thing that the books are advanced in this way.) A Beka is admired for its effort to integrate material from the various subjects: for example, terms learned in science will show up in spelling; facts learned in history will be used in example sentences in language. The teachers also say that A Beka "spirals" from one grade level to the next nicely. Those who have had little teaching experience like the curriculum packages, which spell out a teacher's activities for the day, week, month, and year. (But many teachers say they don't use it, making up their own "lesson plans" instead.) On the other hand, A Beka is criticized for being "drill, drill, drill," and "rote, rote, rote. . . . A Beka has been criticized for being factual but not informative" (Field Notes GCA 11/24/86). Bob Jones University materials are thought to be more oriented toward thinking and integrating.

Almost all teachers in traditional classroom settings criticize the ACE form of instruction, saying that students learn neither to take notes from lectures nor to read and synthesize long amounts of material. Some say that "it works OK for the self-motivated child." On the other hand, those who use it say the students like moving at their own pace, and that they get bored in a traditional classroom setting. (The pastor and principal at Hamlin Christian Academy also noted that it was "quiet.") It has the orderliness the conservative Christians admire. Some who use it decry the amount of recordkeeping it requires. Some don't like the total ACE structure, with students at cubicles using small Christian and American flags to call upon monitors for help, so they use other self-paced instruction booklets (BASIC or Alpha Omega) in a classroom setting, with a teacher. Even those who like self-paced instruction, though, have found that mathematics is better taught in a traditional classroom situation to a whole group at once. "It's easier that way, because they all have the same questions, and with the PACEs, they come up and ask them one at a time; this way you can explain it to all of them at once—or a few times" (Field Notes MCA 5/12/87). In a group situation, "the questions one student asks helps them all" (Field Notes PCA 4/8/87). The advocates of any of the curricula consider achievement test scores proof that the students are learning the subject matter. (Even within the conservative Christian community, it is noted that comparisons of Christian school achievement tests with those of public schools are not really fair, because of the differences in the two populations of children. Public schools can include programs for every kind of child; few Christian schools have provision for special education, for instance.)

2. Table 10.1 summarizes the concerns and influences which are the stuff of which decisions are made.

3. There *is* a conservative Christian epistemology of teaching beyond the often invoked principle that the Bible be integrated into every subject. It is best reflected in Jehle (1984, emphasis his), whose writings are used in what is called the "Principle Approach" to Christian education. He explains the difference in the way the Christian school and the public school ("humanism") would approach various subjects. One of the credos is that the children be taught what, not why (or at least, they are taught that a principle is true before they are taught why it is true). He maintains that the humanists teach the other way around, and that this is dangerous. The Christian way begins with the premise that the "student is the investigator of God's laws and design." The student learns that the "principle or rule is a general fact" and "experience is the practical and precise exercise of principles." This mode helps to teach "*obedience* to authority, that which is absolute, [which] builds *faith* in God's laws." On the other hand, the humanist begins with the premise that the "student is the creator and designer of man's laws about nature," and therefore the teacher "explains *why* before *what*." This is a mode whose danger lies in "*discover(ing)* through intelligence that which is true, build(ing) *doubt* in anything not experienced."

None of the schools I observed used the Principle Approach. Their educational concerns are better understood as cloaked in the priorities and language of the professional education scene. This was true both of administrators and teachers educated in secular colleges (GCA) and those from Christian colleges (DCS and MCA).

Chapter Eleven. Discerning God's Will

1. Of course, Mrs. Sherwood does not take credit for her abilities to lead chapel well. Following the Christocentric philosophy, she gives God the glory. A fellow teacher complimented her at the end of chapel: "Very good, Mrs. Sherwood." Mrs. Sherwood replied, "I told you I was going to be good today; I felt the Spirit on me." Mrs. Turner affirmed, "It was" (Field Notes GCA 3/23/87).

Table 10.1 Anatomy of Curriculum Decisions, Sources of Influence in Making Decisions

TOPIC OF CURRICULUM DECISION	CONCERNS OF DECISION-MAKERS		SOURCES OF INFORMATION	
	CHRISTIAN	SECULAR/EDUCATIONAL	CHRISTIAN	SECULAR
DCS: readers	story content	eye catching analytical, not regurgitation teacher helps cost	publishers' advertising publishers' samples A Beka sales representative	
DCS: reading for pre-kindergarten DCS: A Beka video		motor skills social skills cost		
GCA: supplements	complement what we do	horizontal continuity/comparative phonics cost	Focus on Family tape other Christian school ACSI vendors (some secular)	Open Court representative Readers' conference publishers' advertising summer workshop
GCA: history	content assumed Christian-safe	interesting presentation: stories, cartoons, pictures teacher helps coverage	publishers' samples	
GCA: science		continuity experimental approach cost	ICR Seminar other Christian school	publishers college sci professor
MCA: ACE to A BEKA	content assumed Christian-safe believing teachers	student burnout qualified teachers videos give lesson plans handle students' questions more efficiently (math) cost		

Note: The chart summarizes the concerns and influences which impinge on decisions. The language used to describe these various influences derives from the teachers. However, categorization as Christian, educational, and secular concerns is my own; secular concerns include factors like logistics and cost.

2. The parent who had participated in several kinds of churches, including Methodist, Baptist (American), Southern Baptist, nontraditional Catholic, Church of God (Anderson, Ind.), Church of God (Cleveland, Tenn.), and nondenominational "Word" churches, noted some differences with regard to how open the various churches were to "leadings" and to what degree the scriptures were the sole "criterion for leading." She said that all who were open to leadings used a similar process for discerning God's will.

3. In the Living Waters Christian Community lesson, "circumstantial evidence" and "God's provision" are separated, making six guideposts. However, through listening to other informants I found no clear distinctions between them, and so have condensed them for this discussion.

4. In the wake of the Bakker and Swaggert ministry scandals, the media oversimplified its attempts to sort out "who's who" in the conservative Christian world. Basically, it was said that fundamentalists (for example, Baptists) rely on the authority of the scriptures, and charismatics rely on revelations from the Holy Spirit. Actually, although independent Baptists are (typically) against speaking in tongues, they do make a place for the Holy Spirit's action in their lives. Although charismatics speak in tongues and some believe God speaks to them, they see the Bible as the ultimate authority.

5. The peace of God is not just this release from the effort of having to make a choice, however. For most of us, making *any* choice will bring peace, and in the face of a bad decision, some of us will follow up with the mechanisms to reduce cognitive dissonance. But informants reported times when they had made decisions and acted upon them, and then had *not* had peace. When they reversed themselves, then peace came.

Chapter Twelve. Conclusion: Choice and Compromise

1. For some Christians, those neo-post-millenniallists who abide by what is called "Kingdom Now" or "Dominion Theology" and believe that Christians themselves can *work to cause* the Kingdom of God on earth, the rhetoric becomes "utopian," with the aim of achieving a future "golden age."

2. There are differences among the schools, but the differences seem easier to explain by social class differences than they are by doctrinal differences (see also Rose 1988). They are differences of style. Research to clarify the differences and similarities among schools sponsored by different denominations is underway. Our project, entitled "The Demise of Denominationalism and the Rise of Ecumenism within Educational Voluntary Associations (Christian Schools)" is a part of a study of "Evangelicals, Voluntary Associations and American Public Life," funded by the Lilly Endowment, under the auspices of the Institute for the Study of American Evangelicals.

3. Doctrine, in the dictionary sense and as I am using it, means "a body of principles." But the conservative Christians often use it in the narrower sense

of "church rules for specific behavior." For example, a child-care worker at Dells Christian School, explaining the difference between her nondenominational church and Holiness churches, pointed to an elbow-length sleeve and said, "That's Holiness doctrine."

4. Some Christian schools associated with charismatic Christian communities tend to be different from these schools in various ways. For example, they are more closed to students outside the community (at Rose's [1988] Covenant School 5 percent are from outside the community); are more inclined to teach the ritual practices of their particular church and community within the school; and are characterized by a stronger hierarchical link between church and school (Huntington 1988; Rose 1988). Parents in Southeastern Valley who had scouted all the Christian schools in the area noted that Living Waters Christian Academy, affiliated with a charismatic Christian community, seemed to them less open to enrolling students who were not a part of that community; however, parents whose children were enrolled in the Community's day-care program did not feel this way.

5. Rose (1988, 88ff,139) too, notes that the link between ideology and praxis is attenuated.

References

AACS (American Association of Christian Schools). 1986. *Directory of the American Association of Christian Schools.* Fairfax, Va.: AACS.

Acquaviva, Gary J. 1980. Teaching Philosophy in Appalachia: An Existential Approach. Paper presented at the Appalachian Studies Conference, East Tennessee State University, Johnson City, Tenn. 21–23 March.

ACSI (Association of Christian Schools International). 1983. *Evaluative Criteria for Christian Elementary and Secondary Schools: Accreditation Programs of the Association of Christian Schools International.* Whittier, Calif.: ACSI.

———. 1987. 14 Reasons Why Your School Should be a Member of ACSI. Whittier, Calif.: ACSI.

Ahlstrom, Sydney E. 1975. From Puritanism to Evangelicalism: A Critical Perspective. In *The Evangelicals: What They Believe, Who They Are, Where They Are Changing,* edited by David F. Wells and John D. Woodbridge. Nashville: Abingdon Press.

ALCA (Abundant Life Christian Academy). *Student Handbook.* City: ALCA.

Aleichem, Sholom. 1955. *The Great Fair. Scenes from My Childhood.* Translated by Tamara Kahana. New York: Noonday Press.

Alpha Omega Publications. 1988. Tempe, Ariz. Advertisement.

Amason, Boyd. 1990. Christ is the Greatest Puppeteer. Richmond, Va.: Boyd Amason. Song.

Ammerman, Nancy Tatom. 1987. *Bible Believers.* New Brunswick, N.J.: Rutgers University Press.

Anonymous. "Not I, But Christ." Tract.

Associated Press. 1986a. Researchers Rap Writing in Nation's Textbooks. *(Regional Newspaper),* 2 July.

———. 1986b. Drugs are Biggest Problems Facing Schools, Gallup Poll Finds. *(Regional Newspaper),* 24 August.

Ault, James, and Michael Camerini. 1988. *Born Again: Life in a Fundamentalist Baptist Church.* New York: James Ault Films. Film.

Ballweg, George Edward, Jr. 1980. The Growth in the Number and Population of Christian Schools Since 1966: A Profile of Parental Views Concerning Factors Which led Them to Enroll Their Children in a Christian School. Ed.D. diss., Boston University.

Barr, James. 1978. *Fundamentalism.* Philadelphia: Westminster Press.

Bascom, W. R. 1941. The Sanctions of Ifa Divination. *Journal of the Royal Anthropological Institute* 71:43–54.

Basic Education. 1979. *Self-Pac of Basic Education: Math* #1067. Lewisville, Tex.: Accelerated Christian Education.

————. 1974. *Self-Pac of Basic Education: Social Studies* #3061. Lewisville, Tex.: Accelerated Christian Education.

Beattie, John. 1967. Divination in Bunyoro, Uganda. In *Magic, Witchcraft, and Curing,* edited by J. Middleton. Garden City, N.Y.: Natural History Press.

Bellah, Robert N. 1970. *Beyond Belief.* New York: Harper and Row.

————. 1982. Introduction. In *Religion and America,* edited by Mary Douglas and Steven M. Tipton. Boston: Beacon Press.

Bellah, Robert N., Richard Madsen, William M. Sullivan, Ann Swidler, and Steven M. Tipton. 1985. *Habits of the Heart: Individualism and Commitment in American Life.* New York: Harper and Row.

Beteille, André. 1983. The Idea of Natural Inequality and Other Essays. Oxford: Oxford University Press.

Billings, Henry. 1987. Writing Textbooks Isn't Child's Play. *US News and World Report,* 27 July.

Bogert, Frans van der. 1980. The Cultural Context of Philosophic Criticism. Paper presented at the Appalachian Studies Conference, East Tennessee State University, Johnson City, Tenn., 21–23 March.

Briggs, Jean. 1970. Kapluna Daughter. In *Women in the Field,* edited by Peggy Golde. Chicago: Aldine.

Buchanan, John H. 1987. Creation-Law Ruling Ought to Enliven Content of Textbooks. *(Regional Newspaper),* 23 July.

Burnette, Jacquetta. 1974. *Anthropology and Education: An Annotated Bibliographic Guide.* New Haven: HRAF Press for the Council on Anthropology and Education.

Byrne, H. W. 1977. *A Christian Approach to Education: Educational Theory and Application.* Milford, Mich.: Mott Media.

Calvin, John. 1989. *Institutes of the Christian Religion.* Translated by Henry Beveridge. Grand Rapids, Mich.: Eerdmans. Originally published as *Institutio Christianae Religionis.* Geneva: Oliua Roberti Stephani, 1559.

Carlson, Gerald. 1987. Letters to the Editor. *The Administrator.* American Association of Christian Schools, (Fall/Winter): 23–24.

Carnegie Forum on Education and the Economy. 1986. A Nation Prepared: Teachers for the Twenty-first Century. Washington, D.C.: Carnegie Forum on Education and the Economy.

Carper, James C. 1984. The Christian Day School. In *Religious Schooling in America,* edited by James C. Carper and Thomas C. Hunt. Birmingham, Alabama: Religious Education Press.

Carroll, Jackson W., Douglas W. Johnson, and Martin E. Marty. 1979. *Religion in America: 1950 to the Present.* New York: Harper and Row.

Carter, Pamela. 1986. "Get in Shape with Pamela Carter." Trinity Broadcasting Network, 29 July. Television program.

Castillo, Jean Del. 1986. Garbage Kids Move into S.A. *San Antonio Texas Express News,* 15 February.

CBS. 1987. "Evening News." 25 March. Television program.

CBS. 1988. "48 Hours." 14 April. Television program.

Chamberlain, Jack. 1986. Bennett: Public Schools Should Teach Moral Values. *(Regional Newspaper)*, 24 April.

Chaplin, A. M. 1986. Garbage Pail Kids: Not Just Another Pretty Face. *Baltimore (Maryland) Sun*, 11 February.

Chapman, James A., and Phyllis Rand. 1977. *Language 6: Grammar Work-Text for Christian Schools*. Pensacola, Fla.: A Beka Book Publications.

Chapman, Jim. 1982. *Grammar and Composition Book One: A Work-Text for Christian Schools, Teacher's Edition*. Pensacola, Fla.: A Beka Book Publications.

The Christian Educator. 1987. Arlington Heights, Ill.: Christian Liberty Academy Satellite Schools. September, October.

Christian Light Publications. 1980a. *Mathematics Lightunit, 701, Whole Numbers*. Harrisonburg, Va.: Christian Light Publications.

———. 1980b. *Language Arts Lightunit, 604*. Harrisonburg, Va.: Christian Light Publications.

Cohen, Barbara. 1986. Censoring the Sources. *School Library Journal* (March): 97–99.

Cole, Stewart G. 1931. *The History of Fundamentalism*. New York: Harper and Row.

Combee, Jerry H. 1979. *The History of the World in Christian Perspective, Volume I: Since the Beginning*. Pensacola, Fla.: A Beka Book Publications.

Cooper, Bruce, Donald H. McLaughlin, and Bruno Manno. 1983. The Latest Word on Private School Growth. *Teachers College Record* 85(1):88–98.

Crescenti, Peter. 1982. Interview with Bruce Lockerbie: Boom Times for Christian Schools: Good News and Bad. *Eternity,* June.

Cully, Kendig Brubaker, ed. 1963. *The Westminster Dictionary of Christian Education*. Philadelphia: Westminster.

Cumbey, Constance. 1983. *The Hidden Dangers of the Rainbow: The New Age Movement and Our Coming Age of Barbarism*. Shreveport, La.: Huntington House.

DCS (Dells Christian School). *Home-School Handbook*. Southeastern Valley: DCS.

Desilva, Bruce. 1986. Boring Books. *(Regional Newspaper)*, 5 October.

Dobson, James. n.d. Building Self-Esteem in Your Children. Westchester, Ill.: Good News Publishers, From Dobson, James. *Hide or Seek*. Old Tappan, N.J.: Fleming H. Revell, 1974.

Dollar, George W. 1973. *A History of Fundamentalism in America*. Greenville, S.C.: Bob Jones University Press.

Douglas, Mary. 1982. The Effects of Modernization on Religious Change. In *Religion and America,* edited by Mary Douglas and Steven M. Tipton. Boston: Beacon Press.

D'Souza, Dinesh. 1984. Fundamental Divide Forms Between Falwell, Bob Jones. *(Regional Newspaper)*, 15 July.

Dumont, Louis. 1985. A Modified View of Our Origins: The Christian Beginnings of Modern Individualism. In *The Category of the Person,* edited by Michael Carrithers, Steven Collins, and Steven Lukes. New York: Cambridge University Press.

———. 1986. *Essays on Individualism.* Chicago: University of Chicago Press.

Eastman, Charles A. (Ohiyesa). 1902. *Indian Boyhood.* Boston: Little, Brown and Company.

Ebenezer Christian School. *Parent-Student Handbook.* Region: Ebenezer Christian School.

Eller, Ron. 1982. *Miners, Millhands, and Mountaineers: Industrialization of the Appalachian South, 1880–1930.* Knoxville: University of Tennessee Press.

Erikson, Kai T. 1976. *Everything in its Path.* New York: Simon and Schuster.

Evans-Pritchard, Edward Evans. 1937. *Witchcraft, Oracles, and Magic Among the Azande.* Oxford: Clarendon Press.

———. 1962. *Social Anthropology and Other Essays.* New York: Free Press.

Excel Magazine. 1987. San Diego, Calif.: Private Education Services. Fall: 33.

Fernandez, James W. 1974. The Mission of Metaphor in Expressive Culture. *Current Anthropology* 15:119–145.

———. 1977. The Performance of Ritual Metaphors. In *The Social Use of Metaphor: Essays on the Anthropology of Rhetoric,* edited by J. David Sapir and J. Christopher Crocker. Philadelphia, Pa.: University of Pennsylvania Press.

Fichter, Joseph H. 1958. *Parochial School: A Sociological Study.* South Bend, Ind.: University of Notre Dame Press.

Field Notes AACS. American Association of Christian Schools Affiliate Convention, 9 October 1987.

Field Notes AACS Competition. American Association of Christian Schools. Academic Competition; Regional, 19 March 1987; State, 9 April 1987.

Field Notes A Beka. A Beka In-Service Conference for Teachers, 10 August 1987.

Field Notes ACE. Accelerated Christian Education Convention, 10–11 November 1986.

Field Notes ACSI. Association of Christian Schools International Regional Convention, 28–30 January 1987.

Field Notes ACSI Competition. Association of Christian Schools International Regional Art Festival, 1 May 1987.

Field Notes ALCA. Abundant Life Christian Academy, City, sponsored by an independent Baptist church.

Field Notes CCCA. Calvary Cross Christian Academy, Southeastern Valley, sponsored by a Holiness church.

Field Notes DCS. Dells Christian School, Southeastern Valley, sponsored by a Wesleyan church.

Field Notes ECS. Ebenezer Christian School, Region, sponsored by an independent Baptist church.

Field Notes GCA. Grace Christian Academy, Southeastern Valley, incorporated by parents, mostly charismatic.

Field Notes HCA. Hamlin Christian Academy, Southeastern Valley, sponsored by a nondenominational independent Pentecostal church.

Field Notes HCS. Hope Christian School, Region, sponsored by a Presbyterian Church in America church.

Field Notes Heritage USA. Heritage USA (PTL), Charlotte, N.C., 9 August 1987.

Field Notes ICR. Institute for Creation Research Seminar, 11–15 August 1986.

Field Notes LWCA. Living Waters Christian Academy, Southeastern Valley, sponsored by a charismatic Christian community.

Field Notes MCA. Maranatha Christian Academy, Southeastern Valley, sponsored by an independent Baptist church.

Field Notes NWCA. Narrow Way Christian Academy, Region, sponsored by an independent Baptist church.

Field Notes PCA. Porter Christian Academy, Southeastern Valley, sponsored by a Holiness Pentecostal church.

Field Notes PVCA. Pine Valley Christian Academy, Region, sponsored by an independent Baptist church.

Field Notes RCA. Reedsville Christian Academy, Region, sponsored by an independent Baptist church.

Field Notes SCCS. Springfield City Christian School, City, sponsored by an independent Baptist church.

Field Notes SLCA. Springs of Life Christian School, Region, incorporated by parents, mostly Presbyterian Church in America.

Fiske, Edward B. 1986. U.S. Education Study Recommends the Best Ways to Teach. *(Regional Newspaper)*, 2 March.

Focus on the Family. 1986. *The School Textbook Controversy: Interview with James Dobson and Paul Vitz.* Arcadia, Calif.: Focus on the Family. Cassette tape.

———. 1987a. Feedback. *Focus on the Family,* October: 24.

———. 1987b. "Focus on the Family," 3 November. Radio program.

———. 1988a. Advertisement. *Focus on the Family.* February: 10.

———. 1988b. Worship While You Work. *Clubhouse Jr.,* September: 6–7.

Fowler, Robert Booth. 1982. *A New Engagement: Evangelical Political Thought, 1966–1976.* Grand Rapids: William B. Eerdmans.

"Frontline." 1988. Public Broadcasting Service, 26 January. Television program.

Gaebelein, Frank E. 1968. *The Pattern of God's Truth: Problems of Integration in Christian Education.* 2d ed. Chicago: Moody Press.

Gaither, William J., and Gloria Gaither. 1970. "The Family of God." Alexandria, Ind.: William J. Gaither. Song.

Gallup, George H. 1979. The Eleventh Annual Gallup Poll of the Public's Attitudes Toward the Public Schools. *Phi Delta Kappan* 61(1):33–45.

———. 1983. *Public Opinion 1982.* Wilmington, Del.: Scholarly Resources.

Gallup Organization and Princeton Religion Research Center. 1981. *Religion in America, 1981.* Princeton, N.J.: Princeton Religious Research Center.

Gasper, Louis. 1963. *The Fundamentalist Movement.* The Hague: Mouton & Co.

GCA (Grace Christian Academy). *Handbook*. Southeastern Valley: GCA.

Geertz, Clifford. 1973. *The Interpretation of Cultures*. New York: Basic Books.

Gibbon, Edward. 1960. *The Decline and Fall of the Roman Empire*. 1776 abridgement by D. M. Low. New York: Harcourt, Brace.

Green, Martha Grace. 1987. Pockets for our Aprons, *Daybreak* 41(4):7.

Guth, James L. 1983. The New Christian Right. In *The New Christian Right: Mobilization and Legitimization*, edited by Robert C. Liebman and Robert Wuthnow. New York: Aldine.

Hadden, Jeffrey K., and Charles E. Swann. 1981. *Prime Time Preachers: The Rising Power of Televangelism*. Reading, Mass.: Addison-Wesley.

Hadden, Jeffrey K., and Anson Shupe. 1988. *Televangelism: Power and Politics on God's Frontier*. New York: Henry Holt.

Halévy, Elie. 1928. *The Growth of Philosophic Radicalism*. Translated by Mary Morris. London: Faber and Gwyer. Originally published as *La formation du radicalisme philosophique*. 3 vols. Paris: Alcan, 1900–1904.

Hall, Edward T. 1976. *Beyond Culture*. Garden City, N.Y.: Doubleday.

Harding, Susan F. 1984. World Consuming Rhetoric. Paper presented at the annual meeting of the American Anthropological Association, Denver, Colo. 14–18 November.

———. 1987. Convicted by the Holy Spirit: The Rhetoric of Fundamental Baptist Conversion. *American Ethnologist* 14(1):167–181.

HCS (Hope Christian School). *Handbook*. Region: HCS.

Hechinger, Fred M. 1986. Current Methods "Insult to Intelligence." *(Regional Newspaper)*, 30 October.

———. 1987. Pollster Challenges Conservative Views on Education Issues. *(Regional Newspaper)*, 15 October.

Heinz, Donald. 1983. The Struggle to Define America. In *The New Christian Right: Mobilization and Legitimization*, edited by Robert C. Liebman and Robert Wuthnow. New York: Aldine.

Herskovits, Melville J. 1938. *Dahomey: An Ancient West African Kingdom*. 2 vols. New York: J. J. Augustin.

Hicks, George L. 1976. *Appalachian Valley*. New York: Holt, Rinehart, and Winston.

Hill, Kathie. 1987. *We Like Sheep*. Chatsworth, Calif.: Sparrow Corporation.

Hill, Samuel S., Jr. 1981. The Shape and Shapes of Popular Southern Piety. In *Varieties of Southern Evangelicalism*, edited by David Edwin Harrell, Jr. Macon, Ga.: Mercer University Press.

Hill, Samuel S., Jr., and Dennis E. Owen. 1982. *The New Religious Political Right in America*. Nashville: Abingdon.

Hocking, William Ernest. 1968. A Brief Note on Individuality in East and West. In *The Status of the Individual in East and West*, edited by Charles A. Moore. Honolulu: University of Hawaii Press.

Hoge, Dean R., and David A. Roozen. 1979. *Understanding Church Growth and Decline, 1950–1978*. New York: Pilgrim Press.

Hostetler, John A., and Gertrude Enders Huntington. 1967. *The Hutterites in North America*. New York: Holt, Rinehart and Winston.

Howe, Judy England. 1981. *Arithmetic 6: A Beka Book Traditional Math Series.* Pensacola, Fla.: A Beka Book Publications.

Hsu, Francis L. K. 1972. American Core Values and National Character. In *Psychological Anthropology,* edited by Francis L. K. Hsu. Cambridge, Mass.: Schenkman.

"Humanist Manifesto I." 1933. *The New Humanist* 6(3).

"Humanist Manifesto II." 1973. *The Humanist* 33(5).

Humphrey, Richard. 1980. Academic Philosophy and Appalachian Culture. Paper presented at the Appalachian Studies Conference, East Tennessee State University, Johnson City, Tenn., 21–23 March.

Hunter, James Davison. 1983. *American Evangelicalism: Conservative Religion and the Quandary of Modernity.* New Brunswick, N.J.: Rutgers University Press, 1983.

———. 1986. Humanism and Social Theory: Is Secular Humanism a Religion? Testimony presented in Mobile, Alabama Textbook Case, September.

———. 1987. *Evangelicalism: The Coming Generation.* Chicago: University of Chicago Press.

Huntington, Gertrude Enders. 1988. Personal Communication, 19 November.

ICR (Institute for Creation Research). 1986. TRACS Completes Seventh Year and Joins ACCEA. *Acts and Facts* 15(10):5.

———. 1987. *Days of Praise: Daily Bible Readings and Devotional Commentaries* December–January–February: December 6, 1986.

———. 1988. *Days of Praise: Daily Bible Readings and Devotional Commentaries* June–July–August:June 23; June 25.

Interview DF. Donald Farrell, teacher at GCA, charismatic church, 25 September 1986; 4 November 1986; 24 November 1986.

Interview DR. Delores Raleigh, parent at GCA, Presbyterian, Church of God, charismatic churches, 24 October 1986.

Interview GH. Gail Halsey, teacher at GCA, charismatic church, 21 November 1986.

Interview JB. John Branscom, headmaster at LWCA, charismatic community, 26 February 1987.

Interview LT. Lana Townsend, parent, multiple churches, 5 February 1988; 15 February 1988; 17 February 1988; 14 March 1988.

Interview MR. Marie Riley, teacher at ALCA, independent Baptist church, 21 August 1987.

Interview NS. Nancy Sherwood, teacher at GCA, Brethren, charismatic churches, 23–27 June 1986; 1 July 1986.

Interview PC. Phyllis Clark, parent at GCA, Brethren, charismatic churches, 3 September 1987; 17 September 1986.

Interview SC. Sheila Compton, parent at GCA, Baptist, charismatic churches, 27 August 1987.

Interview SR. Sarah Ramsey, teacher at GCA, Brethren, charismatic churches, 28–30 January 1987.

Jehle, Paul. 1984. *Go Ye Therefore . . . and Teach.* Plymouth, Mass.: New Testament Christian School.

Jenkins, Maureen. 1987. Comedian for Christ. *(Regional Newspaper)*, 10 November.

Johnson, Douglas W., Paul R. Picard, and Bernard Quinn. 1971. *Churches and Church Membership in the United States: An Enumeration by Region, State, and County.* Washington, D.C.: Glenmary Research Center.

Johnson, Frank. 1985. The Western Concept of Self. In *Culture and Self,* edited by Anthony J. Marsella, George DeVos, and Francis L. K. Hsu. New York: Tavistock.

Jones, Chip, and Jack Chamberlain. 1986. Liberal Arts Degrees for New Teachers Advised. *(Regional Newspaper)*, 25 September.

Joosse, Wayne. 1987. Feeling Good About Yourself. *Christian Home and School.* Christian Schools International, April:25–27.

Jordan, Philip D. 1982. *The Evangelical Alliance for the United States of America, 1847–1900: Ecumenism, Identity, and the Religion of the Republic.* Studies in American Religion, vol. 7. New York: The Edwin Mellen Press.

Jorstad, Erling. 1981. *The Politics of Moralism: The New Christian Right in American Life.* Minneapolis: Augsburg.

Katzman, Marilyn. 1986. So Disgusting They're the Rage. *The (Hackensack, N.J.) Record,* 30 January.

Kienel, Paul A., ed. 1977. *The Philosophy of Christian School Education.* Whittier, Calif.: Association of Christian Schools International.

Kirkpatrick, John T. 1977. Person, Hierarchy, and Autonomy in Traditional Yapese Theory. In *Symbolic Anthropology: A Reader in the Study of Symbols and Meanings,* edited by Janet L. Dolgin, David S. Kemnitzer, and David M. Schneider. New York: Columbia University Press.

Kraushaar, Otto F. 1972. *American Nonpublic Schools: Patterns of Diversity.* Baltimore: Johns Hopkins University Press.

LaFontaine, J. S. 1985. Person and Individual: Some Anthropological Reflections. In *The Category of the Person,* edited by Michael Carrithers, Steven Collins, and Steven Lukes. New York: Cambridge University Press.

Lakoff, George, and Mark Johnson. 1980. *Metaphors We Live By.* Chicago: University of Chicago Press.

Larson, Gary. 1986. "The Far Side." Kansas City, Mo.: Universal Press Syndicate. 15 August. Cartoon.

Lawrence, Jill. 1986. Bennett Urges Teaching on Evils of Communism. *(Regional Newspaper)*, 6 December.

Lee, Dorothy. 1959. *Freedom and Culture.* Englewood Cliffs, N.J.: Prentice-Hall.
———. 1986. *Valuing the Self: What We Can Learn from Other Cultures.* 2d ed. Prospect Heights, Ill.: Waveland Press.

Lee, Richard Borshay. 1984. *The Dobe !Kung.* New York: Holt, Rinehart, and Winston.

Lessa, William A., and Evon Z. Vogt. 1965. Magic, Witchcraft, and Divination: An Introduction. In *Reader in Comparative Religion,* edited by William A. Lessa and Evon Z. Vogt. New York: Harper and Row.

Lévi-Strauss, Claude. 1966. *The Savage Mind.* Chicago: University of Chicago Press.

Lewis, Jeanne Gerlach. 1973. Freedom, Authority, and Control in a Catholic Pentecostal Community. Ph.D. preliminary examination paper, Anthropology Department, University of Michigan, Ann Arbor, Mich.

Lockerbie, D. Bruce. 1972. *The Way They Should Go.* New York: Oxford University Press.

————. 1986. Personal Communication, 17 December.

Los Angeles Times. 1986. Poll Shows Common Views Among Religious Denominations. *(Regional Newspaper),* 27 July.

————. 1987. Humanities Leader Seeks Restoration in Classrooms. *(Regional Newspaper),* 5 June.

Lowrie, Roy W., Jr. 1980. *Inside the Christian School: From the Headmaster's Diary.* Whittier, Calif.: Association of Christian Schools International.

Luckmann, Thomas. 1967. *The Invisible Religion: The Problem of Religion in Modern Society.* New York: Macmillan.

LWCC (Living Waters Christian Community). n.d.a. Lesson Guide: *Discerning God's Will.* Southeastern Valley: LWCC.

————. n.d.b. Lesson Guide: *God's Bondservant.* Southeastern Valley: LWCC.

————. 1984. Lesson Guide: *Relationships Among Christians.* Southeastern Valley: LWCC.

MCA (Maranatha Christian Academy). Student Handbook. Southeastern Valley: MCA.

MacFarlane, Alan. 1978. *The Origins of English Individualism.* Oxford: Basil Blackwell.

McKeever, James. 1986. What to Give to Jesus. *END–Times News Digest,* December.

————. 1988. Spiritual War. *END–Times News Digest,* February.

McLoughlin, William G. 1978. *Revivals, Awakenings, and Reform: An Essay on Religion and Social Change in America, 1607–1977.* Chicago: University of Chicago Press.

Marsden, George M. 1980. *Fundamentalism and American Culture: The Shaping of Twentieth-Century Evangelicalism: 1870–1925.* New York: Oxford University Press.

————. 1982. The Religious New Right in Historical Perspective. In *Religion and America,* edited by Mary Douglas and Steven Tipton. Boston: Beacon Press.

Marsella, Anthony J. 1985. Culture, Self, and Mental Disorder. In *Culture and Self,* edited by Anthony J. Marsella, George DeVos, and Francis L. K. Hsu. New York: Tavistock.

Martin, David. 1982. Revived Dogma and New Cult. In *Religion and America,* edited by Mary Douglas and Steven M. Tipton. Boston: Beacon Press.

Marty, Martin E. 1975. Tensions Within Contemporary Evangelicalism: A Critical Appraisal. In *The Evangelicals: What They Believe, Who They Are, Where They Are Changing,* edited by David F. Wells and John D. Woodbridge. Nashville: Abingdon Press.

————. 1976. *A Nation of Behavers*. Chicago: University of Chicago Press.

————. 1981. The Revival of Evangelicalism and Southern Religion. In *Varieties of Southern Evangelicalism*, edited by David E. Harrell. Macon, Ga.: Mercer University Press.

————. 1982. Religion in America since Mid-Century. In *Religion and America*, edited by Mary Douglas and Steven M. Tipton. Boston: Beacon Press.

Mauss, Marcel. 1985. A Category of the Human Mind: The Notion of Person; the Notion of Self. Translated by W. D. Halls. In *The Category of the Person*, edited by Michael Carrithers, Steven Collins, and Steven Lukes. New York: Cambridge University Press.

Melton, J. Gordon. 1977. *A Directory of Religious Bodies in the United States*. New York: Garland.

————. 1978. *The Encyclopedia of American Religions*. Wilmington, N.C.: Mc-Grath Publishing.

Moberg, David O. 1975. Fundamentalists and Evangelicals in Society. In *The Evangelicals: What They Believe, Who They Are, Where They Are Changing*, edited by David F. Wells and John D. Woodbridge. Nashville: Abingdon Press.

Mooers, Michael. 1989. Personal Communication, based on a research report by Barna Research Group, commissioned by Alpha Omega Publications, 14 July.

Moore, Charles A., ed. 1968. *The Status of the Individual in East and West*. Honolulu: University of Hawaii Press.

Moore, Sally Falk. 1976. Epilogue: Uncertainties in Situations, Indeterminacies in Culture. In *Symbol and Politics in Communal Ideology: Cases and Questions*, edited by Sally Falk Moore and Barbara Meyerhoff. Ithaca: Cornell University Press.

National Center for Education Statistics. *Digest of Education Statistics*. Annual or biennial since 1976. Washington, D.C.: U.S. Government Printing Office.

National Commission on Excellence in Education. 1983. *A Nation at Risk: The Imperative for Educational Reform*. Washington, D.C.: U.S. Government Printing Office.

Nicholson, William E. 1987. How Public and Christian School Administrators View Key Issues Affecting the Christian Schools—Part II. *The Administrator*. American Association of Christian Schools 5(2):4–13.

Niebuhr, H. Richard. 1931. Fundamentalism. *Encyclopedia of the Social Sciences*. New York: Macmillan.

————. 1960. *Radical Monotheism and Western Culture*, with "Supplementary Essays." New York: Harper and Row. First ed. published 1943.

Nord, Warren A. 1986. A Liberal Case for Religion in School. *The Washington Post*, 6 July.

Nordin, Virginia Davis, and William Lloyd Turner. 1980. More Than Segregation Academies: The Growing Protestant Fundamentalist Schools. *Phi Delta Kappan* 61(6):391–394.

NWCA (Narrow Way Christian Academy). *Student Handbook*. Region: NWCA.

Ortner, Sherry B. 1984. Theory in Anthropology Since the Sixties. *Comparative Studies in Society and History* 1(1):126–166.

Pardue, Douglas. 1988. A Ministry Seared by Scandal. *(Regional Newspaper)*, 15 May.

Park, George K. 1967. Divination and Its Social Contexts. In *Magic, Witchcraft, and Curing,* edited by John Middleton. Garden City, N.Y.: Natural History Press.

Parsons, Paul F. 1987. *Inside America's Christian Schools.* Macon, Ga.: Mercer University Press.

Parsons, Talcott. 1949. *The Structure of Social Action* 2d ed. Glencoe, Ill.: Free Press.

Pauck, Wilhelm. 1968. *Harnack and Troeltsch: Two Historical Theologians.* New York: Oxford University Press.

Peshkin, Alan. 1986. *God's Choice: The Total World of a Fundamentalist Christian School.* Chicago: University of Chicago Press.

———. 1987. The Truth and Consequences of Fundamentalist Christian Schooling. *Free Inquiry,* Fall:5–10.

Piepkorn, Arthur Carl. 1978–1979. *Profiles in Belief: The Religious Bodies of the United States and Canada.* New York: Harper and Row.

Pinkston, William S. 1984. *Life Science for Christian Schools.* Greenville, S.C.: Bob Jones University Press.

Poole, David M. 1988. Baptists Amend Doctrine. *(Regional Newspaper),* 16 June.

Quebedeaux, Richard. 1974. *The Young Evangelicals.* New York: Harper and Row.

———. 1978. *The Worldly Evangelicals.* New York: Harper and Row.

Radcliffe-Brown, A. R. 1964. *The Andaman Islanders.* New York: Free Press. Originally published 1922.

Randall, Eric. 1988. Ethics, Religion Separable, Professor Believes. *(Regional Newspaper),* 31 March.

Rappaport, Roy A. 1976. Liturgies and Lies. *International Yearbook of Sociology and Religion* 10:75–104.

———. 1979. *Ecology, Meaning, and Religion.* Richmond, Calif.: North Atlantic Books.

Ricoeur, Paul. 1979. *The Rule of Metaphor.* Toronto: University of Toronto Press.

Robison, James. 1986. "Daily Restoration." PTL Network, 20 June. Television program.

Roof, Wade Clark. 1974a. Explaining Traditional Religion in Contemporary Society. In *Changing Perspectives in the Scientific Study of Religion,* edited by Alan Eister. New York: Wiley.

———. 1974b. Religious Orthodoxy and Minority Prejudice: Causal Relationship or Reflection of Localistic World View? *American Journal of Sociology* 80:643–664.

———. 1976. Traditional Religion in Contemporary Society: A Theory of Local-Cosmopolitan Plausibility. *American Sociological Review* 41(2):195–207.

Rose, H. J. 1911. Divination (Introductory). Edinburgh: *Encyclopedia of Religion and Ethics,* vol. 4.

Rose, Susan D. 1988. *Keeping Them Out of the Hands of Satan: Evangelical Schooling in America.* New York: Routledge.

Rosenberger, Nancy. 1989. Dialectic Balance in the Polar Model of Self: The Japan Case. *Ethos* 17(1):88–113.

Rushdoony, Rousas John. 1985. *The Philosophy of the Christian Curriculum.* 2d ed. Vallecito, Calif.: Ross House Books.

Sahlins, Marshall. 1976. *Culture and Practical Reason.* Chicago: University of Chicago Press.

Sandeen, Ernest R. 1970. *The Roots of Fundamentalism: British and American Millenarianism 1800–1930.* Chicago: University of Chicago Press.

SCCS (Springfield City Christian School). *Home-School Guide.* City: SCCS.

———. 1985–1986. *Self-Evaluation in Response to ACSI Evaluative Criteria.* City: SCCS.

Schindler, Claude E., Jr., and Pacheco Pyle. 1979. *Educating for Eternity.* Whittier, Calif.: Association of Christian Schools International.

Schlossmann, Siegmund. 1906. *Persona und prosopon im Recht und im christlichen Dogma.* Leipzig: Lipsius and Tischer.

Shweder, Richard, and Edmund Bourne. 1984. Does the Concept of the Person vary Cross-culturally? In *Culture Theory: Essays on Mind, Self, and Emotion,* edited by Richard Shweder and Robert LeVine. New York: Cambridge University Press.

Simpson, John H. 1983. Moral Issues and Status Politics. In *The New Christian Right: Mobilization and Legitimization,* Edited by Robert C. Liebman and Robert Wuthnow. New York: Aldine.

Skinner, John. 1922. *Prophecy and Religion.* Cambridge: Cambridge University Press.

Smith, John E. 1968. The Individual and the Judeo-Christian Tradition. In *The Status of the Individual in East and West,* edited by Charles A. Moore. Honolulu: University of Hawaii Press.

Smith, M. Brewster. 1985. The Metaphorical Basis of Selfhood. In *Culture and Self,* edited by Anthony J. Marsella, George DeVos, and Francis L. K. Hsu. New York: Tavistock.

Spradley, James P. 1980. *Participant Observation.* New York: Holt, Rinehart, and Winston.

Spradley, James P., and David W. McCurdy. 1972. *The Cultural Experience: Ethnography in Complex Society.* Chicago: Science Research Associates.

Springs of Life Christian School. *The Springs of Life School.* Region: Springs of Life Christian School.

Stern, Aimee L. 1988. Religious Recruiters Put Faith in Madison Avenue. *(Regional Newspaper),* 3 January.

Stipp, David. 1986. Teaching Teaching: Schools of Education Try to Assure Johnny a Decent Instructor. *Wall Street Journal,* 11 November.

Synthesis Project. 1984. "Creation vs. Evolution: Battle in the Classroom." Sponsored by Science in Society, the National Science Foundation. San Diego, Calif.: KPBS–TV. Television program.

Tamney, Joseph B., Stephen D. Johnson, and Sandy Halebsky. 1983. The Christian Right, Social Traditionalism, and Economic Conservatism. Paper presented at the Society for the Scientific Study of Religion meeting, Knoxville, Tenn.

Thomas, Elizabeth Marshall. 1959. *The Harmless People*. New York: Random House.

Thoreau, Henry David. 1988. Walking. Sherman Oaks, Calif.: Ninja Press. (First found in 1851 lecture, "The Wild"; First ed. published as Walking in 1861.)

Time. 1986. Putting Teachers up on Top. *Time*, 26 May.

―――. 1987a. Get Ready, "The Pope is Coming." *Time*, 7 September.

―――. 1987b. TV's Unholy Row. *Time*, 6 April.

Tocqueville, Alexis de. 1969. *Democracy in America*. Translated by George Lawrence; edited by J. P. Mayer. New York: Doubleday. Originally published as *De la démocratie en Amérique*, Paris: Gosselin, 1835–1840.

Toennies, Ferdinand. 1957. *Community and Society: Gemeinschaft und Gesellschaft*. Translated by Charles P. Loomis. New York: Harper Torchbooks. Originally published in German, Leipzig: Reisland, 1887.

Toffler, Alvin. 1970. *Future Shock*. New York: Random House.

Triennial School Census. 1984. State Department of Education.

Troeltsch, Ernst. 1960. *The Social Teaching of the Christian Churches*, 2 vol. Translated by Olive Wyon. Chicago: University of Chicago Press. Originally published in Germany. This translation originally published by Macmillan, 1931.

Turner, William Lloyd. 1979. Reasons for Enrollment in Religious Schools: A Case Study of Three Recently Established Fundamentalist Schools in Kentucky and Wisconsin. Ph.D. diss., University of Wisconsin.

U.S. Bureau of the Census. 1983. *1980 Census of Population, General Social and Economic Characteristics*. Washington, D.C.: U.S. Government Printing Office.

―――. 1988. *County and City Data Book, 1988*. Washington, D.C.: U.S. Government Printing Office.

U.S. Department of Education. 1986. *What Works: Research About Teaching and Learning*. Washington, D.C.: U.S. Department of Education.

Vitz, Paul. 1986. *Censorship: Evidence of Bias in our Children's Textbooks*. Ann Arbor, Mich.: Servant Books. Originally published as *Equity in Values Education: Do the Values Education Aspects of Public School Curricula Deal Fairly with Diverse Belief Systems*. Report, National Institute of Education, 1985.

Vobejda, Barbara. 1987. Broad Ideological Mix of Leaders Urge Restructuring School Curriculum to Extol Democratic Government. *(Regional Newspaper)*, 21 May.

Wagner, Melinda Bollar. 1983. *Metaphysics in Midwestern America*. Columbus, Ohio: Ohio State University Press.

Wallace, Anthony F. C. 1966. *Religion: An Anthropological View.* New York: Random House.

Ward, David L. 1985. *ZOE Health Fitness Program: A Biblical Approach to God-Like Life.* Zoe Ministries.

Weber, Max. 1948. *The Protestant Ethic and the Spirit of Capitalism.* Translated by Talcott Parsons. New York: Scribner. Originally published as *Die protestantische Ethik un der Geist des Kapitalismus*, Tubingen: J. C. B. Mohr, 1920–21.

———. 1963. *The Sociology of Religion.* Translated by Ephraim Fischoff. Boston: Beacon Press. Originally pubished as Religionssoziologie. In *Wirtschaft und Gesellschaft.* 2 vols. Tubingen: J.C.B. Mohr, 1922.

Wei-ming, Tu. 1985. Selfhood and Otherness in Confucian Thought. In *Culture and Self,* edited by Anthony J. Marsella, George DeVos, and Francis L. K. Hsu. New York: Tavistock.

Weller, Jack E. 1965. *Yesterday's People: Life in Contemporary Appalachia.* Lexington: University Press of Kentucky.

Wikse, John. 1977. *About Possession: The Self as Private Property.* University Park: Pennsylvania State University Press.

Wilcox, Clyde. 1986. Evangelicals and Fundamentalists in the New Christian Right: Religious Differences in the Ohio Moral Majority. *Journal for the Scientific Study of Religion* 25(3):255–363.

Will, George F. 1985. American Values Tied to Judeo-Christian Tradition. *(Regional Newspaper),* 16 August.

Willie George Ministries. 1987. Letter. *Deputy Magazine* 7(9), September.

Zborowski, Mark. 1955. The Place of Book Learning in Traditional Jewish Culture. In *Childhood in Contemporary Cultures,* edited by Margaret Mead and M. Wolfenstein. Chicago: University of Chicago Press.

Index

decision-making, influences on, 65, 92t, 93, 97, 99–100, 171–202, 247t. *See also* culture-building process

demographic characteristics: of Christian schools in Southeastern Valley, 25–28, 27t; of conservative Christians, 7, 15–17; of Southeastern Valley, 9–10, 16

denomination as determinant of Christian school culture, 28, 31

dependence on God, as conservative Christian ideal, 80–82

devil, 85, 187, 194, 205

discipleship, 244n2

discipline, 149–150, 161–167, 162–163t, 204. *See also* behavior, ideal

dispensationalism, 234n6

diversity, effect of on school doctrine, 209–210; effect of on school rules, 137–139; of student body, 137–139, 157, 209–210, 233n1; of teachers, 137

divination, 181–182, 215; functions of, 200–202

divine influence on decision-making, 65, 92–93, 97, 99–100, 171, 180–202, 215

Dobson, James, 32, 87, 174, 240n14

doctrinal purity, lack of in Christian schools, 207, 209–210

Dominion theology, *see* Kingdom Now theology

dress: code, 40–41, 60–61, 123–125; of students, 2–3, 49

Dumont, Louis, 74, 81–84, 235n1, 236n2, 236n3, 236n5, 237n6, 237n7, 240n1

Easter bunny, 138

Economy Readers curriculum, 172

education conferences, attended by teachers, 147–151, 148t

education culture, 141–170, 203–204, 229; influence on decision-making, 171–179, 247t; language of, used in Christian schools, 142–143, 145–147, 179, 246n3

educational resources, used by teachers, 151–152

epistemology of teaching, 246n3

ethics, situation, 179

evangelicals, *see* conservative Christians

evangelizing, *see* witnessing

explanations for events, 92t; as coincidence, 195–196, 201; as God's will, 171, 180–202, 241n5

family symbolism, 81, 238n9

fashion, *see* dress

freedom, 89

fruits of the spirit, as conservative Christian ideal, 68–70, 111, 115, 197, 203, 211

fundamentalists, *see* conservative Christians

"Fundamentals, The," 13

Garbage Pail Kids, 125–126, 214

gifts of the spirit, 12, 30, 192

glorifying God, as conservative Christian ideal, 91–97, 202, 246n1

God as locus of power, 91, 92t

God's leading, 248n2; as grounds for making decisions, 92t, 180–202; in discernment process, 185–189. *See also* decision-making

God's provision, 191–196

God's schools, 34, 35, 44, 96

God's will: as explanation for events, 92t, 97–99, 171, 180–202, 241n5; coming under, 34, 35, 79, 80, 80f, 90, 106, 168, 199, 215, 228; discerning, 180–202, 215

golden rule, as conservative Christian ideal, 70

graduation ceremony, 63–67, 143